THE ANCIENT MYSTERIES

THE ANCIENT MYSTERIES

A Sourcebook of Sacred Texts

Edited by
Marvin W. Meyer

PENN

University of Pennsylvania Press

Philadelphia

Originally published 1987 by HarperCollins Publishers
Copyright © 1987 Marvin W. Meyer
First University of Pennsylvania Press edition published 1999 by arrangement
with HarperCollins Publishers
Printed in the United States of America on acid-free paper

10 9 8 7 6 5 4

Published by
University of Pennsylvania Press
Philadelphia, Pennsylvania 19104-4011

Library of Congress Cataloging-in-Publication Data

The ancient mysteries: a sourcebook of sacred texts / edited by Marvin W. Meyer
    p.   cm.
  Includes bibliographies.
  ISBN-13: 978-0-8122-1692-9 (pbk. : alk. paper)
  ISBN-10: 0-8122-1692-X (pbk. : alk. paper)
  1. Mysteries, Religious—Histories—Sources. I. Meyer, Marvin W.
BL 610.A59   1986
291.1'3   86-45022

Designed by Donald Hatch

To Bonnie

nam mihi cum multa eximia divinaque videntur Athenae tuae peperisse atque in vitam hominum attulisse, tum nihil melius illis mysteriis, quibus ex agresti immanique vita exculti ad humanitatem et mitigati sumus, initiaque ut appellantur, ita re vera principia vitae cognovimus; neque solum cum laetitia vivendi rationem accepimus, sed etiam cum spe meliore moriendi.

For it appears to me that among the many exceptional and divine things your Athens has produced and contributed to human life, nothing is better than those mysteries. For by means of them we have been transformed from a rough and savage way of life to the state of humanity, and have been civilized. Just as they are called initiations, so in actual fact we have learned from them the fundamentals of life, and have grasped the basis not only for living with joy but also for dying with a better hope.

Marcus, in Cicero, *On the Laws* (*De legibus*), 2.14.36, with reference to the Eleusinian mysteries

Contents

Preface

This anthology of texts on the Greco-Roman mystery religions marks the coalescence of two interests. For a number of years I have felt the need for a single volume that would include a substantial selection of texts on the ancient mysteries. Such a volume might be employed in the classroom or used for private study, but prior to the present anthology no such volume has been available. For several years I also have considered publishing a translation of a fascinating yet neglected inscription from ancient Greece, the Rule of the Andanian Mysteries. The present book thus is meant to bring these two interests to expression.

In preparing this anthology, I have attempted to collect reliable English translations of approximately forty of the most significant texts concerning the ancient mystery religions. Some of the translations are my own, including a number of passages incorporated into the introductions; many translations are the work of others. In all instances I have tried to produce or select translations that are both accurate and graceful. To some extent I have standardized the translations for the sake of ease of reading, though I have sought to maintain the style and the integrity of the individual translations. Occasionally I have corrected obvious mistakes or typographical errors in the translations. The use of sigla is, in general, a standard use (for a brief discussion of such sigla see *The Nag Hammadi Library in English*, eds. James M. Robinson and Marvin W. Meyer [Leiden: Brill; San Francisco: Harper & Row, 1977], xvi). All parenthetical insertions in the translations introduce explanatory material that is supplied by the editor or the translator but is technically not a part of the translation per se (for example, a key Greek work that underlies the English translation may be inserted within parentheses). Limitations of space have necessitated the exclusion of some texts on the mysteries that I would have preferred to include (e.g., portions of Ovid's *Fasti*, Julian's *Orations*, Iamblichus's *On the Mysteries* [*De mysteriis*], and Sallustius's *Concerning the Gods and the Universe* [*De deis et mundo*], as well as shorter texts, inscriptions, and more fragmentary textual remains bearing witness to such mysteries as those at Phlya, and those of Sabazios and Sarapis). The bibliographies provided refer the reader to additional texts and monuments published elsewhere.

I wish to acknowledge a few of the institutions and individuals who have lent support to this project. Ferrum College generously provided released time and faculty grants for my work; Kathy Spradlin merits special thanks for her skillful word processing. Chapman University awarded me the position of Research Fellow and offered encouragement and support through the final stages of the project. Hans Dieter Betz first led me into the academic study of the mystery religions of Greco-Roman antiquity, and his advice and counsel have always been cherished. Morton Smith, Kurt Rudolph, and Birger Pearson looked through an early draft of the manuscript, and their comments proved especially helpful. John Loudon, Janet Reed, and the staff at HarperCollins gave patient and careful attention to the preparation of the book. The staff at the University of Pennsylvania Press have also done an excellent job of preparing the book as an edition published by their press. To these colleagues and institutions I express my heartfelt appreciation. I reserve my most profound statement of thanks for my wife and children, who have endured my absence and my preoccupation with this book, and who continue to teach me the *principia vitae*.

The present University of Pennsylvania Press edition of this book has been slightly revised and updated, and an Epilogue has been added. The Epilogue was written during a period of time in 2001 when I was in Italy visiting sanctuaries for the observance of the mystery religions, including Mithraea beneath the churches of San Clemente and Santa Prisca in Rome. The inscriptions from the Mithraeum at Santa Prisca, disarmingly reminiscent of Christian confessions, are presented in Chapter 7. I understand this sort of architectural juxtaposition of mystery sanctuaries and Christian churches to be a metaphor for the continuity of ideas and practices within the ancient mysteries and Christianity. Within the ancient mystery religions and Christianity, the *principia vitae* were—and still are—affirmed, and the mysteries of death and life were—and still are—celebrated.

Marvin W. Meyer
Chapman University

1
Introduction

By the time of Alexander the Great and his successors, Olympian Zeus had grown old. Father Zeus, lord of the sky and master of the thunderbolt, had ruled easily and well over the traditional *polis* (plural, *poleis*), or city-state, of pre-classical Greece. The feudal chieftain of the Olympian pantheon, Zeus lived with his queen Hera, his brothers Poseidon and Hades, and the other gods and goddesses in such a way as to recall the proud, heroic days of the Trojan War, when deities and human beings fought gloriously side by side. But for Greeks of the fifth and fourth centuries B.C.E., the heroic days celebrated by the bard Homer in his *Iliad* and *Odyssey* represented the old order of the Greek world, and that old order, with its increasingly anachronistic poleis and its outmoded gods, was giving way to a new, post–Olympian world.

The Hellenistic period, from the time of Alexander the Great through the Ptolemaic, Seleucid, and Antigonid Kingdoms established by his successors, witnessed the transformation of the polis. The Hellenic polis had proved successful in fostering the creative spirit of Greek citizens during an earlier, more parochial era. Ordinarily small in size and homogeneous in character, the autonomous city-states dotted the landscape among the hills and mountains of Greece and integrated the political, social, cultural, and religious lives of the populace to a remarkable extent. Thus, Pericles, the first citizen of Athens during the golden age of that great democratic polis, extolled the virtues of his city-state in a funeral oration he delivered in 430 B.C.E. According to the report of the Greek historian Thucydides (*History of the Peloponnesian War* 2.34–46), Pericles described the polis of Athens as the school of Greece, with a citizenry composed of individuals united in their commitment to law, freedom, beauty—and political life. Hence, claimed Pericles, the quiet, reticent person with no political interests and involvements is not simply apolitical; that person is quite useless. Similarly, Aristotle, the Greek philosopher and tutor of Alexander the Great, defined a human being as a political animal, that is, a person whose life is lived within the corporate context of the Greek polis.

Alexander the Great's conquests of 336 to 323 B.C.E. brought profound changes to the values of the old Greek polis and the Olympian gods and goddesses linked to the polis. In the years before Alexander, the Greek city-states had established significant lines of communication with other peoples, particularly through the exploits of mercenaries and the exchange of goods, but more than anything else, Alexander's triumphant achievements changed the Greek world forever. Alexander marched through Central Asia as far as Bactria and Sogdiana (present-day Afghanistan and the regions around), and even crossed the Indus River in India. Along the way he built cities named after himself, his trusty horse Bucephalus, and even, Plutarch tells us, a beloved dog Peritas, and thus he founded a network of municipalities that aided in the realization of new ecumenical interests. With Alexander and those who came after him, the Greek provincialism of the polis was modified, and in the Hellenistic period there emerged a new sense of the *oikoumene*, the "inhabited" world, as the international stage for human action. The Hellenistic world was not simply another classical world with Greek values and classical deities. Rather, it was more "cosmopolitan": the *kosmos*, or "world," was the polis, and the citizens and gods of this world were not only Greek, but also Anatolian, Asian, African, and Indian.

Doubts had been cast upon the Olympian deities of the Greek polis, however, long before the time of Alexander the Great. In the world of fifth-century Greece, philosophers and playwrights already questioned the virtues and, implicitly, the existence of gods and goddesses who were portrayed, with anthropomorphic vividness, as lustful, jealous, malevolent immortals. The critics demanded to know how one could worship a god like Zeus. According to the Greek myths, Zeus dethroned his titanic father Kronos, pursued and ravished, often while in bestial disguise, many a beautiful woman, and resorted to countless stratagems in order to evade his suspicious wife Hera. Such behavior on the part of the Olympians raised serious theological doubts in the minds of the more reflective Greeks.

Among the philosophers and professional Sophists of the fifth century, a number of freethinkers offered rationalistic interpretations of religion and the gods to explain the existence and nature of the tarnished Olympians. Some philosophers, like Protagoras of Abdera, embraced agnosticism. In his work *On Gods* (*Peri theon*) Protagoras declares that he is unable to say whether the gods actually exist, and if they do, of what sort they might be. For this statement the Athenians brought him to trial and condemned him to death. While Protagoras escaped the Athenians, he could not evade the power of mighty Poseidon, and he died in a shipwreck.

Other students of religion articulated specific theories of religion in their attempts to come to terms with the Greek deities. Prodicus of Ceos, for instance, claimed that ancient peoples considered all the good things of life—sun, moon, rivers, springs—to be divine. Hence, in the development of Greek religion, bread was revered as the goddess Demeter, wine was worshiped as the god Dionysos, water as Poseidon the god of the sea, fire as the divine smith Hephaistos, and so on. Another scholar, the dramatist Critias, wrote a play *Sisyphus* in which he advocated a view of religion very much like that of Marxism. The gods were the invention of politicians who wished to control their subjects by putting the fear of the gods into them. These political officials insisted that the deities saw all and knew all—even plots hatched in secret—and would surely punish lawbreakers. A later scholar of Greek religion, Euhemerus of Messene, was nicknamed the *atheos*, "atheist," (so reports Sextus Empiricus) because of what he wrote in *Sacred Record* (*Hiera anagraphe*). According to Euhemerus, whose theory has been called Euhemerism ever since he proposed it, the Greek gods and goddesses long ago were mere mortals, kings and leaders of people. Those who acknowledged the power and beneficence of Zeus and his friends honored them with sacrifices and proclaimed that they were to be esteemed as gods. Yet in reality Zeus and the other great Olympians were divine only by popular convention.

In sum, the Olympians began to fall from glory for several reasons. Their destiny was linked to that of the Greek polis, which was no longer the basic political unit in the world after Alexander's time. Furthermore, the philosophical criticism of religion that took place before and during the Hellenistic period challenged Greek beliefs and exposed the gods as unworthy of the worship and devotion of thoughtful Greek people. To be sure, the Olympian pantheon maintained itself as a religious and cultural force in the Hellenistic world, and attempts were made to inject new philosophical and religious values into the systems of the Olympian deities. Homer did not relinquish his place at the center of ancient education, and the allegorical exegesis of Homeric texts allowed people to interpret the sacred myths in new, scientific, philosophical ways (for example, see Porphyry, *On the Cave of the Nymphs*). Nonetheless, the hearts of many were turning away from Zeus and the Olympians during this period, and many searched at home and abroad for gods that would satisfy more fully their religious longings.

One type of religion, the so-called "mysteries," flourished during the Hellenistic period and proved very popular among people seeking new and more satisfying religious experiences. These mysteries, involving the worship of deities from Greece, Syria, Anatolia, Egypt, or Persia, were diverse in geographical origin and heterogeneous in historical development and theological orientation. Yet during the Hellenistic period the various mysteries shared a similar response to the religious needs of the day, and they resembled each other sufficiently to warrant being classified and discussed together.

The mysteries were secret religious groups composed of individuals who decided, through personal choice, to be initiated into the profound realities of one deity or another. Unlike the official religions, in which a person was expected to show outward, public allegiance to the local gods of the polis or the state, the mysteries emphasized an inwardness and privacy of worship within closed groups. The person who chose to be initiated joined an association of people united in their quest for personal salvation.

The word *mystery* (*mysterion* in Greek) derives from the Greek verb *myein*, "to close," referring to the closing of the lips or the eyes. This "closed" character of the mysteries may be interpreted in two ways. First of all, an initiate, or *mystes* (plural, *mystai*) into the *mysterion* was required to keep his or her lips closed and not divulge the secret that was revealed at the private ceremony. Vows of silence were meant to ensure that the initiate would keep the holy secret from being revealed to outsiders. Most *mystai* observed their pledge of secrecy, and as a result we possess little information about the central features of the mysteries. However, Christian converts who once had been initiated into the mystery religions sometimes felt no hesitation about betraying the mysteries and readily unveiled what they believed to be godless and shameless secrets. It is commonly supposed that a betrayal of the pledge of silence was the main concern in the case of Alcibiades during the late fifth century B.C.E., shortly before the ill-fated Syracusan Expedition. In Plutarch's *Life of Alcibiades,* it is said that Alcibiades and his friends were accused of having profaned the Eleusinian mysteries of Demeter and Kore in a drunken parody of the sacred rites. Several of the friends mimicked the roles of the officials in the mysteries, and the rest of the inebriated partygoers claimed to be initiates. After the Athenian expedition sailed for Sicily, Alcibiades was recalled to face charges of impiety both for the profanation of the mysteries and for the mutilation of the ithyphallic images of Hermes (cp. Andocides, *On the Mysteries* [*De mysteriis*], a speech Andocides delivered in his own defense).

A second way to interpret the "closed" nature of the mysteries relates to the closing and the opening of the eyes. Closed eyes brought darkness to the prospective initiate both literally and metaphorically, and the opening of the eyes was an act of enlightenment. Just as one of a baby's first responses to the world is the discovery of light through the opening of the eyes, so the initiate, sometimes described as one reborn, also saw the light. Nocturnal initiatory ceremonies, with flickering torches accentuating the contrast between light and darkness, made the primal experience of enlightenment that much more vivid to the eyes and the emotions.

If the experience of seeing was primary in the mystery religions, it may be anticipated that much visual imagery is to be discovered in texts describing these ceremonies. Such is in fact the case. For example, one of the priests in the mysteries was termed a hierophant (*hierophantes*), "one who shows sacred things." The highest stage of initiation in the Eleusinian mysteries is that of *epopteia*, "beholding," and an initiate into the great mysteries was called an *epoptes*, "beholder." A fragment of Pindar, quoted by Clement of Alexandria (*Miscellanies* [*Stromateis*] 3.3.17), further focuses upon the happiness of one who has attained enlightenment through the Eleusinian mysteries: "Blessed is one who goes under the earth after seeing these things. That person knows the end of life, and knows its Zeus-given beginning."

Many of the mystery religions were of great antiquity, and their origins are hidden in the mists of prehistory. Some of the mysteries seem to have developed from agrarian festivals that celebrated the fertility of nature as it manifested itself in the life cycle of crops. At Eleusis, Demeter and Kore were goddesses of grain, and ancient agricultural ceremonies dramatized the planting, growing, and harvesting of the grain. Early worship of Dionysos also reflected concern for the power of nature, but devotees of this god recognized that power not only in the cultivated grapevine and in grain (hence the place of the *liknon*, or winnowing basket, in the worship of Dionysos), but also in the wild vegetation and the pine tree of the woods and mountains—in the moist sap pulsating in plants and all of nature, according to Plutarch (*On Isis and Osiris*, 35, in Chapter 6).

Hellenistic devotion to the Syrian goddess Atargatis (called by the Greek name Hera in the text *The Syrian Goddess*, in Chapter 5), also emerged from earlier Mediterranean concerns for fertility. The second-millennium B.C.E. tablets from Ugarit, Syria, may illustrate the sorts of deities that antedate Hera-Atargatis and her "Zeus": the mighty goddess Anath and her lover, the fertility god Baal, who dies and rises from death with the plants and the earth. The Asian Adonis, the Anatolian Attis, and the Egyptian Osiris similarly were gods who had died and who were linked to the life cycle of vegetation, and the rebirth of fertility in the world of nature is exemplified in the ways these gods were portrayed. Myths about Adonis, Attis, and Osiris hinted at the germination of life in these three gods. Such objects as the "grain Osiris" from a tomb like that of Tutankhamun proclaimed more graphically the resurrection of grain and the power of Osiris. Even though Mithras *tauroktonos*, "bull-slaying" Mithras, shows few real connections with agrarian interests, still the artwork commissioned by initiates of Mithras depicts the creation of life from a living sacrifice: heads of grain, and perhaps the vine, sprout from the body and blood of the sacrificed bull.

This ancient heritage of the agrarian festivals may help explain the prominent place of goddesses in the mystery religions of the Hellenistic world. Through these early agricultural festivals, worshipers expressed concern for the fertility of the earth and are thought to have confessed the earth to be nourished and protected by the divine Mother. It has often been supposed that in some of the earliest religions in human history, the mother goddess reigned alone or nearly alone and embodied the mysterious forces of life and death in the world. As cosmic matriarch and universal source of life, the divine Mother must have been invoked with various names and described in various ways. Aspects of her power and her preeminence may be found in the Magna Mater Kybele, in features of Isis, and even in Demeter and Kore-Persephone, in spite of the patriarchal, Olympian overlay in the Greek myths.

At other times the ancient mother goddess of the earth seems to have shared her throne with a god, and within the Indo-European sphere of thought that god often was a sky god like the Roman Jupiter, Greek Zeus Pater, or Dyaus Pitar, the Indo-European patriarch of heaven. Fertility on the earth, then, could be depicted as the result of a sacred marriage between the sky and the earth: the semen of the sky poured down as rain, penetrated the womb of the earth, and so brought life to the world. This view of the cosmos may account for the use of the enigmatic formula that the Christian heresiologist Hippolytus claims was employed within the mysteries in one form of their reenactment: *Hye kye*, "Rain! Conceive!"

The mystery religions retained this concern for the divine Mother, and many of the mysteries reserved a position of dominance for a great goddess. Such is the case in the Eleusinian mysteries, with the emphasis upon the grain mother Demeter and her daughter Kore; the Andanian mysteries, with the worship of several gods and goddesses, among them Demeter, Hagne, and (in Pausanias) the Great Goddesses; the Mysteries of Isis and Osiris, in which Queen Isis provided maternal constancy in the face of the vicissitudes in the career of Osiris; and the mysteries of the Great Mother, with the Magna Mater as mistress over all, including her dying lover Attis. The mysteries of the Great Mother also celebrated the greatness of Attis, but his ambiguous masculinity served to highlight the female power of the Mother. According to the myths of Attis, he castrated himself, and some of his initiated followers, the Galli, imitated his self-sacrifice and adopted transvestite practices suitable for those who voluntarily had become eunuchs devoted to the Great Mother. Commonly, artwork showing an Attis or a Gallus depicts a soft, feminine figure with no pronounced masculine characteristics. A similar figure appears in depictions of another god said to have Anatolian roots, the Greek Dionysos. Although Dionysos could be described as a divine bull, he also could be portrayed with more feminine features, as in Euripides' play The Bacchae. Further, the worship of Dionysos left room for devotion to a divine mother or a female beloved. Thus, Dionysos was incorporated into the later celebrations of the Eleusinian mysteries, in the company of Demeter and Kore; and Dionysos himself often was shown in the presence of a loving goddess, such as the woman enthroned above the reclining Dionysos in the Villa of Mysteries at Pompeii.

Not all the mystery religions, however, exhibited this concern for the feminine. At times the mysteries of Mithras may have been conducted in conjunction with the worship of the Great Mother, Anahita, or Hecate, but taken by themselves the Mithraic mysteries championed masculine values. It is quite appropriate to describe this religion as a cult of machismo. Only men were allowed to be initiated, and the devotees of Mithras included many Roman soldiers and imperial officers who were attracted to the militant piety of Mithraism. Early Christian sources report that initiates of Mithras held such ranks as Miles (Soldier) or Leo (Lion), and ultimately attained the highest grade of initiation as Pater (Father). These ancient sources also suggest that trials and contests were required of the initiates in order to test their courage and fortitude. Finally, in the mythic cast of characters within Mithraism, males clearly predominate. Mention may be made of the two torch-bearers Cautes and Cautopates, the unconquered Sun, the warrior Mithras, and the slain bull.

The development of early agrarian or fertility festivals into the mystery religions involved, first and foremost, the conviction on the part of the worshipers that the cycle of nature related directly to human life. Plants and animals participated in a cycle of death and life, and so also did human beings. Death came to all the divine forces of nature—Kore, Dionysos, Adonis, Attis, Osiris, the Mithraic bull—but finally life was victorious. Kore returned from the realm of Hades; Dionysos vivified his devotees; Adonis rose from the dead; Attis gave an intimation of new life; Osiris reigned as king of the underworld; and the bull provided life for the world. Hence, if human beings could assimilate the power that made life triumphant in the world of nature, they too might live in a more complete way.

Just how the initiates into the mysteries appropriated this power we do not know, but they may have understood themselves to have experienced an immediate or mystical encounter with the divine. At times this experience seems to have entailed an approach to death and a return to life. Sometimes, as in the Eleusinian and Egyptian mysteries, the *mystai* underwent dramatic rituals of darkness and death and emerged afterward into new light and life. In several texts the initiates are specifically declared to be reborn (Apuleius, *The Golden Ass*, bk. 11; the Mithraic inscriptions from Santa Prisca; the inscription of 376 C.E. on the *taurobolium* and *criobolium*, [the bath in the blood of a bull or a ram]; cp. also the Christian Gospel of John 2–3). In other texts the initiates are acclaimed as children who come from the divine (the Orphic lamella), and are transformed by "immortal birth" (the Mithras Liturgy). Ordinarily the *mystai* partook of food and drink in the ritual celebrations, and sometimes they may have become one with the divine by participating in a sacramental meal analogous to the Christian Eucharist. The wild maenads of Dionysos, for example, were said to have devoured the raw flesh of an animal in their *omophagia*, or feast of flesh. While it is not clear that Greco-Roman women actually took part in the *omophagia*, the descriptions of the raw feast suggest that participants believed they were consuming the god himself, whose divine power was incarnate in the slain animal. In the mysteries of Mithras, the initiates partook of a ceremony that was so reminiscent of the Christian "Lord's Supper" that it proved an embarrassment to the Christian apologist Justin Martyr. According to Justin, the Mithraic *mystai* ate bread and drank water (perhaps a mixed cup of water and wine) at an initiatory meal—in diabolical imitation, he hastily adds, of the Christian Eucharist (see below, Chapter 8). Those who ate and drank of this Mithraic meal thus revitalized themselves with the elements representing the divine body and blood of the slaughtered bull.

In a literary fragment (178) attributed to Plutarch (in Stobaeus, *Anthology* [*Anthologion*] 4.52.49), the experience of death is compared with initiation into great mysteries. Plutarch initially notes the similarity of the Greek verbs *teleutan* (to die) and *teleisthai* (to be initiated) and then observes that people who die and people who are initiated go through comparable transformations. The author most likely was reflecting on the great mysteries of Eleusis in his idealized observations, but the passage may be read in a more general manner as a characterization of the place of death and life in the various mystery religions.

> At first there is wandering, and wearisome roaming, and fearful traveling through darkness with no end to be found. Then, just before the consummation (*telos*), there is every sort of terror, shuddering and trembling and perspiring and being alarmed. But after this a marvelous light (*phos*) appears, and open places and meadows await, with voices and dances and the solemnities of sacred utterances and holy visions. In that place one walks about at will, now perfect and initiated (*memuemenos*) and free, and wearing a crown, one celebrates religious rites, and joins with pure and pious people. Such a person looks over the uninitiated and unpurified crowd of people living here, who are packed together and trample each other in deep mud and murk, but who hold onto their evil things on account of their fear of death, because they do not believe in the good things that are in the other world.

These are the eternal blessings, the joys for this life and the hopes for the next, bestowed upon initiates into the mystery religions.

While a substantial number of ancient *mystai* must have considered themselves changed people after their initiation into the mysteries, many participants surely joined the mystery festivities for reasons other than mystical longings. As Plato so aptly said in the *Phaedo* (69C), many people bore the thyrsus of Dionysos, but relatively few were true *mystai*. Some people sought initiation because they were lonely, alienated, or bored, and they wished to become members of a close-knit social club. Others were attracted to the religious communities that were egalitarian. Free people and slaves, rich and poor, members of one ethnic group or another, and men and women (except within Mithraism) often celebrated the mysteries as brothers and sisters in spirit.

Whatever else the mystery religions were, they were fascinating and delightful occasions for the participants. Several of the textual sources published in this volume (such as Aristophanes, *The Frogs*; the Rule of the Andanian Mysteries; Arnobius, *The Case Against the Pagans*; Apuleius, *The Golden Ass*, bk. 11) describe in detail the public celebrations that preceded the secret ceremonies. A colorful band of people marched together in the parades and processions that took place during the holidays observed for the mystery religions. Some *mystai* sang and danced, others displayed unusual and sometimes bizarre attire, while dignitaries carried the holy shrines or sacred paraphernalia of the deities featured in the mysteries. As portrayed by ancient authors, the processions in honor of the Magna Mater and Isis were carnivals that would rival modern celebrations of Mardi Gras.

Other rituals preliminary to the secret initiations were less spectacular but equally stirring to those taking part. These observances included such rites of purification as fasting, abstaining from specified foods (such as meat or wine), refraining from sexual intercourse, and submitting to cleansings and lustrations. Prayers and sacrifices were offered to the deities, and if the deity was one of the *chthonioi*, the powers of the earth, the worshipers assumed an appropriate posture for prayer and selected a chthonian animal for sacrifice. Ancient worshipers commonly prayed to earth deities with arms lowered and palms opened downward and sacrificed animals such as pigs to the earth gods and goddesses. Libations dedicated to the *chthonioi* were poured into trenches so that the liquid might soak down into the soil.

The secret ceremonies of the mystery religions, however, remain largely hidden from us. We know that the purified devotees, properly attired according to the regulations for a given mystery religion, assembled at a holy site for the rituals of initiation. In the Eleusinian mysteries the *mystai* participated in rites that incorporated three types of sacred observances: *legomena*, "things recited," *deiknymena*, "things shown," and *dromena*, "things performed." Although these three categories of communication apply particularly to the mysteries of Demeter and Kore, they may be employed to describe the rites of the other mystery religions as well.

The *legomena* of the mysteries were statements recited to express the deep truths of the gods. Sometimes the *legomena* may have been sung or chanted by such performers as the Eleusinian priests who were descended from the holy family of the Eumolpidai (named after Eumolpos, "one who sings well"). The *legomena* may have been recitations of the *hieros logos* (the "sacred account" that provided the mythological foundation for the celebration of the mysteries; plural, *hieroi logoi*), interpretations of the stories of the deities, or responses of the initiates to the divine mystery. In the books of the ecclesiastical authors Clement of Alexandria, Hippolytus of Rome, Eusebius of Caesarea, Arnobius of Sicca, and Firmicus Maternus, we read of formulas, or *symbola* ("symbols"), that allegedly were spoken during the mystery rites. The Christian authors reported what the participants in the mysteries said about the accomplishment of the preliminary rituals and the meaning of the secret ceremonies. The *symbola* present us with particular problems of interpretation, and we shall consider them in the appropriate chapters.

In addition to hearing and reciting the *legomena*, the *mystai* beheld the *deiknymena*. The mysteries were replete with visual images, and the sanctuaries where the holy initiations were held frequently housed numerous works of art. The scenes carved or painted in the "apse" of a Mithraeum, for instance, often gave a concise picture of Mithraic themes, and the *mystai* might have viewed these scenes as being among the *deiknymena*. Presumably the beholding of the "things shown" also meant that the initiates saw sacred objects previously hidden from sight. We may suppose that among the *deiknymena* in the mysteries of Dionysos was an unveiling of the mysterious object, barely concealed beneath a protective covering, in the *liknon*. When uncovered, the object would be recognized as an embodiment of Dionysos: an erect phallus set in a basket commonly used as a cradle. (Sometimes a mask of Dionysos, or the infant Dionysos himself, was shown in the *liknon*.) According to Hippolytus, in certain enactments of the mysteries of Demeter and Kore, the initiates glimpsed a single head of grain as the visual climax of the ceremonies (*Refutation of All Heresies*, 5.8.39). Whether the description of this ecclesiastical author pertains to the Eleusinian mysteries remains in question. Nonetheless, this suggested experience of the initiates captures the essence of the mysteries of the Grain Mother and her daughter. The power of Demeter and the resurrected life of Kore are symbolized quietly but powerfully in the ripe grain that grants vitality to the earth and people on the earth.

The third sort of experience in the mystery religions was more dramatic in character. The *dromena* may have included a variety of rituals, such as the actions mentioned briefly and enigmatically in the *symbola* quoted by the church fathers. Clement of Alexandria cites a *symbolon* in which one makes a cryptic declaration of having undertaken a series of tasks with a chest and a basket and of *ergasamenos*, "having done the work" (*Exhortation to the Greeks*, 2.21, in Chapter 8). Yet Clement also states that those initiated into the mysteries of Demeter and Persephone took part in another kind of activity: a *drama mystikon* (mystic drama) that was illumined with the fiery light of torches and that commemorated the rape of Kore and the sad wanderings of Demeter.

Doubtless such productions were staged by priests or *mystai* in many of the mysteries. The actors produced and the audience witnessed a theatrical performance in which the *hieroi logoi* of the mystery religions came to life in liturgical drama. The company of initiates played the roles of mythological characters and sometimes donned masks or costumes in order to reenact the sufferings, sorrows, and joys of the gods and goddesses. Such costuming is known from the presence of masks in representations of the mysteries of Dionysos, from Apuleius's description of initiation into the mysteries of Isis, from occasional texts and monuments depicting the mysteries of Mithras (for example, a bas-relief from Konjica, Bosnia, showing a Raven, a Persian, a Soldier, and a Lion [all Mithraic ranks] in masks at a banquet), and even from the props that are symbolic of the deities and are borne in the processions of initiates.

A usual feature of the ancient mystery religions was the partaking of food and drink, and this communion celebration often reenacted a holy meal established by the gods and goddesses. In the *Homeric Hymn to Demeter* the Mother drinks the *kykeon* instead of red wine, and her devotees likewise drank the ceremonial *kykeon* in their mystic repast. Mithraic monuments show Mithras and Sol (the Sun) sharing a meal on the body or the hide of a bull, and this sacred feast functioned as the prototype for a holy meal eaten by the Mithraic *mystai*. Furthermore, two or three texts discussed in this sourcebook refer to invitations to dine with the gods of the mysteries. Several other texts make mention of sacred banquets and symposia held under the auspices of the deities and suggest that animals were sacrificed and sacrificial meat was consumed at ritual celebrations in some of the mystery religions. One *symbolon* from the mysteries of Attis claims that a *mystes* ate from a tambourine and drank from a cymbal in the initiatory rites. The precise nature and significance of these different meals, however, cannot be known with certainty. The holy meals, like so many other features of the mystery religions, elude our inquiring eyes and remain shrouded in secrecy.

A fragment of Aristotle preserved in Synesius (*Dio* 10) provides the occasion for a final word on the ancient mystery religions. In this fragment Aristotle concludes that initiates into the mysteries do not learn anything (*ou mathein ti*), but rather have an experience (*pathein*) and are put in a certain state of mind (*diatethenai*). There is much to commend this conclusion. While the ancient initiates may have been emotionally affected by the rituals and may have gained insight into divine profundities through the *legomena*, *deiknymena*, and *dromena*, they were not given instruction or taught doctrine in any traditional sense. Initiation was not classroom education, but an eye-opening experience that transcended earthly realities and mundane learning. Just as any mystical experience ultimately cannot be put into words or described adequately in books, so also the blessed *mystai* heard, saw, and performed the ineffa-

2
The Greek Mysteries of the Grain Mother and Daughter, and Related Mysteries

The most influential and popular of the Greek mysteries were those of Demeter and Kore at Eleusis, an important town in Attica some twenty-one kilometers to the northwest of Athens. It was believed from ancient times that there the gods had favored humanity by giving grain for food, so that an early agricultural cult at Eleusis commemorated the yearly sowing of grain around the time of the Greek month Boedromion (September/October). Like this early agrarian cult and like the Thesmophoria (an autumn agricultural festival that was exclusively for women and was somewhat similar to the mysteries), the Eleusinian mysteries also celebrated the fertility and life of grain. Before Athens took control of Eleusis (shortly before 600 B.C.E.?), the mysteries of Demeter and Kore were conducted by an independent Eleusis, and the *Homeric Hymn to Demeter* seems to presuppose such a state of affairs. After Athens assumed jurisdiction of the mysteries, however, Athenian interests naturally predominated in the celebration of the Eleusinian mysteries.

The mysteries at Eleusis focused upon the goddesses Demeter and Kore. Demeter is probably a Cretan goddess by origin (as she is in the *Homeric Hymn*) and is most likely the "Grain Mother" by name, though some scholars suggest that her name means "Earth Mother." Kore is the "Maiden," and because of her sojourn in the realm of Hades, Kore is often identified with Persephone, the queen of the underworld. Both Demeter and Kore are personifications of grain: Demeter, the mature grain with maternal potency, and Kore, the newly planted grain of the autumn sowing.

Our information concerning specific features of the Eleusinian mysteries derives mainly from the mysteries as celebrated during the period of Athenian domination. In the month of Anthesterion (February) the lesser mysteries were conducted near Athens, at Agrai by the Ilissos River, as something of a preparation for the greater mysteries celebrated in Boedromion. The celebration of the greater mysteries can be reconstructed from several sources. On Boedromion 13, Athenian youths carried *kistai* (chests) and *ta hiera* ("the sacred things," the precise identity of which is uncertain; cp. Clement of Alexandria, *Exhortation to the Greeks*, in Chapter 8) from Eleusis to Athens, where they were temporarily stored in the Eleusinion (the Eleusinian temple) until the Iacchos procession. On subsequent days a herald in Athens excluded criminals and *barbaroi* (those who do not speak Greek) from participation in the mysteries; a proclamation declared that the initiates were to bathe in the sea; and the initiates sacrificed a young pig to Demeter and Kore. Boedromion 19 brought with it the Iacchos procession (see the excerpts from Herodotus and Aristophanes in this chapter): the initiates marched along the Sacred Way from Athens to Eleusis, singing, dancing, and carrying the "sacred things" of the goddesses back to the Telesterion (great hall of initiation) in Eleusis.

What happened in Eleusis during the mystery rites themselves remains, in large part, a secret. To be sure, there were *legomena, dromena,* and *deiknymena,* but exactly what was spoken, performed, and shown is unclear.

Christian authors such as Clement of Alexandria, Hippolytus of Rome, and Arnobius of Sicca suggest various rites, frequently sexual in nature, that may have taken place in the Eleusinian mysteries, but their testimonies must be treated with considerable caution. Even if their information is reliable, they may not be commenting on the Greek Eleusinian mysteries at all, but instead may be offering their observations on other, later mysteries, such as the mysteries of Demeter and Kore at Alexandria. Three sets of testimony from the Christian fathers merit our attention:

1)   According to Clement of Alexandria (*Exhortation to the Greeks*, 2.21; cp. Arnobius of Sicca, *The Case Against the Pagans*, 5.26), the initiatory formula of the Eleusinian mysteries is as follows:

> I have fasted;
> I have drunk the *kykeon;*
> I have taken from the chest (*kiste*);
>   having done the work,
> I have placed in the basket (*kalathos*),
>   and from the basket into the chest.

(This translation, by Marvin W. Meyer, differs slightly from that of G. W. Butterworth, in Chapter 8.)

The initiate, writes Clement, thus claims to have accomplished the requisite fast, to have partaken of the ceremonial *kykeon,* and to have performed mysterious rites with sacred objects. Clement believes that the sacred symbols to be found in the *kistai* are various sorts of cakes, a serpent, pomegranates, leaves and stalks, poppies, and a model of a woman's genitals (*Exhortation to the Greeks,* 2.22).

2) According to Hippolytus of Rome, the great mystery of the Eleusinians is the cry *Hye kye,* "Rain! Conceive!" (*Refutation of All Heresies,* 5.7.34; cp. the fifth-century Neoplatonist author Proclus, *In Timaeum,* 293C). Evidently this *symbolon* was intended as a command to the sky to emit rain and to the earth to become fruitful. The uttering of the formula may have been accompanied by such a ritual as the pouring of water into the ground, an act symbolizing the intercourse of the deities and the impregnation of mother nature (Athenaeus, *The Learned Banquet* [*Deipnosophistai*], 496AB). In the context of Eleusinian interests, the male partner would be Father Zeus, and the female partner Mother Demeter or the Maiden Kore. A sacred marriage (*hieros gamos*) also is intimated by two other *symbola.* Hippolytus maintains that the hierophant at Eleusis calls out, under a bright light, "A holy child is born to the Lady Brimo, Brimos" (*Refutation of All Heresies,* 5.8.40). Lady Brimo ("Strong One" or "Terrible One") probably is to be understood to be Kore-Persephone, who had intercourse with Zeus and gave birth to Dionysos, Brimos. (Contrast with Clement, in *Exhortation to the Greeks,* 2.15, where he applies the epithet Brimo to Demeter.) A Dionysian *symbolon* recorded by Clement of Alexandria and several other Christian authors (see the introduction to Chapter 4) proclaims the same holy union between Zeus and partners of the earth: *tauros drakontos kai pater taurou drakon,* "The bull is father of the serpent, and the serpent father of the bull." Clement explains that Zeus, in the form of a bull, had intercourse with Demeter and produced earthy Kore-Persephone; Zeus in the form of a serpent had intercourse with his daughter Kore-Persephone and produced bull-like Dionysos.

3) According to Hippolytus, among the *deiknymena* in the Eleusinian mysteries is a single harvested head of grain that is beheld in silence, apparently as a simple but profound manifestation of the life in the grain and in all things (*Refutation of All Heresies,* 5.8.39).

Whatever happened in the secret ceremonies of Demeter and Kore at Eleusis and elsewhere, the initiates beheld the light literally or metaphorically, and so became *epoptai.*

In this chapter I include three readings from the mysteries of the

Kabeiroi at Samothrace and the mysteries of Glykon and Alexander of Abonoteichos, since these mystery religions also were of considerable significance in antiquity and at times were compared to the Eleusinian mysteries.

Of the numerous works on the Eleusinian mysteries, the following are particularly helpful: Mircea Eliade, *Rites and Symbols of Initiation: The Mysteries of Birth and Rebirth* (New York: Harper & Row, 1958); W. K. C. Guthrie, *The Greeks and Their Gods* (Boston: Beacon, 1955), 277–94; C. Kerényi, *Eleusis: Archetypal Image of Mother and Daughter* (New York: Schocken, 1977); George E. Mylonas, *Eleusis and the Eleusinian Mysteries* (Princeton: Princeton Univ. Press, 1961); Martin P. Nilsson, *Greek Folk Religion* (Philadelphia: Univ. of Pennsylvania Press, 1972); Walter F. Otto, "The Meaning of the Eleusinian Mysteries," in *The Mysteries*, ed. Joseph Campbell, Bollingen Series, no. 30, Papers from the Eranos Yearbooks (Princeton: Princeton Univ. Press, 1955), 83–112; R. Gordon Wasson, Carl A. P. Ruck, and Albert Hofmann, *The Road to Eleusis: Unveiling the Secret of the Mysteries* (New York: Harcourt Brace Jovanovich, 1978).

HOMERIC HYMN TO DEMETER

The most precious extant text of the Eleusinian mysteries is the so-called *Homeric Hymn to Demeter*. Presumably composed around the seventh century B.C.E. before Athens assumed control of the celebration of the Eleusinian mysteries, the *Hymn to Demeter* contains the *hieros logos* of the ancient mysteries at Eleusis. The *Hymn* recounts the myth of the rape of Kore by Hades (or Plouton [Pluto], "Wealthy One"), the grief of Demeter and her quest for her daughter, and the subsequent founding of the Eleusinian mysteries by the Great Mother herself.

The *Hymn to Demeter* proclaims, in mythic form, the mystery of the life cycle of grain: after growing with youthful vigor, the grain becomes the harvest of death. Kore's yearly sojourn in the underworld for a four-month period of time compares well with the period of time, in the Greek agricultural calendar, between the harvest in June and planting in October, during which time the grain fields lie barren and empty. Yet in Greece the fruit of the earth is also the wealth stored under the earth, for during the summer months the harvested grain is kept underground in subterranean silos. In the autumn, then, the grain is carried up to the fields for the next sowing. The grain sown in the fields undergoes still another, culminating ascent to the realm of life: the seed is put beneath the surface of the earth once again, but now it sprouts and grows as the new crop for another season. Thus, life emerges after death in the world of vegetation, and the living Grain Daughter rejoins her Mother in the *Hymn to Demeter*.

As *hieros logos* the account of Demeter and Kore in the *Homeric Hymn to Demeter* formed the basis for the observance of the Eleusinian mysteries during the month Boedromion. Various passages within the hymn describe rituals celebrated by those participating in the mysteries, such as the fast and the partaking of the *kykeon* (the ceremonial drink of barley water).

This translation of the *Homeric Hymn to Demeter* is by David G. Rice and John E. Stambaugh, *Sources for the Study of Greek Religion,* Society of Biblical Literature Sources for Biblical Study, no. 14 (Chico, Calif.: Scholars, 1979), 171–83. A convenient presentation of the Greek text with an English translation of the hymn is that of H. G. Evelyn White, *Hesiod: The Homeric Hymns and Homerica* (Loeb Classical Library, 1959), 288–325. Other helpful studies on the *Hymn to Demeter* include George E. Mylonas, *The Hymn to Demeter and Her Sanctuary at Eleusis,* Washington University Studies in Languages and Literature, no. 13; (St. Louis: Washington University Studies, 1942); and Nicholas J. Richardson, *The Homeric Hymn to Demeter* (Oxford: Clarendon, 1974). On Demeter with Metaneira and Iambe in the house of Keleos, compare the story of Demeter and Baubo in Clement of Alexandria, *Exhortation to the Greeks,* 2.20–21, in Chapter 8.

I begin my song of the holy goddess, fair-haired Demeter, and of her   1
slim-ankled daughter whom Aidoneus snatched away; and Zeus the loud-crashing, the wide-voiced one, granted it. She was playing with the deep-bosomed daughters of Ocean, away from Demeter of the golden   5
weapon and glorious fruit, and she was gathering flowers throughout the luxuriant meadow—roses, saffron, violets, iris, hyacinth, and a narcissus which was a trap planted for the blossoming maiden by Earth (Gaia) in accord with Zeus's plans, a favor to Hades the receiver of many   10
guests; it was radiantly wonderful, inspiring awe in all who saw it, whether immortal god or mortal man; a hundred stems grew from its root; and the whole wide heaven above, the whole earth, and the salt surge of the sea smiled for joy at its fragrance. The girl was charmed by   15
it, and reached out both hands to pluck the pretty plaything—suddenly, the earth split open wide along the plain and from it the lord host of many, Kronos's son of many names, darted out on his immortal horses. He grabbed her, resisting and screaming, and took her away in his   20

golden chariot. She lifted her voice in a cry, calling upon father Zeus, the almighty and good. But no one, god or mortal, heard her voice, not even the glorious-fruited olive trees, except the childish daughter of Perses,
25 Hecate of the glistening veil, who—from her cave—heard, and so did Lord Helios the glorious son of Hyperion, as the maiden calling upon father Zeus, though he was sitting, removed from the other gods, in his much-besought temple, receiving fine sacrifices from mortal men.

30   Her, all unwilling, with the approval of Zeus, he took away on his immortal horses, Kronos's son of many names, brother of her father, designator of many, host of many. As long as the goddess could see the earth and the starry sky, the flowing, fish-filled sea and the rays of the sun,
35 she still had hope that her holy mother and the race of the immortal gods would see her, and there was still much hope in her heart in spite of her distress. . . . The peaks of the mountains and the depths of the sea ech-
40 oed back the immortal voice, and her blessed mother heard her. Then sharp grief seized the mother's heart; she tore the headdress upon her ambrosial hair, and threw her dark veil down from both her shoulders; and like a bird she darted over land and sea, searching. None of the gods
45 or of mortal men would give her a true report, nor would any of the birds come to her as a true messenger.

For nine days then lady Deo wandered the earth, holding blazing torches in her hands; in her grief she touched neither ambrosia nor the
50 sweetness of nectar, nor did she bathe her body with water. But when the tenth day dawned Hecate, bearing light in her hands, encountered her and spoke to her this message: "Lady Demeter, bringer of seasons
55 and glorious gifts, who of the gods of heaven or of mortal men has taken Persephone and pained your own heart? I heard her voice, but did not see who it was. I am telling you everything promptly, and accurately."

60   So spoke Hecate. The daughter of fair-haired Rhea did not answer a word, but she immediately darted off with her, holding blazing torches in her hands, and they came to Helios, the viewer of gods and men. They stood before his horses and the divine goddess said, "Helios, as a
65 god, respect me, as a goddess, if ever in word or deed I have warmed your heart. The maiden whom I bore—sweetest blossom—beautiful—I heard her voice, sobbing, as if she were being raped, but I did not see her. But you survey from the bright heaven all the earth and the sea
70 with your rays; tell me accurately whether you have seen who of gods or mortal men has forced her and taken her away, all unwillingly, in my absence."

So she spoke, and the son of Hyperion answered her: "Lady

Demeter, daughter of fair-haired Rhea, you will know all: I have great re- 75
spect for you and pity you in your grief for your slim-ankled child: none
of the immortals is responsible except Zeus the cloud-gatherer, who has
granted to Hades his own brother that she be called his tender wife; and
he has taken her, screaming a loud cry, away on his horses down into 80
the misty darkness. So, goddess, stop your loud lament; you should not
rashly hold on to this boundless anger; Aidoneus, the designator of
many, is after all not an unsuitable son-in-law for you, since you have
the same mother and father; and his honor he gained when at the begin- 85
ning a division into three parts was made; and he dwells with those over
whom the lot made him king." When he had said this he called to his
horses, and at his command they bore the swift chariot like broad-
winged birds.

Then grief still more horrible and oppressive came upon her heart, 90
and in anger at Zeus, shrouded in clouds, she deserted the gatherings of
the gods and went far from Olympus to the cities and farms of men and
for a long time disguised her appearance. No man, no woman who saw 95
her recognized her, until she arrived at the home of clever Keleos, who
was the king of fragrant Eleusis at the time. At the spring Parthenion
where the citizens draw water in the shade of a towering olive tree she 100
sat by the side of the road in the guise of an old woman, one who is beyond the age of childbearing and the gifts of Aphrodite who bears the
garland of love, one who might be a nurse of royal children or governess
of important households. The daughters of Keleos of Eleusis saw her as 105
they came to draw water and carry it in bronze vessels to their father's
house. There were four of them, like goddesses in youthful bloom—
Kallidike, Klesidike, lovely Demo, and Kallithoe, the eldest of them all. 110
They did not recognize her, for gods are hard for mortals to see. They approached her and said, "Old woman, who are you? Why have you kept
away from the city and not approached the settlement? There in the
dusky houses there are women as old as you and younger, who would 115
treat you kindly in word and deed."

So they spoke, and the goddess mistress said in answer, "Dear children, daughters of womanly mothers, be of good cheer, and I will tell 120
you, for it is right to tell you the truth. The name my lady mother gave to
me is Doso. I have just come across the sea from Crete, forced by pirate
men who abducted me against my will. They brought their swift ship to 125
shore at Thorikos, and a crowd of women came on board from the land
and they all prepared their dinner by the ship's stern-cables. But my heart
had no desire for a pleasant supper; instead I got up secretly and escaped

130 those arrogant overlords across the dark countryside, so that they might
     not enjoy any profit from selling me. I wandered about until I arrived
     here; but I do not know what land it is nor which people dwell here. May
140 all the gods who dwell on Olympus grant you vigorous husbands and all
     the progeny they want; but pity me, maidens; dear children, help me
     come propitiously to some home of a man and a woman where I may pro-
145 vide the services of an aged woman for them: I could hold their infant
     child in my arms and nurse it well, I could keep house, make the master's
     bed in the inmost chamber, and instruct the women in their tasks."

145   So said the goddess, and the maiden Kallidike, most beautiful of
     Keleos's daughters, answered her, "Mother, we humans endure the
     gifts of the gods, even under grievous compulsion, for they are much
     mightier. I will explain it all to you clearly, and tell you the men who
150 hold the power of authority here, and who stand out in the government
     and direct the defense of the city with their counsels and decisions.
     There are Triptolemos the clever, Dioklos, Polyxeinos, Eumolpos the
155 blameless, Dolichos, and our father the manly one. Their wives manage
     everything in their households, and not one of them would dishonor
     you at first sight by making you depart from their houses. They will re-
160 ceive you, for you are godlike. If you wish, wait here while we go to our
     father's house and tell Metaneira our deep-belted mother all these
     things, and see whether she bids you come to our house and not search
     for another's. A favorite son, born to her late, is being nursed in the
165 strongly built palace; she prayed much for him, and rejoiced in him. If
     you would nurse him and he would reach adolescence, any woman
     would envy the sight of you, for she (viz. Metaneira) would give you so
     great a reward for nursing him."

170   So she spoke, and she nodded her head, and then they filled their
     shining jugs with water and carried them proudly. Soon they reached
     their father's great house, and quickly told their mother what they had
     seen and heard. She told them to go quickly and bid her come, at a vast
175 wage. As deer or heifers frolic across the meadow eating to their heart's
     content, so they darted along the road down the gulley, holding up the
     folds of their lovely gowns, and their hair streamed along their shoul-
     ders like saffron blossoms. They reached the spot near the road where
180 they had left the glorious goddess, and they led her to their father's
     house. She, grieved at heart, walked behind them with her head veiled,
     and the dark robe trailed along around the slender feet of the goddess.

         Soon they reached the house of Zeus-descended Keleos, and went
185 through the portico to the place where their lady mother was sitting be-

side a column of the carefully made chamber, holding her new baby in her lap. The girls ran to her, but Demeter trod upon the threshold, and her head reached the roof-beam, and she filled the doorway with a divine radiance. At this awe, reverence, and pale fear seized the woman. **190** She rose from her chair and urged her to be seated, but Demeter the bringer of seasons and glorious gifts did not wish to be seated on the gleaming chair, but silently cast down her beautiful eyes and waited until Iambe understood and set a jointed stool out for her, and threw a shin- **195** ing white fleece upon it. She sat down, holding her veil in front with her hands. For a long time she sat there on the stool sorrowfully, without speaking; and made no contact with anyone in word or gesture. Without smiling, without touching food or drink she sat, consumed with yearn- **200** ing for her daughter, until Iambe understood and made plenty of jokes and jests and made the holy Lady smile with kindly heart, and ever afterward she continues to delight her spirit. Then Metaneira filled a cup of **205** sweet wine and offered it to her, but she refused it, for she said it was not right for her to drink red wine. Instead she asked her to give her barley groats and water mixed with crusted pennyroyal to drink. She made the compound, the *kykeon,* as she commanded, and offered it to the god- **210** dess. Deo the greatly revered accepted it for the sake of the ceremony. . . . Fair-belted Metaneira began with these words, "Be of good cheer, woman; I do not expect that you are sprung from base stock, but from good; dignity and grace are manifest in your eyes, like those of **215** kings, stewards of the right. But we humans endure the gifts of the gods, even under grievous compulsion, for a yoke lies upon our neck. But now that you have come here, all that is mine shall be yours. Nurse this child for me, whom the immortals have given me, late-born and un- **220** expected, but much prayed for. If you would nurse him and he would reach adolescence, any woman would envy the sight of you, for I would give you so great a reward for nursing him."

Then Demeter of the fair crown said to her, "May you also be of good **225** cheer, woman, and may the gods grant you all good things; I willingly accept the child, as you bid me. I will nurse him, and I do not expect that he will be injured by nurse's incompetence, supernatural attacks, nor magical cuttings, for I know an antidote more mighty than the woodcut- **230** ter, and I know a fine preventative against malignant attacks."

When she had said this she received him with her immortal hands in her fragrant lap, and the mother's heart rejoiced. So she nursed the glorious son of clever Keleos, Demophon, whom fair-belted Metaneira bore, and he grew like a god, eating no food, being suckled on no milk, for **235**

Demeter would [feed and] anoint him with ambrosia, like the progeny of a god, and she breathed sweetly on him and held him in her lap. At night she would hide him like a fire-brand within the might of the flame,
240 without his parents' knowledge. It made them wonder greatly how he was so precocious, and why his appearance was like the gods'. She would have even made him ageless and deathless, if it had not been that fair-belted Metaneira foolishly kept watch one night and watched her
245 from her fragrant bed-chamber. She screamed and struck both her thighs in fear for her child and in a frenzy of mindlessness. Wailing, she said, "My child Demophon, the stranger woman is hiding you in the blazing fire, and is making grief and bitter sorrow for me."
250 So she spoke, lamenting, and the divine goddess heard her. Demeter of the beautiful crown was amazed at her; with her immortal hands she put from her the dear child whom Metaneira had borne, all unexpected, in the palace, and threw him at her feet, drawing him out of the fire, terri-
255 bly angry at heart, and at the same time she said to fair-belted Metaneira, "Humans are short-sighted, stupid, ignorant of the share of good or evil which is coming to them. You by your foolishness have hurt him beyond curing. Let my witness be the oath of the gods sworn by the intractable
260 water of Styx, that I would have made your son deathless and ageless all his days, and given him imperishable honor. But now it is not possible to ward off death and destruction. Still he will have imperishable honor for-ever, since he stood on my knees and slept in my arms; in due season, as
265 the years pass around, the children of the Eleusinians will conduct in his honor war (games) and the terrible battle-cry with each other for ever and ever. I am Demeter, the Venerable, ready as the greatest boon and
270 joy for immortals and mortals. So now let the whole people build me a great temple, and an altar beneath it, below the city and the towering wall, above Kallirhoe on the ridge which juts forth. I myself will estab-lish rites so that henceforth you may celebrate them purely and propiti-ate my mind."
275 With these words the goddess altered size and form and sloughed off old age; beauty wafted about her. A lovely fresh smell radiated from her lovely gown and the radiance from the skin of the immortal goddess shone afar. Her blonde hair flowed down over her shoulders, and the
280 sturdy house was filled with light like a flash of lightning. She went out through the palace. As for the other, her knees gave way, and for a long time she was speechless. She did not even remember the child, her favor-ite, to pick him up from the floor. His sisters heard his piteous crying,
285 and they leapt down from their well-covered beds. Then one of them

took the child in her hands and put him in her lap, one kindled a fire,
and another hurried on gentle feet to rouse her mother out of the fragrant chamber. Crowding around they washed him, covering him with
love as he squirmed; his heart was not comforted, however, for less skill-   290
ful nurses and nurse maids were holding him now.

All night long the women, quaking with fear, propitiated the glorious
goddess. As soon as dawn appeared they gave a full report to wide-
ruling Keleos, as Demeter of the beautiful garlands commanded. He   295
summoned the people from their many boundaries and ordered them to
build an elaborate temple to fair-haired Demeter and an altar on the
ridge which juts forth. They obeyed him straightway, and hearkened to
him as he spoke, and started to build as he commanded. And it   300
grew at the dispensation of the divinity. When they finished and ceased
from their toil, each person went back to his home. Blonde Demeter
stayed there, seated far from all the blessed gods, wasting with grief for
her deep-belted daughter.

She made the most terrible, most oppressive year for men upon the   305
nourishing land, and the earth sent up no seed, as fair-garlanded
Demeter hid it. Cattle drew the many curved plows in vain over the
fields, and much white barley seed fell useless on the earth. By now she
would have destroyed the entire race of men by grievous famine, and de-   310
prived those who dwell on Olympus of the glorious honor of offerings
and sacrifices, if Zeus had not taken notice and taken counsel with his
mind. First he roused gold-winged Iris to summon fair-haired Demeter,   315
of the very desirable beauty. So he spoke, and she obeyed Zeus wrapped
in clouds, the son of Kronos. She rushed down the middle and arrived at
the citadel of fragrant Eleusis. In the temple she found Demeter dark-
clad, and addressed her with winged words. "Demeter, father Zeus who   320
understands imperishable things summons you to come among the race
of the immortal gods. So come, and let my message from Zeus not be
fruitless."

So she spoke in supplication, but her heart was not persuaded. Therefore the Father sent out the blessed, ever-living gods one after another,   325
and they went in turn and implored her, and offered her many fine gifts
and whatever honors she might choose among the immortal gods.
None, however, was able to persuade the heart and mind of the angry
goddess. She rejected their speeches firmly, and claimed that she would   330
never set foot upon fragrant Olympus, nor allow any fruit to grow on the
earth, until she saw with her eyes the beautiful face of her daughter.

When Zeus the loud-crashing, the wide-voiced one, heard this, he

335 sent Hermes the slayer of Argos with his golden wand to Erebos, to use smooth words on Hades and lead pure Persephone out of the misty darkness into the light to join the deities, in order that her mother might see

340 her with her eyes and turn from her anger. Hermes obeyed, and eagerly rushed down under the recesses of the earth, leaving the seat of Olympus. He found the Lord inside his house, seated on couches with his modest and very unwilling wife, yearning for her mother. . . .

345 The mighty slayer of Argos came near and said, "Dark-haired Hades, ruler of the departed, Father Zeus has ordered me to lead glorious Persephone out of Erebos to join them, in order that her mother might

350 see her with her eyes and cease from her anger and terrible wrath, since she is contriving a tremendous deed, to destroy the fragile race of earthborn men, hiding the seed under the earth and obliterating the honors of the immortals. Her anger is terrible, she has no contact with the gods,

355 but sits apart inside her fragrant temple, holding the rocky citadel of Eleusis."

So he spoke, and Aidoneus the lord of the underworld smiled with his brows, and did not disobey the injunctions of Zeus the king.

360 Promptly he gave the command to diligent Persephone: "Go, Persephone, to your dark-clad mother, and keep gentle the strength and heart in your breast. Do not be despondent to excess beyond all others. I shall not be an inappropriate husband for you among the immortals; I

365 am a brother of Father Zeus. Being there, you will rule over all that lives and moves, enjoying the greatest honors among the immortals. And there shall be punishment forever on those who act unjustly and who do not propitiate your might with sacrifices, performing the pious acts and offering appropriate gifts."

370 So he spoke, and Persephone the discreet was glad, and swiftly leapt up for joy. But he gave her a honey-sweet pomegranate seed to eat, having secretly passed it around (himself?), so that she might not stay forever there by modest dark-clad Demeter. Aidoneus, designator of many,

375 harnessed the immortal horses in front of the golden chariot, and she stepped on the chariot; beside her the mighty slayer of Argos took the reins and a whip in his hands and drove out of the palace. The pair of

380 horses flew willingly. They finished the long journey quickly. Neither sea nor rivers nor grassy glens nor mountain peaks held back the rush of the immortal horses; they went above them, and cut through the high air. He drove them where Demeter of the fair crown waited in front of

385 her fragrant temple, and he stopped them there. Seeing them, she darted up like a maenad in the woods on a thick-shaded mountain. . . .

(Demeter asked Persephone if she had eaten anything in the under-

world. If not,) "you will come up and dwell with me and Zeus of the   395
dark clouds and be honored by all the immortals. But if you have tasted
anything, then you shall go back down and dwell there for the third part
of the season, and for the other two, here with me and the other immor-   400
tals. Whenever the earth blossoms with all the sweet-smelling flowers of
spring, then you will come back up from the misty darkness, a great wonder to gods and to mortal men. But what trick did the powerful host of
many use to deceive you?"

Persephone, the exceedingly beautiful, gave her this response: "I will   405
tell you, Mother, everything accurately. When the swift slayer of Argos
came to me from Father Zeus and the others in heaven with the message
to come out of Erebos, so that seeing me with your eyes you might cease   410
from your anger and terrible wrath, I leapt up for joy. But he secretly in-
sinuated a pomegranate seed, honey-sweet food, and though I was unwilling, he compelled me by force to taste it. How he snatched me away
through the clever plan of Zeus and carried me off, down into the re-   415
cesses of the earth, I will tell you and I will go through it all as you ask.
We were all there in the lovely meadow—Leukippe, Phaino, Elektre
(Electra), Ianthe, Melite, Iache, Rhodeia, Kallirhoe, Melobosis, Tyche,   420
Okyrhoe of the flowering face, Chryseis, Ianeira, Akaste, Admete,
Rhodope, Plouto, charming Kalypso, Styx, Ouranie, lovely Galaxaure,
Pallas the inciter of battles, Artemis the shooter of arrows—playing and   425
picking the lovely flowers, a profusion of gentle saffron blossoms, iris,
hyacinth, rose buds, and lilies, a marvel to see, and narcissus, which the
broad land grew like saffron. Full of joy, I was picking them, but the
earth under me moved, and the powerful Lord, the host of many, leapt   430
out. And he took me under the earth on his golden chariot, against my
will, and I screamed loudly with my voice. Grieved though I am, I am
telling you the whole truth."

Then with minds in concord they spent the whole day warming their
hearts and minds, showering much love on each other, and her mind   435
found respite from its griefs, as they gave and received joys from each
other. And there came near them Hecate of the glistening veil, and she
also showered much love on the daughter of holy Demeter, and ever
since she has been her attendant and lady-in-waiting.   440

Zeus the loud-crashing, the wide-voiced one, sent fair-haired Rhea as
a messenger to them, to bring dark-gowned Demeter among the race of
the gods; he promised to give her whatever honors she might choose
among the immortal gods. He granted that her daughter should spend   445
the third portion of the year in its cycle down in the misty darkness, but
the other two with her mother and the other immortals.

So he spoke, and the goddess obeyed the biddings of Zeus. Promptly
450 she darted along the peaks of Olympus, and came to the Rarian plain,
the life-bringing udder of plough-land formerly, but at that time not life-
bringing at all, as it stood all barren and leafless. The white barley was
concealed according to the plans of fair-ankled Demeter, but at this time
455 it was about to grow shaggy with waves of grain as it became spring. In
the field the rich furrows were to be loaded with the grain, and they
were to be bound in sheaves. Here she first alighted from the boundless
aether, and they saw each other gladly, and rejoiced in their hearts.

460 Rhea of the glistening veil said to her, "Come here, child. Zeus the
loud-crashing, the wide-voiced one, summons you to come among the
race of the immortal gods, and he has promised to give whatever honors
you might choose among the immortal gods. He has granted that your
daughter will spend the third portion of the year in its cycle down in the
465 misty darkness, but the other two with you and the other immortals. So
has he promised, and nodded his head in affirmation. Go, now, my
child, and obey; do not be obdurately angry at Zeus of the dark clouds
but give prompt increase to the fruit, bringer of life to men."

470 So she spoke, and Demeter of the fair crown obeyed. Promptly she
sent up fruit on the rich-soiled fields, and the whole broad land was
loaded with leaves and flowers. She went to the royal stewards of the
right and to Triptolemos, Diokles the driver of horses, mighty
475 Eumolpos, and Keleos the leader of the people. She showed the
tendance of the holy things and explicated the rites to them all, to
Triptolemos, to Polyxeinos, and to Diokles—sacred rites, which it is forbidden to transgress, to inquire into, or to speak about, for great rever-
480 ence of the gods constrains their voice. Blessed of earthbound men is he
who has seen these things, but he who dies without fulfilling the holy
things, and he who is without a share of them, has no claim ever on such
blessings, even when departed down to the moldy darkness.

When the divine goddess had ordained all this, she went to Olympus
485 among the assembly of the other gods. And there they dwell, sacred and
reverent, with Zeus who revels in thunder. Greatly blessed of earthbound men is he whom they propitiously love: to him they promptly
send to the hearth of his great house Ploutos (Wealth), who gives abundance to mortal men.

490 Now, ye that hold the people of fragrant Eleusis, and sea-girt Paros
and rocky Antron, Lady mistress Deo, bringer of seasons and glorious
gifts, thou thyself and Persephone, the exceedingly beautiful, do ye be-
495 stow a heartwarming livelihood in exchange for my song. Now I shall recall thee and also another song.

HERODOTUS, *HISTORY*, Book 8.65

The fifth-century B.C.E. Greek historian Herodotus (d. ca. 425) has been both acclaimed as the father of history and damned as the falsifier of history for his work on the history of the Persian Wars. Born within a family from Halicarnassus in Asia Minor, young Herodotus lived through many of the events he later described in his *History*. The book he created is artful and entertaining, a delightful narration based upon travel and research and enlivened through humor and legend.

In Book 8 of his *History*, Herodotus recounts a story concerning the Iacchos procession in the Eleusinian mysteries. After Athens assumed jurisdiction over the mysteries, the celebration included a parade along the Sacred Way from Athens to Eleusis. The joyful initiates, in ritual garb, bore the sacred objects back to Eleusis and uttered the cry of Iacchos on the way. Iacchos sometimes was personified as a god and even identified with Bacchos (Dionysos), probably because of the similarity of their names.

This translation of the *History* is from Aubrey de Sélincourt, *Herodotus: The Histories* (Baltimore: Penguin, 1954).

There is a story which used to be told by Dicaeus, the son of 65
Theocydes, an Athenian exile who had made a name for himself in Persia. After the evacuation of Attica, when the Persian troops were devastating the countryside, this person happened to be in the plain of Thria with Demaratus the Spartan. Noticing a cloud of dust, such as might have been raised by an army of thirty thousand men on the march, coming from the direction of Eleusis, they were wondering what troops they could be, when they suddenly heard the sound of voices. Dicaeus thought he recognized the Iacchos song, which is sung at the mysteries, but Demaratus, who was unfamiliar with the religious ceremonial of Eleusis, asked his companion whose voices they were. "Sir," Dicaeus answered, "without any doubt some dreadful disaster is about to happen to the king's army. There is not a man left in Attica; so the voice we heard must clearly be not of this world—it is a divine voice, coming from Eleusis to bring help to the Athenians and their friends. If it descends upon the Peloponnese, there will be danger for the king and for his army; if it moves towards the ships at Salamis, Xerxes may well lose his fleet. Every year the Athenians celebrate a festival in honor of the Mother and the Maid, and anyone who wishes, from Athens or elsewhere, may be initiated in the mysteries; the sound you heard was the Iacchos song which is always sung at that festival."

"Do not breathe a word of this to anybody," said Demaratus. "If it should reach the ears of the king, you would lose your head, and neither I nor anyone else in the world could save you. So hold your tongue—the gods will see to the king's army."

While Demaratus was speaking, the cloud of dust, from which the mysterious voice had issued, rose high into the air and drifted away towards Salamis, where the Greek fleet was stationed. By this the two men knew that the naval power of Xerxes was destined to be destroyed. Such was Dicaeus's story, and he used to appeal to Demaratus and others to witness the truth of it.

ARISTOPHANES, *THE FROGS*, Lines 311–459

The comic playwright Aristophanes produced his play *The Frogs* in 405 B.C.E., when Athens was caught in the last vicious throes of the Peloponnesian War (431–404 B.C.E.) Awarded first prize in the Lenaia (the Athenian festival of Dionysos that was celebrated in the Greek month Gamelion, or January/February), *The Frogs* presents Dionysos, the god of drama, visiting the great departed playwrights Aeschylus and Euripides in the underworld and judging a dramatic contest between the two eminent poets. Dionysos declares Aeschylus the winner, and at last he escorts the playwright from his chair of tragedy in the underworld back to Athens, so that the poet may restore artistic excellence to the beleaguered literary life of late fifth-century Athens.

Among those Dionysos encounters in the realm of Hades are initiates into the Eleusinian mysteries, who are still celebrating the mysteries in death as they did in life. Robed in white and bearing torches, the initiates are depicted singing and dancing together in the Iacchos procession and enticing the slave Xanthias with the smell of pork from the pigs sacrificed in the mysteries.

This translation is by Richard Lattimore, *The Frogs* (New York: New American Library, Mentor, 1962).

(Flute within.)

DIONYSOS

Hey, you.

XANTHIAS
    What is it?

DIONYSOS
        Did you hear?

XANTHIAS

        Did I hear what?

DIONYSOS

Flutes being blown.

XANTHIAS

      I heard them too, and there's a crackle and smell of torches.
Seems like it's mysteries going on.

DIONYSOS

Let's just quietly squat where we are, and listen in.   **315**

CHORUS

(Off.)
Iacchos Iacchos
Iacchos O Iacchos

XANTHIAS

That's what I thought it was, master. The Initiates.
Remember, he told us, their playground's hereabouts.
They sing the Iacchos song by that noted theologian,   **320**
Diagoras.

DIONYSOS

I think you're right, but still we'd better sit quiet here
until we find out just exactly what goes on.

CHORUS

(In white, as Initiates.)
Iacchos! Well beloved in these pastures O indwelling
Iacchos O Iacchos   **325**
come to me come with dance steps down the meadow
to your worshiping companions
with the fruited, the lifebursting,
the enmyrtled and enwreathed garland on your brows,   **330**
and bold-footed stamp out the sprightly measure
of the dancing that's your pleasure,
of the dancing full of graces, full of light and sweet and
sacred for your dedicated chosen ones.   **335**

XANTHIAS

Demeter's daughter, Persephone, holy lady and queen,
ineffable fragrance wafts upon me. Roasting pigs!

DIONYSOS

If I promise you a handful of tripes, will you shut up?

CHORUS

340 Let flames fly as the torch tosses in hand's hold
     Iacchos O Iacchos
     star of fire in the high rites of the night time.
     And the field shines in the torch light,
345 and the old men's knees are limber,
     and they shake off aches and miseries,
     and the years of their antiquity drop from them
     in the magical measure.
350 Oh, torch-in-hand-shining.
     Iacchos go before us to the marsh flowers and the meadow
     and the blest revel of dances.
     (*Parabasis. The Chorus advances down stage and the leader addresses the
     audience directly.*)

LEADER

     All now must observe the sacred silence: we ban from our choruses any
355 whose brain cannot fathom the gist of our wit; whose hearts and feelings
          are dirty;
       who never has witnessed and never partaken in genuine cult of the
          Muses,
       who knows not the speech of bullgobble Kratinos, who knows not the
          Bacchic fraternity,
       who laughs at cheap jokes that should not have been made, who writes
          such stuff at the wrong time,
       who stirs up sedition dissension and hate, who does not like the Athe-
          nians,
360 who hopes to make money out of our quarrels and lights them and fans
          them to fury,
       who holds high office and then takes bribes when the city is tossed in the
          tempest,
       who sells out a ship or a fort to the enemy, smuggling our secret intelli-
          gence
       from Aegina over to Epidauros, like any goddam taxcollecting
       Thorykion, with the oarpads and sails and pitch that was meant for our
          navy,
365 who goes on his rounds and collects contributions to finance the
          enemy's war fleet,
       who, humming his cyclical verses the while, uses Hecate's shrine as a
          backhouse,
       who gets up to speak in the public assembly and nibbles at the fees of the
          poets

just because they once made a fool of him in the plays that our fathers established.
Such men I forbid, and again I forbid, and again I forbid them a third
time,
let them get up and go from our choral mysteries.   370
               All others, strike up the singing
and dance of our holy and nightlong revels befitting this solemn occasion.

CHORUS
(*Slowly.*)
Advance all now, firmly
into the flower strewn hollows
of meadow fields. Stamp strongly
and jeer and sneer
and mock and be outrageous.   375
For all are well stuffed full with food.

Advance advance, sing strongly
our Lady of Salvation
and march to match your singing.   380
She promises
to save our land in season
for all Thorykion can do.

LEADER
Come now and alter the tune of the song for the queen of the bountiful
seasons;
sing loud, sing long, and dance to the song for Demeter our lady and
goddess.

CHORUS
Demeter, mistress of grave and gay,
stand by now and help me win.   385
Protect this chorus. It is your own.
Let me in safety all this day
play on and do my dances.
Help me say what will make them grin.
Help me say what will make them think.   390
Help me say what will make me win
in your own festival today
and wear the victor's garland.

LEADER
Change the tune.
395 Sing to the pretty god of the time   summon him to join us.
We have a sacred way to go   and he goes with us.

CHORUS
Iacchos, well-beloved spirit of song, O be
my leader and march along with me
this holy way.
400 Bring me to Eleusis swift and musically.
To you I pray.
Iacchos lover of dancing help me on my way.

You split my shirt to make them laugh and boo.
405 You cut my cheap little shoes in two.
My rags flap on me.
You know how to make do.
Wartime economy.
Iacchos lover of dancing help me on my way.

I saw a sweet little girl in the crowd down there.
410 As she leaned forward, her dress, I swear,
bust open a trifle
and I was happy to stare
at a bosomy eyeful.
Iacchos lover of dancing help me on my way.

DIONYSOS
I've always been a fellow who's good
at follow-my-leader; I gladly would
go down and help you play with her.

XANTHIAS
415   I would if I could.

CHORUS
Shall we now, all together
make fun of Archedemos?
Seven years he tries to naturalize and still he hasn't made it.

Now he's a leading citizen
420 among the upworld corpses.
Nobody up there can claim a similar fame—for being a bastard.

And Kleistenes, they tell me,
sits mourning among the tombstones,
and tears the hair from his you-know-where, and batters his jawbones.

He was seen, in his usual posture   425
in tears for his vanished sweetheart—
the dear little friend of his after-end, Sebinos of Anaphlystos.

And Kallias they say,
the son of Ponyplay,
wears a panoply and has gone to sea and the ships with a lionskin over   430
    his hips.

DIONYSOS
Can any of you guys tell
me where Pluto happens to dwell?
We're visiting firemen. Never been here before.

CHORUS
Stop bothering me so.
You haven't got far to go.   435
He lives right here. Walk up and knock at the door.

DIONYSOS
Boy! Pick up the stuff again.

XANTHIAS
What's the matter with this guy?
Pick up, pick up, it's nothing but pick up bundles.

CHORUS
Forward, now   440
to the goddess's sacred circle-dance to the grove that's in blossom
and play on the way for we belong to the company of the elect,
and I shall go where the girls go and I shall go with the women   445
who keep the nightlong rite of the goddess and carry their sacred torch.

Let us go where the roses grow
and fields are in flower,
in the way that is ours alone,   450
playing our blessed play
which the prosperous Fates today
ordain for our playing.

On us alone the sun shines here
and the happy daylight,   455

for we are Initiates, we
treat honorably
all strangers who are here
and our own people.
(*The white-robed Chorus file off.*)

PLUTARCH OF CHAERONEA, *PROGRESS IN VIRTUE (DE PROFECTU IN VIRTUTE)*, 10 (81DE)

One of the most significant sources of information about cultural and religious affairs in the world of Greco-Roman antiquity is the prolific author Plutarch of Chaeronea (b. before 50–d. after 120 c.e.). A writer and lecturer of note, Plutarch also was a well-educated, well-traveled student of ancient religion, and he functioned as priest at Delphi for some three decades.

In the following excerpt from his moral essay on *Progress in Virtue*, Plutarch compares progress in philosophy with initiation into the mysteries (by which he means the Eleusinian mysteries in particular). At the beginning of the ceremonies, the crowd of initiates is quite disorderly, but when the *dromena* and the *deiknymena* commence, the initiates become silent, filled with awe. So also with those who gain insight into philosophy: they enter an inner sanctum and behold a great light (*mega phos*).

This translation of Plutarch is from Frank Cole Babbitt, *Plutarch's Moralia: I* (Loeb Classical Library, 1927).

10 Just as persons who are being initiated into the mysteries throng together at the outset amid tumult and shouting, and jostle against one another, but when the holy rites are being performed and disclosed the people are immediately attentive in awe and silence, so too at the beginning of philosophy: about its portals also you will see great tumult and talking and boldness, as some boorishly and violently try to jostle their way towards the repute it bestows; but he who has succeeded in getting inside, and has seen a great light, as though a shrine were opened, adopts another bearing of silence and amazement, and "humble and orderly attends upon" reason as upon a god.

DIODORUS SICULUS, *LIBRARY OF HISTORY*, Book 5.47.1–49.6

At Samothrace, an island in the northern part of the Aegean Sea, the mysteries of the Kabeiroi were celebrated. The Kabeiroi were fertility gods whose worship was linked, variously, to that of Demeter, Dionysos, Hermes, and the Dioskouroi ("sons of Zeus," Kastor and Polydeukes [Pollux]). They were also called the Great Gods; compare the use of this title in the Rule of the Andanian Mysteries in Chapter 3. According to one tradition, the names of the Kabeiroi are Axieros, Axiokersa, Axiokersos, and Kadmilos, and they are identified with Demeter, Persephone, Hades, and Hermes, respectively (scholiast on Apollonius Rhodius, *Argonautica*, 1.917). The first three of these words seem to be formed with the honorific epithet *Axios*, "worthy," prefixed to the names Eros, Kersa, and Kersos.

In Book 5 of his *Library of History*, written in the first century B.C.E., Diodorus Siculus gives his description of the island of Samothrace. According to Diodorus the native deities offered protection to seafarers from early times, and hence the mythical inhabitants of the island began the custom of venerating the Samothracian gods. Particularly noteworthy in Diodorus's account is the syncretistic manner in which he introduces a variety of divine figures into the story of Iasion and the founding of the mysteries.

This translation of Diodorus Siculus is from C. H. Oldfather, *Diodorus of Sicily: III* (Loeb Classical Library, 1939). For an elegant report of the archaeological excavations at Samothrace undertaken by the Institute of Fine Arts of New York University, see Karl Lehmann, ed., *Samothrace*, Bollingen Series, no. 60 (New York: Pantheon, 1958–). The first volume, edited by Naphtali Lewis, contains a convenient collection of the ancient literary sources that discuss Samothrace.

W e shall now give an account of the islands which lie in the neighbor- 47.1 hood of Greece and in the Aegean Sea, beginning with Samothrace. This island, according to some, was called Samos in ancient times, but when the island now known as Samos came to be settled, because the names were the same, the ancient Samos came to be called Samothrace from the land of Thrace which lies opposite it. It was settled by men who were 2 sprung from the soil itself; consequently no tradition has been handed down regarding who were the first men and leaders on the island. But some say that in ancient days it was called Saonnesus and that it received the name of Samothrace because of the settlers who emigrated to it from both Samos and Thrace. The first and original inhabitants used 3 an ancient language which was peculiar to them and of which many words are preserved to this day in the ritual of their sacrifices. And the Samothracians have a story that, before the floods which befell other peoples, a great one took place among them, in the course of which the outlet at the Cyanean Rocks was first rent asunder and then the Hellespont.

4 For the Pontus, which had at the time the form of a lake, was so swollen by the rivers which flow into it, that, because of the great flood which had poured into it, its waters burst forth violently into the Hellespont and flooded a large part of the coast of Asia and made no small amount of the level part of the land of Samothrace into a sea; and this is the reason, we are told, why in later times fishermen have now and then brought up in their nets the stone capitals of columns, since even cities

5 were covered by the inundation. The inhabitants who had been caught by the flood, the account continues, ran up to the higher regions of the island; and when the sea kept rising higher and higher, they prayed to the native gods, and since their lives were spared, to commemorate their rescue they set up boundary stones about the entire circuit of the island and dedicated altars upon which they offer sacrifices even to the present day. For these reasons it is patent that they inhabited Samothrace before the flood.

48.1 After the events we have described one of the inhabitants of the island, a certain Saon, who was a son, as some say, of Zeus and Nymphe, but, according to others, of Hermes and Rhene, gathered into one body the peoples who were dwelling in scattered habitations and established laws for them; and he was given the name Saon after the island, but the multitude of the people he distributed among five tribes which he

2 named after his sons. And while the Samothracians were living under a government of this kind, they say that there were born in that land to Zeus and Electra, who was one of the Atlantids, Dardanus and Iasion

3 and Harmonia. Of these children Dardanus, who was a man who entertained great designs and was the first to make his way across to Asia in a make-shift boat, founded at the outset a city called Dardanus, organized the kingdom which lay about the city which was called Troy at a later time, and called the peoples Dardanians after himself. They say also that he ruled over many nations throughout Asia and that the Dardani who dwell beyond Thrace were colonists sent forth by him. But Zeus desired

4 that the other of his two sons might also attain to honor, and so he instructed him in the initiatory rite of the mysteries, which had existed on the island since ancient times but was at that time, so to speak, put in his hands; it is not lawful, however, for any but the initiated to hear about the mysteries. And Iasion is reputed to have been the first to initiate strangers into them and by this means to bring the initiatory rite to high

5 esteem. And after this Cadmus, the son of Agenor, came in the course of his quest for Europe to the Samothracians, and after participating in the initiation he married Harmonia, who was the sister of Iasion and not, as the Greeks recount in their mythologies, the daughter of Ares.

This wedding of Cadmus and Harmonia was the first, we are told, for **49.1** which the gods provided the marriage-feast, and Demeter, becoming enamored of Iasion, presented him with the fruit of the grain, Hermes gave a lyre, Athena the renowned necklace and a robe and a flute, and Electra the sacred rites of the Great Mother of the Gods, as she is called, together with cymbals and kettledrums and the instruments of her ritual; and Apollo played upon the lyre and the Muses upon their flutes, and the rest of the gods spoke them fair and gave the pair their aid in the celebration of the wedding. After this Cadmus, they say, in accordance with **2** the oracle he had received, founded Thebes in Boeotia, while Iasion married Kybele and begat Korybas. And after Iasion had been removed into the circle of the gods, Dardanus and Kybele and Korybas conveyed to Asia the sacred rites of the Mother of the Gods and removed with them to Phrygia. Thereupon Kybele, joining herself to the first Olympus, **3** begat Alke and called the goddess Kybele after herself; and Korybas gave the name of Korybantes to all who, in celebrating the rites of his mother, acted like men possessed, and married Thebe, the daughter of Kilix. In like manner he also transferred the flute from Samothrace to **4** Phrygia and to Lyrnessus the lyre which Hermes gave and which at a later time Achilles took for himself when he sacked that city. To Iasion and Demeter, according to the story the myths relate, was born Ploutos (Wealth), but the reference is, as a matter of fact, to the wealth of the grain, which was presented to Iasion because of Demeter's association with him at the time of the wedding of Harmonia. Now the details of the **5** initiatory rite are guarded among the matters not to be divulged and are communicated to the initiates alone; but the fame has traveled wide of how these gods appear to mankind and bring unexpected aid to those initiates of theirs who call upon them in the midst of perils. The claim is **6** also made that men who have taken part in the mysteries become more pious and more just and better in every respect than they were before. And this is the reason, we are told, why the most famous both of the ancient heroes and of the demi-gods were eagerly desirous of taking part in the initiatory rite; and in fact Jason and the Dioskoroi, and Heracles and Orpheus as well, after their initiation attained success in all the campaigns they undertook, because these gods appeared to them.

HERODOTUS, *HISTORY*, Book 2.51

In another excerpt Herodotus provides a few observations on the mysteries of the Kabeiroi at Samothrace. Herodotus articulates his familiar theory of the Egyptian origin of Greek religious practice but suggests that the Greek custom of portraying Hermes in an ithyphallic fashion is an exception to this theory. Herodotus's reference to the ithyphallic statues at Samothrace is confirmed by the Christian author Hippolytus in his *Refutation of All Heresies*, 5.8.10, in which he claims that at Samothrace there stand two statues of naked men with hands stretched upward and phalli erect.

This translation is from Aubrey de Sélincourt, *Herodotus: The Histories* (Baltimore: Penguin, 1954).

51 These practices, then, and others which I will speak of later, were borrowed by the Greeks from Egypt. This is not the case, however, with the Greek custom of making images of Hermes with the phallus erect; it was the Athenians who took this from the Pelasgians, and from the Athenians the custom spread to the rest of Greece. For just at the time when the Athenians were assuming Hellenic nationality, the Pelasgians joined them, and thus first came to be regarded as Greeks. Anyone will know what I mean if he is familiar with the mysteries of the Kabeiroi—rites which the men of Samothrace learned from the Pelasgians, who lived in that island before they moved to Attica, and communicated the mysteries to the Athenians. This will show that the Athenians were the first Greeks to make statues of Hermes with the erect phallus, and that they learned the practice from the Pelasgians—who explained it by a certain religious doctrine, the nature of which is made clear in the Samothracian mysteries.

LUCIAN OF SAMOSATA, *ALEXANDER THE FALSE PROPHET*, 38–43

During the second century C.E. a self-acclaimed prophet, Alexander of Abonoteichos (a small town near Paphlagonia, in northern Asia Minor), brought forward a new incarnation of the Greek god Asklepios in the form of a marvelous snake, Glykon. Glykon appeared as a large serpent that had a face with human features, and he functioned as the divine sponsor of an oracular cult and mystery religion of considerable fame.

Alexander's contemporary, Lucian of Samosata, was asked by a friend to write an account of the career of Alexander, and Lucian proceeded to compose a scathing, satirical indictment of the man in *Alexander the False Prophet*. Alexander was a fraud and an imposter who used bogus religion to deceive the gullible and obtain for himself wealth and sexual pleasure. The divine Glykon in the bosom of Alexander (cp. Clement of Alexandria, *Exhortation to the Greeks*, 2.16) was only the body of a snake with a lifelike mask, and the supposed revelations of Asklepios were nothing more than the statements of an associate of Alexander who was hidden outside and was speaking through a tube.

This selection from *Alexander the False Prophet* is from Lionel Casson, *Selected Satires of Lucian* (New York: Norton, 1968). This excerpt portrays the mystery ceremonies of Alexander and Glykon with images and terms familiar from the Eleusinian mysteries. As in the Eleusinian rites at Athens, a public proclamation banned certain people from the ceremonies, and those who did participate in the torchlit parades were led by priests ("garlic-reeking Paphlagonian clodhoppers") vaguely reminiscent of the sacred dignitaries from the Eleusinian families of the Eumolpidai and the Kerykes.

Also aimed at the Italian trade was the following scheme. He worked 38 up a mystery ceremony of his own, complete with torchbearers and presiding priests. It lasted three whole days in a row. On the first there was, as at Athens, an initial proclamation. Here it took the form: "If any atheist, Christian, or Epicurean has come here to spy, let him be gone. And may the true believers of the god conduct their rites with heaven's blessing." Immediately thereafter the ceremony led off with an expulsion ritual. Alexander opened it with the words, "Christians, begone!" and the crowd responded with one voice, "Epicureans, begone!" Then came the acting out of Leto in labor, of the birth of Apollo, his mating with Coronis, and the birth of Asklepios. On the second day there was the birth and presentation of the god Glykon. On the third day came the 39 marriage of Podalirius and Alexander's mother; this was called Torch Day, so torches were burned. The finale was Alexander's love affair with Selene and the birth of Rutilianus's wife. Alexander alias Endymion was torchbearer (*dadouchos*) and officiating priest (hierophant). He lay in the center of the scene, ostensibly asleep. Flying down to him from the roof, as if from heaven, came, not Selene, but Rutilia, a beauty married to one of the imperial procurators. She was actually in love with Alexander and he with her, so there, with everybody around, before her poor husband's very eyes, the pair exchanged kisses and embraces. And, if there hadn't been lots of torches burning, Alexander probably would have carried on some under-the-dress lovemaking as well. A little later he reappeared in the officiating priest's regalia and, amid a dead silence, cried in a loud voice, "Hail, Glykon!" Whereupon the garlic-reeking Paphlagonian clodhoppers who were presumably his Eumolpidai and Kerykes responded with, "Hail, Alexander!"

At frequent intervals during the torchlight parades and mystic jig- 40 ging he made sure his thigh was bared so everyone could see it was golden; apparently he had wrapped around it a piece of gilded leather which glittered in the lamplight. A pair of brainless academes once undertook to do research on whether his golden thigh meant he actually had Pythagoras's soul or one similar to it. They brought the problem to Alexander himself, and Lord Glykon settled all difficulties with an oracle:

> Sometimes the soul of Pythagoras waxeth and sometimes it waneth.
> Prophets, however, are blessed with a fragment of heavenly spirit
> Sent by the father of gods as an aid to all god-fearing mortals.
> Homeward to Zeus doth it hasten when Zeus's swift thunderbolt strikes it.

41   Alexander used to issue warnings to the public to refrain from pederasty on the grounds that it was a sin. Yet he himself, noble soul, worked out the following scheme. He ordered the cities in Paphlagonia and Pontus to send choirboys who for a three-year period would be quartered at his house and sing for the god. They were to be carefully screened, and only those judged perfect in family qualifications and age, and unrivaled in looks, were to be sent. Alexander kept those boys behind closed doors and used them like so many slaves, sleeping with them and behaving like a drunken degenerate with them. He had made it a general rule never to greet anyone over eighteen on the lips or welcome them with a kiss. They got his hand to kiss; his mouth was reserved for the fresh flowers, to whom he gave the official title "Receivers
42   of the Kiss." Such were the pleasures he enjoyed at the expense of the poor dupes about him; life was a continuous round of ruining young women and sleeping with young boys. All husbands without exception considered it a most desirable mark of distinction to have the prophet notice their wives, and, if he decided they were worth a kiss, the poor devils were sure their households would be swamped by a wave of good fortune. Many of the wives boasted of having had children by him—and their own husbands were willing to testify they spoke the truth.

43   I'd like to quote for you a dialogue that took place between Glykon and a certain Sacerdos from Tium, whose intellectual capacity you'll gauge from the questions he asked. The whole thing was inscribed in letters of gold on a wall of Sacerdos's house in Tium, which is where I read it:

> "Tell me, Lord Glykon, who are you?"
> "I am the new Asklepios."
> "What do you mean? Different from the former one?"
> "You are not allowed to know that."

"How many years will you remain with us and give us your prophecies?"

"One thousand and three."

"Then where will you go?"

"To Bactria and the lands there. For foreigners, too, must reap the benefits of my presence among them."

"Does your forefather Apollo still abide in the other seats of prophecy, at Didyma and Clarus and Delphi, or are the oracles now issued from there all false?"

"Do not seek to know this either. It is forbidden."

"What will I become after this life?"

"A camel, then a horse, and then a wise man and prophet as great as Alexander."

3
The Andanian Mysteries of Messenia

3
The Andanian Mysteries of Messenia

The ancient town of Andania was located in the region of Messenia in the southwestern part of the Greek Peloponnesus. Here the Andanian mysteries were celebrated. The traveler and geographer Pausanias depicts the topography, history, and religion of Messenia in the fourth book of his *Description of Greece* (in this chapter). His account declares that the Andanian mysteries were of great antiquity and "second only to the Eleusinian in sanctity" (4.33.5). The celebration of the mysteries was interrupted by the warfare that raged in the region but was reinstated with the liberating efforts of Epaminondas, the Theban general who fought against the Spartans and brought about Messenian independence in 369 B.C.E., when the city of Messene also was established as the capital of the region. The evidence of the Rule of the Andanian Mysteries indicates that the mysteries were reinstated yet again in 92/91 B.C.E., some fifty-five years after the Romans took control of the region.

Our limited knowledge of the rites of the Andanian mysteries comes from Pausanias and the Andanian Rule. In the mid-second century C.E., Pausanias mentions the Karnasian cypress grove, with a spring nearby, as the site of the Andanian worship of several gods: Apollo Karneios, Hermes, Hagne, and the Great Goddesses. Pausanias understands Hagne ("Pure One") to be a title of Kore, daughter of Demeter, and refers in this context to the Eleusinian mysteries, so that Pausanias's account may imply some sort of Athenian influence. Two and one half centuries earlier, the Andanian Rule also mentioned the Karnasian grove as the site at which the gods and goddesses of the mysteries were worshiped, but this earlier text enumerated a slightly different list of deities: Demeter, Hermes, Apollo Karneios, Hagna (Hagne), and the Great Gods. (On the question of the identity of the Great Gods, a matter of considerable debate, see the introduction to the excerpt from Diodorus Siculus in Chapter 2.) Hagna also is said to be the ancient name of the spring or fountain (Andanian Rule 17), so that Hagna might be understood to be a water nymph.

For a brief introduction to the Andanian mysteries, with bibliography, see Martin P. Nilsson, *Geschichte der griechischen Religion*, Handbuch der Altertumswissenschaft (Munich: Beck, 1955–1961), 1.449, note 4; 2.96–98.

PAUSANIAS, *DESCRIPTION OF GREECE*, Book 4: *MESSENIA*, 33.3–6

The geographer Pausanias, who wrote in the mid-second century c.e., here describes Andania and the grove of Karneios in a manner that agrees rather well with the earlier and more detailed evidence of the Rule of the Andanian Mysteries. Pausanias refers to the Great Goddesses and probably means to identify them with Demeter and Kore (equated by Pausanias with Hagne), but he does not make mention of the Great Gods of the Andanian Rule.

The following translation is by W. H. S. Jones and H. A. Ormerod, *Pausanias: Description of Greece: II* (Loeb Classical Library, 1926). For more of Pausanias's observations on Andania, see 1–2, 3.10, 14.1, 15.7, 16.2, and 26.6–27.6, all in his fourth book, on Messenia. *Description of Greece*, 4.1.5–7 is particularly instructive on the mysteries at Phlya and the Andanian mysteries.

3 At the Arcadian gate leading to Megalopolis is a Herm of Attic style; for the square form of Herm is Athenian, and the rest adopted it thence. After a descent of thirty stades from the gate is the watercourse of Balyra. The river is said to have got its name from Thamyris throwing *(ballein)* his lyre away here after his blinding. He was the son of Philammon and the nymph Argiope, who once dwelt on Parnassus, but settled among the Odrysae when pregnant, for Philammon refused to take her into his house. Thamyris is called an Odrysian and Thracian on these grounds. The watercourses Leucasia and Amphitos unite to form one stream.

4   When these are crossed, there is a plain called the plain of Stenyclerus. Stenyclerus was a hero, it is said. Facing the plain is a site anciently called Oechalia, in our time the Karnasian grove, thickly grown with cypresses. There are statues of the gods Apollo Karneios (and Hagne), also Hermes carrying a ram. Hagne is a title of Kore the daughter

5 of Demeter. Water rises from a spring close to the statue. I may not reveal the rites of the Great Goddesses, for it is their mysteries which they celebrate in the Karnasian grove, and I regard them as second only to the Eleusinian in sanctity. But my dream did not prevent me from making known to all that the brazen urn, discovered by the Argive general, and

the bones of Eurytus the son of Melaneus were kept there. A river **6**
Charadrus flows past the grove; about eight stades along the road to the
left are the ruins of Andania. The guides agree that the city got its name
from a woman Andania, but I can say nothing as to her parents or her
husband. On the road from Andania towards Cyparissiae is Polichne, as
it is called, and the streams of Electra and Coeus. The names perhaps are
to be connected with Electra the daughter of Atlas and Coeus the father
of Leto, or Electra and Coeus may be two local heroes.

RULE OF THE ANDANIAN MYSTERIES

The Rule of the Andanian Mysteries is a public record of the specific
regulations to be followed in the celebration of the Andanian mysteries.
The inscription may be dated with confidence to 92/91 B.C.E., "the fifty-
fifth year" after Achaea became a Roman province in 146 B.C.E.; thus the
rule establishes the celebration of these ancient mysteries in Hellenistic
times. The honors to be bestowed upon Mnasistratos, the chief benefac-
tor of the Andanian mysteries, may stem from the fact that he recovered
and donated the sacred books and chest that were indispensable for the
reinstitution of the mysteries (cp. Pausanias, *Description of Greece*, bk. 4,
26.8, on Epaminondas recovering a similar book).

Nothing secret or forbidden is divulged in the Andanian Rule. When
the inscription makes mention of things that must not be revealed, it
does so with guarded and obscure language and hence employs such
cryptic phrases as "the things pertaining to the initiation" and "the
things pertaining to the sacrifices." The rule decrees in minute detail the
regulations to be followed by all the participants and the penalties to be
assessed for transgressions. The sacred men and women designated to
participate in the mysteries are to take the necessary oaths, dress in the
appropriate manner, and be properly observant with regard to the procession, the sacrifices, the sacred meal, the tents, and the furnishings. Because large amounts of money are involved in the Andanian mysteries,
the financial affairs are to be administered with great care. In one instance, at the end of section 19 ("Regarding the sacred meal"), blank
space is left in the inscription where the specific figure limiting spending
was to be inscribed. The text closes with the statement that "the rule is to
be authoritative for all time." Yet provisions are made for the administra-
tors to meet the needs of circumstances not covered by the rule.

This translation is by Marvin W. Meyer from the Greek text published in Wilhelm Dittenberger, ed., *Sylloge Inscriptionum Graecarum*, 3d
ed. (Leipzig: Hirzel, 1915–24; reprint, Hildesheim: Georg Olms, 1960),

2.401–11 (number 736). An English translation of a small portion of the
rule is given in Frederick C. Grant, *Hellenistic Religions: The Age of
Syncretism* (Indianapolis: Bobbs-Merrill, 1953), 31–32. Three valuable
studies of the Andanian Rule are those of Otto Kern, *Die Religion der
Griechen* (Berlin: Weidmann, 1963), 3.188–90; Charles T. Newton, *Essays
on Art and Archaeology* (London: Macmillan, 1880), 177–84; and Ernst
Sauppe, *Die Mysterieninschrift aus Andania* (Göttingen: Königliche
Gesellschaft der Wissenschaften, 1860).

1   Concerning] sacred men and sacred women. The scribe of the magistrates is to administer the following oath, then and there, to those who
have been designated sacred men, who pour the blood and wine when
the [offerings] are kindled, that no one may be remiss: "I swear, by the
gods for whom the mysteries are celebrated: I shall be careful that the
things pertaining to the initiation are done reverently and in a fully lawful manner; I myself shall do nothing shameful or wrong at the conclusion of the mysteries, nor shall I confide in anyone else; rather, I shall
obey what is written; and I shall administer the oath to the sacred
women and the priest in accordance with the rule. May I, by keeping the
oath, experience what is in store for the pious, but may one who breaks
the oath experience the opposite." If someone does not wish to take the
oath, he is to pay a fine of one thousand drachmai, and in his place he is
to appoint by lot another person from the same clan. The priest and the
sacred men are to administer the same oath to the sacred women in the
sacred area of Karneios on the day before the mysteries, and they are to
administer an additional oath as well: "I also have lived purely and lawfully with my husband." The sacred men are to fine one who does not
wish to take the oath one thousand drachmai and not allow her to celebrate the things pertaining to the sacrifices or participate in the mysteries. Rather, the women who have taken the oath are to celebrate. But in
the fifty-fifth year those who have been designated sacred men and sacred women are to take the same oath in the eleventh month before the
mysteries.

2   Regarding transferral. The sacred men are to hand over, to those appointed as successors, the chest and the books that Mnasistratos donated; they also are to hand over whatever else may be furnished for the
sake of the mysteries.

3   Regarding wreaths. The sacred men are to wear wreaths, the sacred
women a white felt cap, and the first initiates among the initiated a tiara.
But when the sacred men give the order, they are to take off their tiara,
and they are all to be wreathed with laurel.

Regarding clothing. The men who are initiated into the mysteries are **4**
to stand barefoot and wear white clothing, and the women are to wear
clothes that are not transparent, with stripes on their robes not more
than half a finger wide. The independent women are to wear a linen tunic and a robe worth not more than one hundred drachmai, the daughters an Egyptian or linen tunic and a robe worth not more than a mina,
and the female slaves an Egyptian or linen tunic and a robe worth not
more than fifty drachmai. The sacred women: the ladies are to wear an
Egyptian tunic or an undergarment without decoration and a robe worth
not more than two minas, and the [daughters] an Egyptian tunic or a
robe worth not more than one hundred drachmai. In the procession the
ladies among the sacred women are to wear an undergarment and a
woman's wool robe, with stripes not more than half a finger wide, and
the daughters an Egyptian tunic and a robe that is not transparent. None
of the women are to wear gold, or rouge, or white makeup, or a hair
band, or braided hair, or shoes made of anything but felt or leather from
sacrificial victims. The sacred women are to have curved wicker seats
and on them white pillows or a round cushion, without decoration or
purple design. The women who must be dressed in the manner of the
gods are to wear the clothing that the sacred men specify. But if anyone
somehow has clothing contrary to the rule, or anything else of what is
prohibited, the supervisor of the women is not to allow it, but the supervisor is to have the authority to inflict punishment, and it is to be devoted to the gods.

Oath of the supervisor of the women. When the sacred men them- **5**
selves take the oath, they also are to administer the oath to the supervisor of the women, before the same sacred men: "I truly shall be careful
concerning the clothing and the rest of the things assigned to me in the
rule."

Regarding the procession. In the procession Mnasistratos is to lead **6**
the way, then comes the priest of the gods whose mysteries are being
held, together with the priestess, then the director of the games, the
priests of the sacrifices, and the flute players. After them the sacred virgins, as they are assigned by lot, draw the carts bearing the chests that
contain the sacred things of the mysteries; then come the mistress of the
banquet for the worship of Demeter and the assistants who have begun
their duties, then the priestess of Demeter of the Hippodrome, then the
priestess of Demeter in Aigila. Then come the sacred women, one by
one, as assigned by lot, then the sacred men, as assigned by the council
of ten. The supervisor of the women is to appoint by lot the sacred
women and the virgins and is to be careful that they take their places in

the procession as assigned by lot. Animals for sacrifice also are to be led in the procession, and they are to be sacrificed: a pregnant pig for Demeter, a ram for Hermes, a young pig for the Great Gods, a boar for Apollo Karneios, a sheep for Hagna.

7   Regarding tents. The sacred men are not to allow anyone to have a tent larger than thirty feet square or to put curtains or screens around the tents; nor is anyone not of the sacred men to have a tent within the area that the sacred men mark off. No uninitiated person is to go into the area that they mark off. They also are to set out vessels for water. They also are to record publicly from what one must be pure and what one must not have in order to enter.

8   What one must not have in the tents. No one is to have in the tent couches or silver plate worth more than three hundred drachmai. If someone does, the sacred men are not to allow it, and what is in excess is to be devoted to the gods.

9   Regarding those who are disorderly. When the sacrifices and the mysteries are celebrated, all are to be still and attend to the orders that are given. The sacred men are to scourge anyone who is disobedient or who behaves improperly toward what is holy and exclude such a one from the mysteries.

10   Regarding rod-bearers. There are to be twenty rod-bearers from the sacred men. They are to be obedient to those who oversee the mysteries, and they are to be careful that everything is done in a decent and orderly manner by those in attendance, as those appointed over them order. They are to scourge those who are disobedient or who behave improperly. If one of the rod-bearers does not do as it is written, or commits some other wrong, or does something else at the conclusion of the mysteries, he is not to participate in the mysteries, once he has been tried by the sacred men and condemned.

11   Concerning funds. Five people appointed by the popular assembly are to manage the funds accruing from the mysteries. The rulers together must nominate people each having a fortune of not less than a talent, and never the same person twice; the council of elders is to record the fortune of those who are appointed and in like manner also that of those who nominated them. The assessor of silver is to offer public assistance to those collecting the funds. When the mysteries are concluded, they are to give account of everything at the first regular meeting of the magistrates and make a report to the officer in charge, then and there. They are to report, item by item, the funds that accrued from the rite of purification; the entrance fee from the first initiates, and whatever else accrued; and the disbursement that was made, and whatever might be left.

They are to make payment to the treasurer, then and there, and if they are found to have done anything wrong, they are to be held liable for double the amount plus a fine of one thousand [drachmai]; and the judges are not to reduce the amount whatsoever. But those appointed in the fifty-fifth year are also to contribute to Mnasistratos the sum of money granted [to him] by the city for the crown, six thousand drachmai. They also are to pay the treasurer whatever funds are spent [by] the treasurer, in [the fifty-fifth] year, [for] the preparations in [the] grove of Karneios or the expenditures on behalf of the mysteries. [The five appointees] are to pay what [remains of the expenses of this year for the] restorations in the grove of Karneios. If there is still a need for something [in addition to these] revenues, they are to bring the matter up and report [precisely] on what is needed, and the rulers and the magistrates are to make a decree that the treasurer must be [given] the funds. The funds from what accrues from the mysteries are to be handed over to the treasurer, and they are to make a report to the officer in charge concerning whatever they manage. If they have done anything wrong, they are to be held liable, as it is written above. The treasurer is to report, in an additional notation, whatever remaining money he receives from them for the restoration of the things in the grove of Karneios, and he is not to use it for anything else until he pays for whatever is needed for the completion of the mysteries. Nor is anyone to propose a decree that these funds must be used for something else. If someone does, the proposal is to be disallowed and the one making the proposal is to be fined two thousand drachmai, and likewise also the treasurer is to be fined double the amount that he paid out, plus two thousand drachmai, and the judges are not to reduce the amount whatsoever. The funds accruing from these judgments are to go for the restoration of the things in the grove of Karneios. When he has paid for whatever is needed for completing the mysteries, the funds accruing from the mysteries are to go to the revenue of the city.

Regarding the furnishing of animals for sacrifice. After being ap- 12
pointed, the sacred men are to issue a public proclamation and permit the furnishing of the animals that must be sacrificed and supplied for the mysteries, as well as the things for the rites of purification. Whether it seems advantageous for all the animals for sacrifice to be obtained in the same purchase or separately, they are to permit the one submitting the lowest bid to receive the money. This is what must be provided before the opening of the mysteries: two white lambs; at the rite of purification, a ram with a fine color; when one is purified in the theater, three piglets; for the first initiates, one hundred lambs; in the

procession, a pregnant pig for Demeter, a two-year-old pig for the Great Gods, a ram for Hermes, a boar for Apollo Karneios, a sheep for Hagna. Once the contractor has given the sacred men a guarantee, he is to take the funds, supply animals that are sound, pure, and fit for sacrifice, and show them to the sacred men ten days before the mysteries. The sacred men are to place a mark on the animals that have been examined, and the contractor is to supply the animals that are thus marked. If he does not supply them for examination, the sacred men are to demand that the guarantors pay back the money plus half the amount. Then they themselves are to provide the animals for sacrifice and recover the money designated for the animals from the funds that are paid back.

13   Regarding artists for the dances. Each year the sacred men are to appoint, for religious service in the sacrifices and mysteries, as many capable performers on the flute and the lyre as they may find. Those appointed are to provide religious service to the gods.

14   Regarding offenses. If anyone is caught stealing or committing some other offense during the days on which the sacrifices and the mysteries take place, that person is to be brought before the sacred men. If a free man is convicted, he is to repay twice the amount; a slave is to be scourged, and repay twice the amount stolen; and the fine for the other offenses is twenty drachmai. If one does not make payment then and there, the master is to hand over the slave to the one against whom the offense was committed to work off the debt; otherwise, he is to be liable for twice the amount.

15   Concerning those cutting wood in the sacred area. No one is to cut wood from the sacred place. One who is caught doing so is to be scourged by the sacred men, if he is a slave, or he is o repay whatever the sacred men decide, if he is a free man. The one who finds such people is to bring them before the sacred men and is to receive one-half the amount.

16   There being a place of refuge for slaves. The sacred area is to be a place of refuge for slaves, as the sacred men may designate the place. No one is to harbor the fugitive slaves nor offer food or provide goods. One who acts contrary to what is written is to be liable to the master for twice the value of the person, plus a fine of five hundred drachmai. The priest is to decide about whatever fugitives may be in hiding (or: may be) from our city: he is to hand over whomever he convicts to their masters; but if he does not hand someone over, the fugitive is to be allowed to leave the master in charge of him.

17   Concerning the fountain. Mnasistratos is to have the custody of the

fountain named Hagna in the ancient writings and the statue that is near the fountain as long as he lives. He is to participate with the sacred men in the sacrifices and the mysteries. Mnasistratos is to receive whatever those who sacrifice at the fountain offer, as well as the hides of the animals for sacrifice. Mnasistratos also is to receive one-third of whatever funds those who sacrifice at the fountain offer or contribute to the treasury, when it is prepared. If some offering of dedication is set up by those who sacrifice, the other two-thirds is to be devoted to the gods. The priest and the sacred men are to be careful that the offerings of dedication decreed by the magistrates are prepared for the gods from the funds.

Regarding the preparation of the treasuries. The sacred men ap- **18** pointed in the fifty-fifth year, along with the director of building, are to be careful that two stone treasuries, that can be closed, are prepared; they are to place one in the temple of the Great Gods and the other near the fountain at whatever place seems to them to be safe. They are to provide keys: for the treasury by the fountain Mnasistratos is to have one key and the sacred men the other; for the treasury in the temple the sacred men are to have the key; and they are to open them every year for the mysteries. They are to bring forth and record the money, which is to be counted out from each treasury separately; they also are to give Mnasistratos the money coming to [him], as it is written in [the] rule.

Regarding the sacred meal. After the sacred men remove the custom- **19** ary allotments for the gods from each of the sacrificial animals led in the procession, they, together with the sacred women and the virgins, are to use [the rest] of the meat for the sacred meal. They are to invite the priest [and the] priestess, [the] priestess of Karneios, Mnasistratos and his wife and children, the artists providing their services [in the] dances, and the assistants serving them. And as for the remaining expenses, they are to spend no more than ___ drachmai.

Regarding the market. The sacred men are to designate a place in **20** which everything may be sold. The supervisor of the market for the city is to be careful that the dealers deal honestly and honorably and use weights and measures agreed upon by the community. He is not to set the price at which something must be sold, nor is anyone to fix the time or charge the dealers anything for the place. He is to scourge the slaves who do not deal as it is written, and fine the free men twenty drachmai, and the judgment is to rest with the sacred [men].

Regarding water. The supervisor of the market also is to be careful **21** concerning the water, that at the festival time no one harms [the] sluice or the conduits or contrives anything else in the sacred area with regard to the water; and that the water flows just as it is apportioned, and [no] one hinders those using it. If he catches someone doing something that is prohibited, he is to scourge him if he is a slave or [fine] him twenty drachmai if he is a free man, and the judgment is to rest with the sacred men.

22   Regarding anointing and bathing. The supervisor of the market is to be careful that those who wish [to provide public baths] in the sacred area not charge the bathers more than two copper coins, and provide heat, a lukewarm bathtub, and lukewarm water for those washing [themselves]; and that the contractor furnishing the supply of wood for the place of anointing provide enough dry wood for those anointing [themselves], day by day, from the fourth hour until the seventh. No slave is to anoint himself. The sacred men are to permit the furnishing of wood [for] the place of anointing. If any one of the contractors or the dealers in baths does not do as it is written, the supervisor of the market is to scourge him if he is a slave or fine him twenty drachmai for each offense if he is a free man; and the judgment is to rest with the sacred men.

23   Regarding the reporting of a decision. The sacred [men] are to give a report on whatever they managed during the festival, or the people they convicted, to the town hall. They also are to record [on] the building in the sacred area those whom they convicted, and for what offense.

24   Having a copy of the rule. Those appointed to transcribe the rule as approved are to give a copy to the legal advisors, and those who receive it are to show it to anyone who has [need] of it. And the herald, flute player, seer, and director of building are to share with the sacred men the religious duties during the mysteries.

25   Regarding [the] appointment of the council of ten. On the twelfth day of the sixth month before the time (viz. for the selection) of the sacred men and the sacred women, the officials are to permit the popular assembly to hold an election that it may appoint, from all the citizens, ten men at least forty years old, and never the same person twice, for the same year. The rulers and anyone else who wishes are to propose nominations, nominating people from those recorded as sacred men appointed by lot. The scribe of the magistrates is to administer to those who are appointed the oath that the sacred men swear. Those appointed are to be careful concerning everything that must be accomplished during the mysteries and be attentive to what is needed for the celebration of the mysteries. They also are to announce the appointment, from the sacred men, of most capable rod-bearers and likewise also mystagogues. If they find some capable people who are not from the sacred men, they are to announce their appointment to share the religious duties with

Mnasistratos; and those appointed are to be obedient to authority and accomplish whatever they assign. They are to condemn anyone not doing this with a fine of twenty drachmai and report him to the officers. The rod-bearers are to scourge those whom the council of ten commands to be scourged, and those appointed to the council of ten are to adjudicate [all the judgments].

If [there needs] to be a meeting for some deliberation, the whole council of ten is to assemble the sacred men and reach the conclusion as the majority decides. The members of the council of ten are to wear a purple headband during the mysteries. **26**

Regarding what is not written. If there are some things not written in the rule for the accomplishment of the mysteries and the sacrifices, the magistrates are to take council—but not alter anything of what is in accordance with the rule—at the conclusion of the mysteries; if they do, the proposal is to be disallowed. The rule is to be authoritative for all time. **27**

4
The Greek Mysteries of Dionysos

4
The Greek Mysteries of Dionysos

The Greek god Dionysos, also termed Bacchos (Bacchus), had numerous manifestations and his worship was incredibly diverse. He may have originated in Thrace, though he also had connections with Phrygia and possibly even Crete (compare with the Cretan Zeus). Sometimes he was depicted as assuming the form of a mighty bull, the embodiment of animal maleness, but he also could appear in a more effeminate form, with fair skin and long curls. At times his followers roamed the forests and the mountains, clothing themselves in fawn skins and wielding thyrsi (the long shafts, topped with ivy or vine leaves, that are symbols of the god), but actors also appeared in the official festivals and theaters of Dionysos, the god of drama, and wore their masks in the public performances of Greek plays.

The worshipers of Dionysos acknowledged his presence in the raw flesh of wild beasts as well as the goblet of wine, in the phallus concealed in the *liknon* (a winnowing basket that may be used as a cradle for a baby), and also (among the Orphics) in the immortal human soul. Thus, one who was confronted with the presence of Dionysos and possessed by him might feel his power variously: in ecstasy, in inebriation, in sexuality, in spiritual bliss. Such a person became one with Dionysos, and in fact might be called Bacche (feminine) or Bacchos (masculine) after the god himself.

Little is known of the actual mysteries of Dionysos, but presumably they were as diverse as the manifestations of the god. It seems likely that the Dionysian mysteries usually included eating and drinking. At least in the archaic and savage mysteries of Dionysos, as portrayed in Euripides' play *The Bacchae*, the initiates were said to tear animals to pieces *(sparagmos)* and eat the flesh raw *(omophagia)* as a way of assimilating the Dionysian power embodied within the animal. In more serene Bacchic rites, such as those of the Iobacchoi in Athens, the meal was a banquet. The holy drink that initiates of Dionysos consumed was ordinarily wine, since wine was the special gift of the god. Sexual practices must have been a part of some Bacchic festivals.

A house often termed the Villa of the Mysteries (the Villa Item) in Pompeii contains a wall-painting that provides important evidence for sexual ceremonies in the context of the Dionysian mysteries. Ten enig-matic scenes on the walls of a room in the villa present Dionysian motifs, though the interpretation remains difficult:

1) A nude boy reads a papyrus scroll as two mature women assist.

2) A young woman, apparently pregnant, carries a tray toward three other women whose position around a table obscures their activity.

3) A silenus (old spirit of the wild) plays the lyre while staring in rap-ture at the central scene in the series described in (6); a satyr (young goat-man of the wild) plays a syrinx (panpipe) and a satyress nurses a goat.

4) A frightened woman flees, perhaps from the flagellation scene de-scribed in (8).

5) A silenus and a satyr hold a bowl and a silenus mask so that an-other satyr, looking for his reflection in the concave bowl, instead will see the likeness of a silenus.

6) The centerpiece of the series, this scene (partially damaged) shows Dionysos reclining voluptuously across the lap of a seated woman, most likely his beloved Ariadne; a thyrsus falls across his body.

7) A woman is about to reveal the phallus covered in the *liknon*, and a winged female figure threatens with a whip.

8) A woman bows for the flagellation; another, nearly nude, whirls in dance and plays cymbals; a third holds a thyrsus.

9) A young woman prepares herself, apparently for a wedding.

10) The matron (of the house or of the mysteries) oversees the prepara-tions depicted in the scenes.

However we interpret the details of these frescoes, they focus upon the mysteries of Dionysos as the mysteries of sexuality. Love and sexuality, with their attendant joys and pains, are presented as the culminating ex-perience of Dionysian power.

About the Orphic mysteries of Dionysos we know somewhat more. Named after their founder Orpheus, whose myths depict him as a Thracian singer who tried to liberate his departed Eurydice from death and who was torn to pieces by Bacchantes (women maddened by Dionysos), the Orphics laid special claim to the god Dionysos, but did so in a peculiar manner. For the Orphics the Dionysian practice of *omophagia* became the original transgression, and they recounted the myth of Dionysos Zagreus in order to show the enormity of the sin of *omophagia*. (A version of the myth is given in Clement of Alexandria, *Ex-hortation to the Greeks*, 2.17–18, in Chapter 8; cp. the allusion to the story in Plutarch, *On Isis and Osiris*, 35, in Chapter 6.) According to the myth of

Zagreus, it was the evil Titans who consumed Dionysos. Yet after Zeus incinerated the Titans for their wicked deed, human beings were created from the ashes. Thus, human beings are bipartite, according to the Orphics: they are composed of a Titanic nature (the fleshly body) and a Dionysian nature (the immortal soul). Although the Dionysian soul is imprisoned in a Titanic body (the *soma*, or body, is termed a *sema*, or tomb, by the Orphics), the soul may be delivered from its shackles by means of a life devoted to purity and realize its true Dionysian destiny.

Two *symbola* related to the mysteries of Dionysos are noteworthy, and both come from Christian authors. The first ("The bull is father of the serpent, and the serpent father of the bull") is cited by Clement of Alexandria (*Exhortation to the Greeks*, 2.16), Eusebius of Caesarea (*Preparation for the Gospel [Praeparatio Evangelica]* 2.3.21), Arnobius of Sicca (*The Case Against the Pagans*, 5.21), and Firmicus Maternus (*The Error of the Pagan Religions*, 26.1). Its meaning is explained in the introduction to Chapter 2. The second *symbolon* (*aiai dikeros dimorphe*, "Alas, O two-horned one, O two-formed one!") is known from Firmicus Maternus (ibid., 21.2) and probably refers to Dionysos as a divine bull in some traditions and a god of human and sometimes effeminate appearance in others. Compare this with the Orphic hymn 30 in this chapter.

For further material on the mysteries of Dionysos see W. K. C. Guthrie, *The Greeks and Their Gods* (Boston: Beacon, 1955), 145–82; K. Kerényi, *Dionysus: Archetypal Image of Indestructible Life* (Princeton: Princeton Univ. Press, 1976); Martin P. Nilsson, *The Dionysiac Mysteries of the Hellenistic and Roman Age* (New York: Arno, 1975); W. F. Otto, *Dionysus: Myth and Cult* (Bloomington: Indiana Univ. Press, 1965). On Orphism see also W. K. C. Guthrie, *Orpheus and Greek Religion: A Study of the Orphic Movement*, 2d ed. (London: Methuen, 1952); Otto Kern, *Orphicorum Fragmenta* (Berlin: Weidmann, 1922). On the Villa of the Mysteries, see Richard Brilliant, *Pompei A.D. 79* (New York: Potter, 1979); Elaine K. Gazda, ed., *The Villa of the Mysteries in Pompeii: Ancient Ritual, Modern Muse* (Ann Arbor: Kelsey Museum of Archaeology and University of Michigan Museum of Art, 2000); Amedeo Maiuri, *Pompeii* (Rome: Istituto Poligrafico dello Stato, 1970). For an ancient equation of Dionysos with the Jewish god, see Plutarch, *Table Talk*, Book 4, Question 6, in Chapter 8.

EURIPIDES, SELECTIONS FROM *THE BACCHAE*

Near the end of the fifth century B.C.E., the elderly poet Euripides wrote an extraordinary play that was destined to win a prize when it was produced posthumously in Athens by his son. *The Bacchae* is a tragedy about the raw, inexorable power of Dionysos, a divine power that erupts in nature and in people, and that brings with it violence and ecstasy, death and life. *The Bacchae* thus tells the sacred story of Dionysos and reflects a *hieros logos* of Dionysian religion.

As the play opens, Dionysos, son of Zeus and Semele, reveals himself as "a god incognito, disguised as man" (lines 4-5). Claiming to have set forth from Lydia and Phrygia and to have journeyed through Asia, Dionysos has come to the Greek city of Thebes, attended by his train of divinely possessed women, the Bacchae. The king of Thebes, Pentheus, expresses alarm at the Dionysian madness that is sweeping through the city: already he has arrested some of the Bacchae, and now he determines also to take into custody the divine stranger in town. The Bacchae who were arrested escape, miraculously, but a prophet of Dionysos—or the god himself, disguised as a man—is captured and brought before Pentheus. The prisoner too escapes, as earthquakes, lightning, and thunder shatter the stronghold of Pentheus. All of this does not dissuade Pentheus from his campaign against Dionysos, nor is he dissuaded by the report of the miracles performed by the women devoted to Dionysos. (On the one hand, the women are described nursing wild animals in a most tender manner and producing cool water, wine, milk, and honey with their hands or their thyrsi. On the other hand, they are said to tear calves, heifers, and bulls to pieces and use their thyrsi as weapons of destruction.) Indeed, Pentheus is about to take up arms against the Bacchae when the prophet reappears and suggests that Pentheus disguise himself as a woman in order to spy upon them. The Theban prince falls under the spell of Dionysos: he dons the clothing of a Bacchante, makes his way to the woods of Cithaeron, and climbs a tree to spy on the activities of the maenads of the god—only to be discovered by the women. As a horrified messenger tells the story, the divine madness of Dionysos bursts forth in the company of the Bacchae, and, led by Agave, the mother of Pentheus, they take vengeance upon the impious king by ripping him apart, limb from limb, with their bare hands. Thus is fulfilled the word of Dionysos: Pentheus, and all people, "shall come to know Dionysos, son of Zeus, consummate god, most terrible, and yet most gentle, to mankind" (lines 859–61).

The following excerpts from *The Bacchae* are translated by William Arrowsmith, *Euripides: V* (Chicago: Univ. of Chicago Press, 1959). Note also should be taken of the commentary by E. R. Dodds, ed., *Euripides: Bacchae* (Oxford: Clarendon, 1960); and the provocative study by Rene Girard, *Violence and the Sacred* (Baltimore: Johns Hopkins Univ. Press, 1977), esp. 119–42.

SCENE: *(Before the royal palace at Thebes. On the left is the way to Cithaeron; on the right, to the city. In the center of the orchestra stands, still smoking, the vine-covered tomb of Semele, mother of Dionysos.*

Enter Dionysos. He is of soft, even effeminate, appearance. His face is beardless; he is dressed in a fawn-skin and carries a thyrsus. On his head he wears a wreath of ivy, and his long blond curls ripple down over his shoulders. Throughout the play he wears a smiling mask.)

DIONYSOS

I am Dionysos, the son of Zeus,   1
come back to Thebes, this land where I was born.
My mother was Cadmus's daughter, Semele by name,
midwived by fire, delivered by the lightning's
blast.
   And here I stand, a god incognito,
disguised as man, beside the stream of Dirce   5
and the waters of Ismenus. There before the palace
I see my lightning-married mother's grave,
and there upon the ruins of her shattered house
the living fire of Zeus still smolders on
in deathless witness of Hera's violence and rage
against my mother. But Cadmus wins my praise: 10
he has made this tomb a shrine, sacred to my mother.
It was I who screened her grave with the green
of the clustering vine.
     Far behind me lie
those golden-rivered lands, Lydia and Phrygia,
where my journeying began. Overland I went,
across the steppes of Persia where the sun strikes hotly
down, through Bactrian fastness and the grim waste   15
of Media. Thence to rich Arabia I came;
and so, along all Asia's swarming littoral
of towered cities where Greeks and foreign nations,
mingling, live, my progress made. There
I taught my dances to the feet of living men,
establishing my mysteries and rites
that I might be revealed on earth for what I am:
a god.
  And thence to Thebes.
       This city, first   20
in Hellas, now shrills and echoes to my women's cries,

their ecstasy of joy. Here in Thebes
I bound the fawn-skin to the women's flesh and armed
25 their hands with shafts of ivy. For I have come
to refute that slander spoken by my mother's sisters—
those who least had right to slander her.
They said that Dionysos was no son of Zeus,
but Semele had slept beside a man in love
30 and fathered off her shame on Zeus—a fraud, they sneered,
contrived by Cadmus to protect his daughter's name.
They said she lied, and Zeus in anger at that lie
blasted her with lightning.
                            Because of that offense
I have stung them with frenzy, hounded them from home
up to the mountains where they wander, crazed of mind,
and compelled to wear my orgies' livery.
35 Every woman in Thebes—but the women only—
I drove from home, mad. There they sit,
rich and poor alike, even the daughters of Cadmus,
beneath the silver firs on the roofless rocks.
Like it or not, this city must learn its lesson:
40 it lacks initiation in my mysteries;
that I shall vindicate my mother Semele
and stand revealed to mortal eyes as the god
she bore to Zeus.
                    Cadmus the king has abdicated,
leaving his throne and power to his grandson Pentheus;
45 who now revolts against divinity, in *me*;
thrusts *me* from his offerings; forgets *my* name
in his prayers. Therefore I shall *prove* to him
and every man in Thebes that I am god
indeed. And when my worship is established here,
and all is well, then I shall go my way
50 and be revealed to other men in other lands.
But if the men of Thebes attempt to force
my Bacchae from the mountainside by threat of arms,
I shall marshal my Maenads and take the field.
To these ends I have laid my deity aside
and go disguised as man.
(*He wheels and calls offstage.*)
55   On, my women,
women who worship me, women whom I led

out of Asia where Tmolus heaves its rampart
over Lydia!
        On, comrades of my progress here!
Come, and with your native Phrygian drum—
Rhea's drum and mine—pound at the palace doors   **60**
of Pentheus! Let the city of Thebes behold you,
while I return among Cithaeron's forest glens
where my Bacchae wait and join their whirling dances.
*(Exit Dionysos as the Chorus of Asian Bacchae comes dancing in from the
right. They are dressed in fawn-skins, crowned with ivy, and carry thyrsi,
timbrels, and flutes.)*

CHORUS
Out of the land of Asia,
down from holy Tmolus,   **65**
speeding the service of god,
for Bromios we come!
Hard are the labors of god;
hard, but his service is sweet.
Sweet to serve, sweet to cry:
        Bacchus! Evohe!
–You on the streets!
        —You on the roads!
            —Make way!
–Let every mouth be hushed. Let no ill-omened words   **70**
profane your tongues.
        —Make way! Fall back!
            —Hush.
–For now I raise the old, old hymn to Dionysos.

–Blesséd, blesséd are those who know the mysteries of god.
–Blesséd is he who hallows his life in the worship of god,
    he whom the spirit of god possesseth, who is one
    with those who belong to the holy body of god.   **75**
–Blesséd are the dancers and those who are purified,
    who dance on the hill in the holy dance of god.
–Blesséd are they who keep the rite of Kybele the Mother.
–Blesséd are the thyrus-bearers, those who wield in their
    hands the holy wand of god.   **80**
–Blesséd are those who wear the crown of the ivy of god.
–Blesséd, blesséd are they: Dionysos is their god!

–On, Bacchae, on, you Bacchae,

bear your god in triumph home!
Bear on the god, son of god,
85   escort your Dionysos home!
Bear him down from Phrygian hill,
attend him through the streets of Hellas!

      –So his mother bore him once
in labor bitter; lightning-struck,
90   forced by fire that flared from Zeus,
consumed, she died, untimely torn,
in childbed dead by blow of light!
Of light the son was born!

95   –Zeus it was who saved his son;
with speed outrunning mortal eye,
bore him to a private place,
bound the boy with clasps of gold;
in his thigh as in a womb,
concealed his son from Hera's eyes.

100   –And when the weaving Fates fulfilled the time,
the bull-horned god was born of Zeus. In joy
he crowned his son, set serpents on his head—
wherefrom, in piety, descends to us
the Maenad's writhing crown, her *chevelure* of snakes.

105   –O Thebes, nurse of Semele,
crown your hair with ivy!
Grow green with bryony!
Redden with berries! O city,
110   with boughs of oak and fir,
come dance the dance of god!
Fringe your skins of dappled fawn
with tufts of twisted wool!
Handle with holy care
the violent wand of god!
And let the dance begin!
115   He is Bromios who runs
    to the mountain!
             to the mountain!
where the throng of women waits,

driven from shuttle and loom,
possessed by Dionysos!

–And I praise the holies of Crete,   120
the caves of the dancing Kyretes,
there where Zeus was born,
where helmed in triple tier
around the primal drum
the Korybantes danced. They,   125
they were the first of all
whose whirling feet kept time
to the strict beat of the taut hide
and the squeal of the wailing flute.
Then from them to Rhea's hands
the holy drum was handed down;
but, stolen by the raving Satyrs,   130
fell at last to me and now
accompanies the dance
which every other year
celebrates your name:
                    Dionysos!
–He is sweet upon the mountains. He drops to the earth   135
    from the running packs.
He wears the holy fawn-skin. He hunts the wild goat
    and kills it.
He delights in the raw flesh.
He runs to the mountains of Phrygia, to the mountains
    of Lydia he runs!   140
He is Bromios who leads us! *Evohe!*

–With milk the earth flows! It flows with wine!
It runs with the nectar of bees!

–Like frankincense in its fragrance
is the blaze of the torch he bears.   145
Flames float out from his trailing wand
    as he runs, as he dances,
    kindling the stragglers,
    spurring with cries,
and his long curls stream to the wind!   150

–And he cries, as they cry, *Evohe!*—

On, Bacchae!
On, Bacchae!
Follow, glory of golden Tmolus,
155   hymning god
    with a rumble of drums,
with a cry, *Evohe!* to the Evian god,
with a cry of Phrygian cries,
160 when the holy flute like honey plays
the sacred song of those who go
to the mountain!
165   *to the mountain!*
–Then, in ecstasy, like a colt by its grazing mother,
the Bacchante runs with flying feet, she leaps!

                     *   *   *   *

PENTHEUS
                 Untie his hands.
We have him in our net. He may be quick,
but he cannot escape us now, I think.
(*While the servants untie Dionysos's hands, Pentheus attentively scrutinizes
his prisoner. Then the servants step back, leaving Pentheus and Dionysos face
to face.*)
                 So,
you *are* attractive, stranger, at least to women—
which explains, I think, your presence here in Thebes.
455 Your curls are long. You do not wrestle, I take it.
And what fair skin you have—you must take care of it—
no daylight complexion; no, it comes from the night
when you hunt Aphrodite with your beauty.
                 Now then,
who are you and from where?

DIONYSOS
460   It is nothing
to boast of and easily told. You have heard, I suppose,
of Mount Tmolus and her flowers?

PENTHEUS
              I know the place.
It rings the city of Sardis.

DIONYSOS
              I come from there.
My country is Lydia.

PENTHEUS
>Who is this god whose worship
you have imported into Hellas?

DIONYSOS
>Dionysos, the son of Zeus.   465
He initiated me.

PENTHEUS
>You have some local Zeus
who spawns new gods?

DIONYSOS
>He is the same as yours—
the Zeus who married Semele.

PENTHEUS
>How did you see him?
In a dream or face to face?

DIONYSOS
>Face to face.
He gave me his rites.

PENTHEUS
>What form do they take,   470
these mysteries of yours?

DIONYSOS
>It is forbidden
to tell the uninitiate.

PENTHEUS
>Tell me the benefits
that those who know your mysteries enjoy.

DIONYSOS
I am forbidden to say. But they are worth knowing.

PENTHEUS
Your answers are designed to make me curious.

DIONYSOS
>No: 475
our mysteries abhor an unbelieving man.

PENTHEUS
You say you saw the god. What form did he assume?

DIONYSOS
Whatever form he wished. The choice was his,

not mine.

PENTHEUS

You evade the question.

DIONYSOS

Talk sense to a fool
and he calls you foolish.

PENTHEUS

480   Have you introduced your rites
in other cities too? Or is Thebes the first?

DIONYSOS

Foreigners everywhere now dance for Dionysos.

PENTHEUS

They are more ignorant than Greeks.

DIONYSOS

In this matter
they are not. Customs differ.

PENTHEUS

Do you hold your rites
during the day or night?

DIONYSOS

485   Mostly by night.
The darkness is well suited to devotion.

PENTHEUS

Better suited to lechery and seducing women.

DIONYSOS

You can find debauchery by daylight too.

PENTHEUS

You shall regret these clever answers.

DIONYSOS

And you,
your stupid blasphemies.

*   *   *   *

MESSENGER

Pentheus, king of Thebes,   660
I come from Cithaeron where the gleaming flakes of snow
fall on and on forever—

PENTHEUS

Get to the point.
What is your message, man?

MESSENGER

Sir, I have seen
the holy Maenads, the women who ran barefoot   665
and crazy from the city, and I wanted to report
to you and Thebes what weird fantastic things,
what miracles and more than miracles,
these women do. But may I speak freely
in my own way and words, or make it short?
I fear the harsh impatience of your nature, sire,   670
too kingly and too quick to anger.

PENTHEUS

Speak freely.
You have my promise: I shall not punish you.
Displeasure with a man who speaks the truth is wrong.
However, the more terrible this tale of yours,
that much more terrible will be the punishment   675
I impose upon that man who taught our womenfolk
this strange new magic.

MESSENGER

About that hour
when the sun lets loose its light to warm the earth,
our grazing herds of cows had just begun to climb
the path along the mountain ridge. Suddenly
I saw three companies of dancing women,   680
one led by Autonoe, the second captained
by your mother Agave, while Ino led the third.
There they lay in the deep sleep of exhaustion,
some resting on boughs of fir, others sleeping
where they fell, here and there among the oak leaves—   685
but all modestly and soberly, not, as you think,
drunk with wine, nor wandering, led stray
by the music of the flute, to hunt their Aphrodite
through the woods.
                    But your mother heard the lowing
of our hornéd herds, and springing to her feet,   690
gave a great cry to waken them from sleep.

and they too, rubbing the bloom of soft sleep
from their eyes, rose up lightly and straight—
a lovely sight to see: all as one,
the old women and the young and the unmarried girls.
695   First they let their hair fall loose, down
over their shoulders, and those whose straps had slipped
fastened their skins of fawn with writhing snakes
that licked their cheeks. Breasts swollen with milk,
new mothers who had left their babies behind at home
700   nestled gazelles and young wolves in their arms,
suckling them. Then they crowned their hair with leaves,
ivy and oak and flowering bryony. One woman
struck her thyrsus against a rock and a fountain
705   of cool water came bubbling up. Another drove
her fennel in the ground, and where it struck the earth,
at the touch of god, a spring of wine poured out.
Those who wanted milk scratched at the soil
710   with bare fingers and the white milk came welling up.
Pure honey spurted, streaming, from their wands.
If you had been there and seen these wonders for yourself,
you would have gone down on your knees and prayed
to the god you now deny.
                      We cowherds and shepherds
715   gathered in small groups, wondering and arguing
among ourselves at these fantastic things,
the awful miracles those women did.
But then a city fellow with the knack of words
rose to his feet and said: "All you who live
upon the pastures of the mountain, what do you say?
720   Shall we earn a little favor with King Pentheus
by hunting his mother Agave out of the revels?"
Falling in with his suggestion, we withdrew
and set ourselves in ambush, hidden by the leaves
among the undergrowth. Then at a signal
all the Bacchae whirled their wands for the revels
to begin. With one voice they cried aloud:
725   "O Iacchos! Son of Zeus!" "O Bromios!" they cried
until the beasts and all the mountain seemed
wild with divinity. And when they ran,
everything ran with them.
                      It happened, however,

that Agave ran near the ambush where I lay
concealed. Leaping up, I tried to seize her,   730
but she gave a cry: "Hounds who run with me,
men are hunting us down! Follow, follow me!
Use your wands for weapons."
                           At this we fled
and barely missed being torn to pieces by the women.
Unarmed, they swooped down upon the herds of cattle   735
grazing there on the green of the meadow. And then
you could have seen a single woman with bare hands
tear a fat calf, still bellowing with fright,
in two, while others clawed the heifers to pieces.
There were ribs and cloven hooves scattered everywhere,   740
and scraps smeared with blood hung from the fir trees.
And bulls, their raging fury gathered in their horns,
lowered their heads to charge, then fell, stumbling
to the earth, pulled down by hordes of women   745
and stripped of flesh and skin more quickly, sire,
than you could blink your royal eyes. Then,
carried up by their own speed, they flew like birds
across the spreading fields along Asopus's stream
where most of all the ground is good for harvesting.   750
Like invaders they swooped on Hysiae
and on Erythrae in the foothills of Cithaeron.
Everything in sight they pillaged and destroyed.
They snatched the children from their homes. And when
they piled their plunder on their backs, it stayed in place.   755
untied. Nothing, neither bronze nor iron,
fell to the dark earth. Flames flickered
in their curls and did not burn them. Then the villagers,
furious at what the women did, took to arms.
And *there*, sire, was something terrible to see.   760
For the men's spears were pointed and sharp, and yet
drew no blood, whereas the wands the women threw
inflicted wounds. And then the men *ran*,
routed by women! Some god, I say, was with them.
The Bacchae then returned where they had started,   765
by the springs the god had made, and washed their hands
while the snakes licked away the drops of blood
that dabbled their cheeks.
                           Whoever this god may be,

sire, welcome him to Thebes. For he is great
770 in many other ways as well. It was he,
or so they say, who gave to mortal men
the gift of lovely wine by which our suffering
is stopped. And if there is no god of wine,
there is no love, no Aphrodite either,
nor other pleasure left to men.
(*Exit messenger.*)

*   *   *   *

MESSENGER
There were three of us in all: Pentheus and I,
attending my master, and that stranger who volunteered
his services as guide. Leaving behind us
the last outlying farms of Thebes, we forded
1045 the Asopus and struck into the barren scrubland
of Cithaeron.
      There in a grassy glen we halted,
unmoving, silent, without a word,
1050 so we might see but not be seen. From that vantage,
in a hollow cut from the sheer rock of the cliffs,
a place where water ran and the pines grew dense
with shade, we saw the Maenads sitting, their hands
busily moving at their happy tasks. Some
1055 wound the stalks of their tattered wands with tendrils
of fresh ivy; others, frisking like fillies
newly freed from the painted bridles, chanted
in Bacchic songs, responsively.
      But Pentheus—
unhappy man—could not quite see the companies
of women. "Stranger," he said, "from where I stand,
1060 I cannot see these counterfeited Maenads.
But if I climbed that towering fir that overhangs
the banks, then I could see their shameless orgies
better."
      And now the stranger worked a miracle.
Reaching for the highest branch of a great fir,
1065 he bent it down, down, down to the dark earth,
till it was curved the way a taut bow bends
or like a rim of wood when forced about the circle
of a wheel. Like that he forced that mountain fir

down to the ground. No mortal could have done it.
Then he seated Pentheus at the highest tip   1070
and with his hands let the trunk rise straightly up,
slowly and gently, lest it throw its rider.
And the tree rose, towering to heaven, with my master
huddled at the top. And now the Maenads saw him
more clearly than he saw them. But barely had they seen,   1075
when the stranger vanished and there came a great voice
out of heaven—Dionysos's, it must have been—
crying: "Women, I bring you the man who has mocked
at you and me and at our holy mysteries.   1080
Take vengeance upon him." And as he spoke
a flash of awful fire bound earth and heaven.
The high air hushed, and along the forest glen
the leaves hung still; you could hear no cry of beasts.   1085
The Bacchae heard that voice but missed its words,
and leaping up, they stared, peering everywhere.
Again that voice. And now they knew his cry,
the clear command of god. And breaking loose
like startled doves, through grove and torrent,   1090
over jagged rocks, they flew, their feet maddened
by the breath of god. And when they saw my master
perching in his tree, they climbed a great stone   1095
that towered opposite his perch and showered him
with stones and javelins of fir, while the others
hurled their wands. And yet they missed their target,
poor Pentheus in his perch, barely out of reach   1100
of their eager hands, treed, unable to escape.
Finally they splintered branches from the oaks
and with those bars of wood tried to lever up the tree
by prying at the roots. But every effort failed.   1105
Then Agave cried out: "Maenads, make a circle
about the trunk and grip it with your hands.
Unless we take this climbing beast, he will reveal
the secrets of the god." With that, thousands of hands
tore the fir tree from the earth, and down, down   1110
from his high perch fell Pentheus, tumbling
to the ground, sobbing and screaming as he fell,
for he knew his end was near. His own mother,
like a priestess with her victim, fell upon him
first. But snatching off his wig and snood   1115

so she would recognize his face, he touched her cheeks,
screaming, *"No, no, Mother! I am Pentheus,*
your own son, the child you bore to Echion!
1120 *Pity me, spare me, Mother! I have done a wrong,*
but do not kill your own son for my offense."
But she was foaming at the mouth, and her crazed eyes
rolling with frenzy . She was mad, stark mad,
possessed by Bacchus. Ignoring his cries of pity,
1125 she seized his left arm at the wrist; then, planting
her foot upon his chest, she pulled, wrenching away
the arm at the shoulder—not by her own strength,
for the god had put inhuman power in her hands.
Ino, meanwhile, on the other side, was scratching off
1130 his flesh. Then Autonoe and the whole horde
of Bacchae swarmed upon him. Shouts everywhere,
he screaming with what little breath was left,
they shrieking in triumph. One tore off an arm,
another a foot still warm in its shoe. His ribs
1135 were clawed clean of flesh and every hand
was smeared with blood as they played ball with scraps
of Pentheus's body.
                    The pitiful remains lie scattered,
one piece among the sharp rocks, others
lying lost among the leaves in the depths
1140 of the forest. His mother, picking up his head,
impaled it on her wand. She seemed to think it is
some mountain lion's head which she carries in triumph
through the thick of Cithaeron. Leaving her sisters
at the Maenad dances, she is coming here, gloating
1145 over her grisly prize. She calls upon Bacchus:
he is her "fellow-huntsman," "comrade of the chase,
crowned with victory." But all the victory
she carries home is her own grief.
                    Now,
before Agave returns, let me leave
this scene of sorrow. Humility,
1150 a sense of reverence before the sons of heaven—
of all the prizes that a mortal man might win,
these, I say, are wisest; these are best.
(Exit Messenger.)

CHORUS
–We dance to the glory of Bacchus!
We dance to the death of Pentheus,
the death of the spawn of the dragon! 1155
  He dressed in woman's dress;
  he took the lovely thyrsus;
  it waved him down to death,
    led by a bull to Hades.
Hail, Bacchae! Hail, women of Thebes! 1160
Your victory is fair, fair the prize,
  this famous prize of grief!
Glorious the game! To fold your child
in your arms, streaming with his blood!

LIVY, *HISTORY OF ROME*, Book 39.8–19

In 186 B.C.E. the Roman Senate met the increasing suspicion about the Bacchanalia with decisive action. The official worship of Dionysos in the Greco-Roman world was ordinarily more domesticated and respectable than the frenzied revels of the Maenads in *The Bacchae*, but the orgies (Greek *orgia*) did continue in some circles. Such apparently was the case in Rome during the early second century B.C.E. Men had joined with the women in secret Bacchic ceremonies held in the evening, and according to the testimony of the witness Hispala, all sorts of criminal and immoral behavior transpired under the cover of darkness. Upon hearing about this, the Senate adopted a decree that called for the destruction of most Bacchic shrines and the strict control of all Bacchic worship in Italy. A copy of the decree, *Senatus Consultum de Bacchanalibus*, still survives; see Frederick C. Grant, *Ancient Roman Religion* (New York: Liberal Arts Press, 1957), 54–56.

The detailed account of this affair given here is that of the Roman historian Livy (Titus Livius, who lived from the first century B.C.E. into the second decade of the first century C.E.) The translation is from Henry Bettenson, *Livy: Rome and the Mediterranean* (New York: Penguin, 1976).

The following year diverted the consuls, Spurius Postumius Alburius 8 and Quintus Marcius Philippus, from the command of armies and the conduct of campaigns abroad to the crushing of conspiracy at home. The praetors drew lots of their spheres of office: Titus Maenius received the jurisdiction in Rome, and Marcus Licinius Lucullus was appointed judge

in suits between citizens and foreigners; the province of Sardinia fell to
Gaius Aurelius Scaurus, Sicily to Publius Cornelius Sulla, Hither Spain
to Lucius Quinctius Crispinus, Further Spain to Gaius Calpurnius Piso.
A senatorial decree entrusted both the consuls with an inquiry into secret conspiracies.

The trouble had started with the arrival in Etruria of a Greek of humble origin, a man possessed of none of those numerous accomplish-
ments which the Greek people, the most highly educated and civilized
of nations, has introduced among us for the cultivation of mind and
body; he dealt in sacrifices and soothsaying. But his method of infecting
people's minds with error was not by the open practice of his rites and
the public advertisement of his trade and his system; he was the
hierophant of secret ceremonies performed at night. There were initiations which at first were imparted only to a few; but they soon began to
be widespread among men and women. The pleasures of drinking and
feasting were added to the religious rites, to attract a larger number of followers. When wine had inflamed their feelings, and night and the mingling of the sexes and of different ages had extinguished all power of
moral judgment, all sorts of corruption began to be practiced, since each
person had ready to hand the chance of gratifying the particular desire to
which he was naturally inclined. The corruption was not confined to one
kind of evil, the promiscuous violation of free men and of women; the
cult was also a source of supply of false witnesses, forged documents
and wills, and perjured evidence, dealing also in poisons and in whole-
sale murders among the devotees, and sometimes ensuring that not
even the bodies were found for burial. Many such outrages were committed by craft, and even more by violence; and the violence was concealed
because no cries for help could be heard against the shriekings, the bang-
ing of drums and the clashing of cymbals in the scene of debauchery and
bloodshed.

9   This evil, with all its disastrous influence, spread from Etruria to
Rome like an epidemic. At the start, the very size of the city concealed it,
giving ample room for such evils and making it possible to tolerate them;
but at length information reached the ears of the consul Postumius, and
the manner of its coming was much as follows.

Publius Aebutius, whose father had served in the select class of cavalry provided with horses by the State, was left a ward; and later, on the
death of his guardians, he was brought up under the protection of his
mother Durenia and his stepfather Titus Sempronius Rutilus. His
mother was under the sway of her husband, and his stepfather had so
performed his guardianship that he was unable to render an account to

the court. The stepfather was therefore desirous that his ward should either be removed or made dependent on him by some tie. The Bacchanalia offered the one way of destroying the young man; and so the mother appealed to her son, saying that when he was ill she had vowed on his behalf that as soon as he got better she would initiate him into the Bacchic rites; now, by the kindness of the gods, she was due to pay her vow, and she wished to fulfill this obligation. She explained that he would have to observe continence for ten days; at the end of that period she could conduct him to a banquet, then, after ceremonial washing, to the shrine.

Now there was a well-known harlot, a freedwoman named Hispala Faecenia, who was worthy of a better life than the business to which she had become accustomed while a mere slave: but even after her manumission she had supported herself by the same occupation. A liaison had started between this woman and Aebutius, a relationship not at all harmful either to the young man's financial resources or to his reputation. He had been loved and courted without any overtures on his part; and since his own family made but grudging provision for all his needs, he was in fact supported by the generosity of the courtesan. Her relationship with Aebutius had brought the woman to the point of applying to the tribunes and the praetor for a guardian, after the death of her patron, since she then had no legal protector, so that she could make her will, in which she named Aebutius as her sole heir.

Since there were these pledges of love between the pair, and they **10**
had no secrets from each other, the young man light-heartedly told his mistress not be surprised if he did not sleep with her for several nights, explaining that he intended to undergo initiation into the Bacchic rites as a matter of religious obligation, in fulfilment of a vow made to obtain recovery from illness. When the woman heard this, she exclaimed, in consternation: "Heaven forbid! Better for you and me to die rather than that you should do that!" And she called down the vengeance of heaven on the heads of those who had prompted him to this course. Amazed at her language and at her distress of mind, the young man bade her forgo her curses; it was his mother, he told her, who had prescribed this, with the approval of his stepfather. "That means," she retorted, "that your stepfather—for perhaps it would be wicked to accuse your mother—is in a hurry to destroy by this action your virtue, your reputation, your prospects, and your life."

All the more amazed at this outburst the young man asked what it was all about; and then, after imploring the gods and goddesses for mercy and forgiveness if under compulsion of her love for him she uttered what should be kept secret, she told him that when she was a maid-servant she had accompanied her mistress to that shrine, but she had never been near it since she gained her freedom. She knew it, she said, as the workshop of corruptions of every kind; and it was common knowledge that for the past two years no one had been initiated who was over the age of twenty. As each one was introduced, he became a kind of sacrificial victim for the priests. They led the initiate to a place which resounded with shrieks, with the chanting of a choir, the clashing of cymbals and the beating of drums, so that the victim's cries for help, when violence was offered to his chastity, might not be heard. She went on to beg and beseech him to put a stop to the whole project by any means, and not to rush into a situation where every kind of enormity would have first to be suffered and then to be practiced. And she refused to let him go until the young man gave her his word that he would have nothing to do with those ceremonies.

11   When he reached home, and when his mother brought up the subject of what had to be done on that day and on the following days in connection with the ceremonies, he told her that he would not do any of these things, and that he had no intention of being initiated. His stepfather was present at this conversation. His mother instantly shouted at him that the trouble was that he could not deprive himself of Hispala's embraces for ten nights; he was so infected with the poisonous charms of that serpent that he had no respect for his mother or his stepfather—or even for the gods. Scolding him in this fashion, his mother on one side, his stepfather with four slaves on the other, they drove him from the house. The young man then went to his aunt Aebutia and explained to her the reason why his mother had thrown him out; and on her suggestion he went next day to the consul Postumius and told him the whole story, with no witnesses present.

The consul sent him away with instructions to come back in two days' time; and he himself meanwhile asked his mother-in-law Sulpicia, a lady of the highest character, whether she knew an elderly lady from the Aventine, named Aebutia. She replied that she knew her as a woman of integrity, one of the old school. The consul then told her that he needed to have an interview with the lady; and he asked Sulpicia to send her an invitation to come over. Aebutia arrived to see Sulpicia, in response to the summons, and in a short while the consul came in, as if by chance, and introduced into the conversation a mention of her nephew Aebutius. Tears sprang to her eyes, and she started to lament the plight of a young man who had been robbed of his fortune by those who should have been the last persons to treat him thus. "He is at this moment," she said, "staying at my house; he has been thrown out of his home by his mother just because—heaven preserve us!—the upright young man has refused to be initiated into ceremonies which, according to all reports, are nothing short of obscene."

Having satisfied himself by this investigation that Aebutius was a reli- **12** able witness, the consul said good-bye to Aebutia; and he asked his mother-in-law to invite a freedwoman named Hispala to visit her; she also was from the Aventine, quite well known in the neighborhood, and he would like to ask her also a few questions. Hispala was disconcerted at receiving the message, for she could not imagine why she had been summoned to such a well-known and respected lady; and she nearly fainted when she saw the lictors in the vestibule, the consul's entourage, and the consul himself.

Postumius conducted her into the inner part of the house, and in the presence of his mother-in-law, he told Hispala that if she could bring herself to tell him the facts she had no cause for alarm. She could take the pledged word of Sulpicia, a lady of such high position, or his own promise; and she would reveal to them the ceremonies that were habitually performed in the nocturnal rites of the Bacchanalia in the grove of Stimula. On hearing this, the woman was panic-stricken, and such trembling seized every part of her body that for a long time she could not open her mouth. When at last she came to herself, she told the consul that when she was a mere girl and a slave she had been initiated with her mistress; but for a good many years, now that she had been manumitted, she had no knowledge of what happened at these rites.

The consul praised her for her conduct so far, in not denying the basic fact that she had been initiated; but he told her to reveal all the rest of the facts, under the same pledge. She denied any further knowledge; and the consul went on to warn her that if she were proved to be lying by the evidence of another witness, she could not expect the same forgiveness or indulgence as she would receive if she made a voluntary confession. He added that the man who had heard the story from her had given him a full account of the facts.

Thinking without a doubt, as was in fact the case, that Aebutius had **13** revealed the secret, the woman fell at Sulpicia's feet and began to beg her not to allow something said by a freedwoman to her lover to be turned into a serious, even a fatal, statement; what she had said was designed to frighten Aebutius—it was not based on any knowledge. At this point Postumius, blazing with anger, told her that she imagined she was at the moment bantering with her lover Aebutius, instead of speaking in the house of a lady of the highest reputation and in conversation with a consul. Sulpicia for her part lifted the terrified creature and tried to comfort her, while endeavoring to assuage the anger of her son-in-law. Hispala eventually pulled herself together and after complaining bitterly about the treachery of Aebutius, who had returned such thanks for all she had done for him, she declared that she was exceedingly afraid of the wrath of the gods whose secret rites she was about to disclose, but far more afraid of the vengeance of the men who would tear her limb from limb with their own hands, if she gave evidence against them. Accordingly she besought Sulpicia and the consul that they would send her into exile somewhere outside Italy, where she could pass the rest of her life in safety.

The consul bade her to keep her spirits up, assuring her that he would make it his business to see that she could live in safety at Rome. Hispala then explained the origin of the ceremonies. They had started as a rite for women, and it was the rule that no man should be admitted. There had been three fixed days in a year on which initiations took place, at daytime, into the Bacchic mysteries; and it was the custom for the matrons to be chosen as priestesses in rotation. But when Paculla Annia of Campania was priestess she altered all this, ostensibly on the advice of the gods. She had been the first to initiate men, her sons, Minius and Herennius Cerrinius; and she had performed the ceremonies by night instead of by day, and in place of three days in a year she had appointed five days of initiation in each month. From the time when the rites were held promiscuously, with men and women mixed together, and when the license offered by darkness had been added, no sort of crime, no kind of immorality, was left unattempted. There were more obscenities practiced between men than between men and women. Anyone refusing to submit to outrage or reluctant to commit crimes was slaughtered as a sacrificial victim. To regard nothing as forbidden was among these people the summit of religious achievement. Men, apparently out of their wits, would utter prophecies with frenzied bodily convulsions: matrons, attired as Bacchantes, with their hair dishevelled and carrying blazing torches, would run down to the Tiber, plunge their torches into the water and bring them out still alight—because they contained a mixture of live sulphur and calcium. Men were said to have been carried off by the gods—because they had been attached to a machine and whisked away out of sight to hidden caves; they were people who refused to enter the conspiracy or to join in the crimes, or to submit to violation. There was, she alleged, a vast number of initiates, and by this time they almost made up a second people; some men and women of rank were to be found among them. She added that in the last two years it had been laid down that no one over twenty should be initiated; they were looking for young people of an age open to corruption of mind and body.

When she had finished giving her information, she again fell at their **14** feet and repeated her prayers that the consul should remove her to some place of retirement. Postumius then asked his mother-in-law to vacate some part of the house, so that Hispala could move into it. A room on the upper floor was given her; the stairs leading down to the street were barred up, and access to the inside of the house was provided instead. All the possessions of Faecenia were at once transferred to this apartment, her domestics were sent for, and Aebutius was bidden to move into the house of one of the consul's clients.

Both witnesses being now under his control, Postumius brought the matter to the attention of the Senate, with all the facts set out in order, beginning with the first reports and then giving the later information resulting from his own inquiries. The Fathers were seized with extreme panic, as well on account of the community, fearing that these conspiracies and nocturnal meetings might lead to some secret treachery or hidden peril, as on private considerations, since each one feared on his own behalf, afraid that he might have some connection with this horrid business. However, the Senate passed a vote of thanks to the consul for having investigated the matter with remarkable thoroughness and without creating any disturbance.

The Fathers then empowered the consuls to hold a special inquiry into the Bacchic ceremonies and these nocturnal rites, bidding them to make sure that the informers Aebutius and Faecenia did not come to any harm in consequence, and to invite other witnesses by the offer of rewards. The Senate decreed that the priests of these rites, male and female, were to be sought out, not only in Rome but in all market-towns and centers of population, so that they should be available for the consuls; furthermore, that it should be proclaimed in the city of Rome—and edicts should be sent throughout Italy to the same effect—that no one who had been initiated into the Bacchic rites should attempt to assemble or meet for the purpose of holding these ceremonies or to perform any such religious rite. More especially, it was decreed that an inquiry should be held regarding those persons who had assembled or conspired for the furtherance of any immoral or criminal design.

Such was the decree of the Senate. The consuls ordered the curule aediles to search out all the priests of this cult, and to keep them under house-arrest for the inquiry; the plebian aediles were to see to it that no celebration of the rites should take place in secret. The *triumviri capitales* were authorized to arrange watches throughout the city, to make sure that no nocturnal assemblies were held, and to take precautions against outbreaks of fire; while five regional officers were to act as assistants to the *triumviri*, each of them being responsible for the buildings in his own district.

15   When the magistrates had been sent off to assume their responsibilities, the consuls mounted the Rostra and called an informal assembly. After reciting the customary form of prayer, regularly said by magistrates before addressing the people, Postumius began as follows:

"Citizens of Rome, there has never been an assembly for which this customary appeal to the gods was so apt—indeed so necessary—as it is for this present meeting. It is a prayer that reminds us that these are the gods who, according to the institutions of your ancestors, are to receive your worship, your veneration, your prayers—not those gods who would drive on to every sort of crime, to every form of lust, those persons whose minds have been taken captive by degraded and alien rites, whipping them on as if with the scourges of the Furies. For my part I confess myself unable to decide what I should cloak in silence or how far I should speak out. If you are kept in ignorance of anything, I fear I may give occasion for negligence; if I lay bare the whole story, I am afraid that I may spread excessive alarm. But whatever I tell you, you may be sure that my words are inadequate to the horror and the seriousness of the actual situation. Our energies will be devoted to the taking of adequate precautions.

"The Bacchic rites have for a long time been performed all over Italy, and recently they have been celebrated even in many places in Rome itself; I am quite sure that you have been made aware of this not only by rumors but also by the bangings and howlings heard in the night, which echo throughout the city. But I am equally sure that you do not know what this thing really is. Some believe it to be a kind of worship of the gods; others suppose it a permitted sport and relaxation; and that, whatever kind of thing it may be, it involves only a few people. As for their number, if I tell you that there are many thousands of them, you are bound to be scared out of your wits straightway, unless I go on to describe who they are and what kind of people they are. In the first place, then, a great part of them are women, and they are the source of this evil thing; next, there are males, scarcely distinguishable from females. Debauched and debauchers, frenzied devotees, bereft of their senses by lack of sleep, by drink, by the hubbub and the shouting that goes on through the night. Up to now this conspiracy has no strength, but it is gaining a vast increase in strength in that its followers grow more numerous as the days go by.

"Your ancestors did not wish that even the citizens should assemble fortuitously, without good reason: they did not wish you to assemble except when the standard was set up on the citadel, or when the army was called out for an election, or when the tribunes had proclaimed a council of the plebs, or one of the magistrates had summoned you to an informal meeting; and they held that whenever a crowd collected there should also be an authorized person in control of the crowd. What kind of gatherings do you suppose these to be, gatherings, in the first place, held at night, and, secondly, gatherings where men and women meet promiscuously? If you knew at what age male persons are initiated you would feel pity for them—yes, and shame. Citizens of Rome, do you feel that young men, initiated by this oath of allegiance, should be made soldiers? That arms should be entrusted to men called up from this obscene shrine? These men are steeped in their own debauchery and the debauchery of others; will they take the sword to fight to the end in defense of the chastity of your wives and your children?

"And yet it would be less alarming if their evil courses had merely **16** rendered them effeminate—that was in great measure their own personal disgrace—and if they had kept their hands from crime and their thoughts from evil purposes. Never has there been so much wickedness in this commonwealth, never wickedness affecting so many people, nor manifesting itself in so many ways. Whatever wrongdoing there has been in these years, whether in the form of lust, or of fraud, or of violent crime, all of it, you may be sure, has its origin in this one shrine. And they have not yet put into practice all the crimes towards which they have conspired. Their impious conspiracy still confines itself to private outrages, because it has not yet strength enough to overthrow the state. But the evil grows with every passing day, and it creeps abroad. It is already too serious for private resources to deal with it; it aims at the supreme power in the state.

"Unless you are on your guard, Citizens of Rome, this present meeting, held in the daylight, legally summoned by a consul, can be paralleled by another meeting held in the night. Now, as individuals, they are afraid of you, as you stand assembled in a united body; but presently, when you have scattered to your houses in the city or to your homes in the country, they will have assembled, and will be making plans for their own safety and at the same time for your destruction; and then you as individuals will have to fear them as a united body. That is why each one of you ought to hope that all those whom you care for may be of sound mind. If lust, if madness, has snatched off any of them into that whirlpool, then the person concerned should deem such a one to belong not to himself but to those with whom he has conspired to commit every kind of wrongdoing and crime.

"I cannot even rest assured that none of you, my fellow-citizens, will be led astray with disastrous error. Nothing is more deceptive and plausible than a perverse scrupulosity in religious matters. When the will of the gods is made an excuse for criminal acts, there comes into the mind the fear that in punishing human misconduct we may be doing violence to something of divine sanction that is mixed up with the offenses. But you are set free from such scrupulosity by countless decisions of the pontiffs, resolutions of the Senate, and, for good measure, responses of the soothsayers. How often in the times of our fathers and grandfathers, have the magistrates been given the task of forbidding the performance of foreign ceremonies, of excluding the dealers in sacrifices and soothsaying from the Forum, the Circus, and the city, of searching out and burning prophetical books, and of abolishing every system of sacrifice except the traditional Roman method? For men of the deepest insight in all matters of divine and human law came to the decision that nothing tended so much to the destruction of religion as a situation where sacrifices were offered not with the traditional ritual but with ceremonies imported from abroad.

"I have thought it right to give you this warning, so that no superstitious fear may agitate your minds when you observe us suppressing the Bacchanalia and breaking up these criminal gatherings. All this we shall do, with the favor and approval of the gods; it is they who have dragged these matters out of the shadows into the light of day, because they were indignant that their divine majesty should be polluted by deeds of crime and lust; and it was not their will that this wickedness should be brought to light in order to be left unpunished, but in order that vengeance might be done upon it and that it might be crushed. The Senate has entrusted to myself and my colleague a special commission of inquiry into this affair. The task assigned to us we, for our part, shall diligently fulfill; the responsibility of keeping watch throughout the city we have committed to the lesser magistrates. You citizens likewise have your duties; and it is incumbent on you, whatever the tasks laid upon you, that you should give ready obedience to your orders, in whatever place each one of you is stationed, and you must use your best efforts to ensure that no danger or disturbance of the public peace is occasioned by the malignity of these criminals."

17   The consuls then ordered the resolutions of the Senate to be read out, and announced the reward to be paid to an informer who brought any suspect before them or gave them the name of any absent offender. If

anyone so named had made his escape, the consuls would fix a day for the hearing and if the accused did not answer to his name on that day he would be condemned in his absence. For those named who were away from Italy at that time a less rigid date would be given, in case any of them wished to come to stand trial. Next followed an edict prohibiting any attempt to sell or buy anything for the purpose of escaping, and forbidding anyone to harbor or conceal any fugitives, or to assist them in any way.

After the dismissal of the assembly there was extreme terror in the whole city, and this was not confined within the walls of the city or the boundaries of Rome; the panic began to spread far and wide throughout the whole of Italy, as letters were received from friends telling of the decree of the Senate, and describing the assembly and the edict of the consuls. In the course of the night following the day on which the matter was disclosed at the public meeting, many people were caught trying to escape; they were arrested and taken back by the guards posted at the gates by the *triumviri*. The names of many suspects were reported to the authorities; and some of these, men and women, committed suicide. It was said that more than 7,000 men and women were involved in the conspiracy; but it was generally agreed that the ringleaders were Marcus and Gaius Atinius, members of the Roman plebs, Lucius Opicernius of the *Falisci*, and Minius Cerrinius of Campania. These men, it was said, were the source of all the crimes and immoralities: they were the chief priests and the founders of the cult. Energetic steps were taken to ensure their arrest at the first opportunity; they were brought before the consul; they confessed, and made no attempt to delay their trial.

But there was such a flight from the city that in many instances the le- **18** gal proceedings and indictments were rendered void; accordingly, the praetors Titus Maenius and Marcus Licinius were compelled, through the action of the Senate, to postpone the hearings for thirty days, until the consuls had completed their inquiries. This depopulation of the city also compelled the consuls to go to the local towns and conduct their inquiries and hold the trials there, since those who had been informed against did not answer to their names at Rome and were not to be found in the city. There were some who had simply been initiated and had made their prayers according to the ritual form, repeating the words after the priest—those prayers being the vows comprising the abominable conspiracy to practice every kind of crime and lust—but had not committed, either against themselves or against others, any of those acts to which they had bound themselves by their oath; such people were left in custody. But those who had polluted themselves by debauchery or murder, who had defiled themselves by giving false witness, by counterfeiting seals, by forging wills, or by other kinds of fraud, were condemned to death. The people executed outnumbered those who were thrown into prison; but there was a large number of men and women in both categories. Condemned women were handed over to their families or to those who had control of them, for punishment in private; if there was no suitable person to inflict punishment in this way, punishment was exacted by the authorities.

The next task entrusted to the consuls was the destruction of all shrines of Bacchic worship, first at Rome and then throughout Italy, except in places where an ancient altar or statue had been consecrated. For the future it was provided by decree of the Senate that there should be no Bacchanalia in Rome or in Italy. If any person regarded such ceremonies as hallowed by tradition and as essential for him, and believed himself unable to forgo them without being guilty of sin, he was to make a declaration before the city praetor, and the praetor would consult the Senate. If permission were granted to the applicant, at a meeting attended by at least a hundred members of the Senate, he would be allowed to perform the rite, provided that not more than five people took part; and there was to be no common fund of money, no president of the ceremonies, and no priest.

19   A further decree of the Senate, connected with this, was then passed on the proposal of the consul Quintus Marcius, providing that the whole question of those who had served as informers for the consuls should be brought before the Senate when Spurius Postumius had completed his investigation and returned to Rome. The Senate voted that Minucius Cerrinius of Campania should be sent to Ardea for imprisonment, and that the authorities there should be warned to keep him in specially close custody, not only to prevent his escape but also to allow him no chance of committing suicide.

It was some considerable time before Spurius Postumius returned to Rome. He brought in a motion about the reward to be paid to Publius Aebutius and Hispala Faecenia, on the grounds that it was thanks to their information that the facts about the Bacchanalia had been discovered; and the Senate decreed that the city quaestors should pay them 100,000 *asses* out of the public treasury; and that the consuls should discuss with the tribunes the suggestion that they should bring before the popular assembly, at the earliest possible moment, a proposal that Publius Aebutius should be counted as having performed his military service, that he should not serve in the army unless of his own volition, and that the censor should not assign him a horse at the public expense without his consent; that Hispala Faecenia should have the right of giving away or alienating property, of marriage outside her *gens*, and of choice of a guardian, just as if a husband had bestowed these rights in his will; that she should be allowed to marry a man of free birth, and that no slur or disgrace on account of the marriage should attach to the man who married her; that the consuls and praetors at this time in office, and their successors, should make sure that no harm should be done to this woman, and that she should live in safety. The tribunes were to tell the people that the Senate wished and deemed it right that this should be done.

All these proposals were put before the popular assembly, and were passed in accordance with the resolution of the Senate. The question of the impunity of the other informers, and the rewards to be paid them, was left for the consuls to decide.

ACHILLES TATIUS, *THE ADVENTURES OF LEUCIPPE AND CLITOPHON*, Book 2.2–3

While Dionysos was not simply a god of wine, one of the plants with which he is most closely associated is the vine. During the second century c.e. (in all likelihood), Achilles Tatius of Alexandria composed a romantic novel, *The Adventures of Leucippe and Clitophon*, which includes, in book 2, a Tyrian tale about Dionysos and his great gift to humanity: "purple water," "blood so sweet," "the blood of the grape," that is, wine. As Achilles Tatius notes, after the fashion of good romance, Cupid (Eros) fires the impassioned flames of love, but Dionysos adds fuel to the fire by providing the wine.

This translation is by S. Gaselee, *Achilles Tatius* (Loeb Classical Library, 1917).

Hardly had she ended when the time of dinner was again at hand. It 2 happened at that season to be the festival of Dionysos Lord of the Vintage; for the Tyrians claim him as their own proper deity, singing on the subject Cadmus's myth, which they relate as the origin of the festival; and this is it. In early days men had no wine; neither the dark, fragrant kind, nor that from the Biblian vine, not Maron's Thracian sort, not the white Chian kind, not the island wine of Icarus, but all these, they said, were derived from Tyrian vines, the original mother of all wines being a plant of their country. There was a certain shepherd noted for his hospitality, just as the Athenians describe Icarus, from whom this Tyrian story derives its origin, so that it almost seems an Attic tale. Dionysos once paid a visit to this herdsman, who set before him the produce of the earth and the result of the strength of his oxen: but their drink was the same as that of the oxen, since vines did not yet exist. Dionysos thanked the herdsman for his kindly cheer, and pledged him in a friendly cup; but his drink was wine. The herdsman, drinking of it, danced for joy, and said to the god: "Where did you get this purple water, my friend? Wherever did you find blood so sweet? For it is not that water which flows on the ground—that, as it descends into the midriff, affords but a faint pleasure, while this delights the sense of smell before ever it reaches the mouth; when you touch it, it is cold, but it leaps down into the belly and there, far down, lights up the fires of delight." "This," said Dionysos, "is harvest water, the blood of the grape": then the god led the herdsman to the vine, and took hold of the clusters and squeezed them; and then, pointing to the vine, "Here is your water," said he, "this is its source." That is the way in which wine came to men, as the Tyrian story goes, and they keep that day as Dionysos's festival.

3   My father, wishing to celebrate it with splendor, had set out all that was necessary for the dinner in a rich and costly fashion; but especially a precious cup to be used for libations to the god, one only second to the famous goblet of Glaucus of Chios. The material of it was wrought rock-crystal; vines crowned its rim, seeming to grow from the cup itself, their clusters drooped down in every direction: when the cup was empty, each grape seemed green and unripe, but when the wine was poured into it, then little by little the clusters became red and dark, the green crop turning into the ripe fruit; Dionysos too was represented hard by the clusters, to be the husbandman of the vine and the vintner. As we drank deeper, I began to look more boldly and with less shame at my sweetheart: Cupid (Eros) and Dionysos are two of the most violent of the gods, they can grasp the soul and drive it so far towards madness that it loses all restraint; Cupid fires it with the flames which are his attribute, while Dionysos supplies wine which is as fuel to the fire: for wine is the very sustenance of love. She too became more hardy, and scrutinized me more curiously. In this state of affairs ten days passed, but we made no other progress nor ventured further than this duel of eyes.

PAUSANIAS, *DESCRIPTION OF GREECE*, Book 6: *ELIS 2*, 26.1–2

As a god associated with the vine, grapes, and wine, Dionysos naturally was believed to perform wonders in connection with wine. Ancient worshipers of Dionysos from various locales claimed that Dionysos effected miracles with wine on holy days. It was said, for instance, that a fountain of wine flowed by itself from the ground and that spring water from the temple of Liber (identified with Dionysos) had the flavor of wine on festival days (Diodorus Siculus, *Library of History*, 3.66.1–2; Pliny the Elder, *Natural History*, 2.106, 31.13; cp. the springs of cool water and wine that come forth when a Bacchante strikes the ground with her thyrsus in Euripides' *Bacchae*).

According to this passage from Pausanias, a miracle took place at a festival of Dionysos at Elis. The priests brought empty jars into a shrine sacred to the god, and the next day the jars miraculously were filled with wine. This translation of Pausanias is by W. H. S. Jones, *Pausanias: Description of Greece: III* (Loeb Classical Library, 1933). For a discussion of Pausanias's account of wine flowing from a shrine, see Campbell Bonner, "A Dionysiac Miracle at Corinth," *American Journal of Archaeology* 33 (1929): 368–75. For a parallel in Christian literature, see John 2 (the story of Jesus changing water to wine at Cana); and Morton Smith, "On the Wine God in Palestine" (Gen. 18, Jn. 2), and "Achilles Tatius," in *Salo Wittmayer Baron Jubilee Volume*, ed. Saul Lieberman (Jerusalem: American Academy for Jewish Research; New York: Columbia Univ. Press, 1974), 2.815–29.

Between the market-place and the Menius is an old theater and a shrine   1
of Dionysos. The image is the work of Praxiteles. Of the gods the Eleans worship Dionysos with the greatest reverence, and they assert that the god attends their festival, the Thyia. The place where they hold the festival they name the Thyia is about eight stades from the city. Three pots are brought into the building by the priests and set down empty in the presence of the citizens and of any strangers who may chance to be in the country. The doors of the building are sealed by the priests themselves and by any others who may be so inclined. On the morrow they   2
are allowed to examine the seals, and on going into the building they find the pots filled with wine. I did not myself arrive at the time of the festival, but the most respected Elean citizens, and with them strangers also, swore that what I have said is the truth. The Andrians too assert that every other year at their feast of Dionysos wine flows of its own accord from the sanctuary.

RULE OF THE IOBACCHOI

Clubs of various kinds proved to be popular voluntary organizations in Greco-Roman antiquity, and one club is especially significant for our understanding of the worship of Dionysos. At Athens a cultic club of Iobacchoi, or followers of Bacchos, was thriving in the second century

C.E. The Rule of the Iobacchoi is a Greek inscription, dated just before 178 C.E. (according to Marcus N. Tod), that recounts the minutes of a general meeting of the club, and records the regulations adopted at the meeting. The rule contains statutes regarding the admission of members into the Bacchic Society (*Bakcheion;* such a Bacchic Society commonly was called a *thiasos*), as well as the dates and occasions of the meetings, the fees and fines to be assessed, the observance of order and decorum at the meetings, and the ceremonies (e.g., sermons, dramatic performances, offerings, libations, banquets, funerary honors) in which the Iobacchoi participate. Noteworthy also are the titles of officials enumerated in the Rule.

This text is translated by Marcus N. Tod, *Ancient Inscriptions: Sidelights on Greek History* (Chicago: Ares, 1974), 86–91. For the Greek of the inscription see Wilhelm Dittenberger, ed., *Sylloge Inscriptionum Graecarum*, 3d ed. (Leipzig: Hirzel, 1915–24, reprint, Hildesheim: Georg Olms, 1960), 3.267–75 (number 1109).

1   To good luck. In the archonship of Arrius Epaphroditus, on the eighth day of the month Elaphebolion, a meeting was convened for the first
5   time by the priest who had been nominated by Aurelius Nicomachus, who had served as vice-priest for seventeen years and as priest for twenty-three years and had in his lifetime resigned his position, for the honor and glory of the Bacchic Society, in favor of the most excellent Claudius Herodes.
10   Nicomachus, nominated by Herodes as vice-priest, read aloud the statutes drawn up by the ex-priests Chrysippus and Dionysius, and after the priest and the arch-bacchos and the patron had expressed their approval there were shouts of "These are what we always observed," "Hur-
15   rah for the priest!," "Revive the statutes: you ought to," "Long life to the Bacchic Society, and good order!," "Engrave the statutes," "Put the question." The priest then said: "Since my colleagues and I and all of you
20   agree, we shall put the question as you demand." Then the chairman, Rufus son of Aphrodisius, put the question: "Whoever wishes the statutes which have been read to be ratified and engraved on a column will
25   raise his hand." All hands were raised. There were shouts of "Long life to the most excellent priest Herodes!," "Now you are in fortune: now we are the first of all Bacchic Societies," "Hurrah for the vice-priest!," "Let the column be made!" The vice-priest said: "The column shall rest upon
30   the pillar, and the statutes shall be engraved; the officers will take care to prevent any infringement of them."

No one may be an Iobacchos unless he first lodge with the priest the

usual notice of candidature and be approved by a vote of the Iobacchoi as   35
being clearly a worthy and suitable member of the Bacchic Society. The
entrance-fee shall be fifty denarii and a libation for one who is not the
son of a member, while the sons of members shall lodge a similar notice   40
and pay, in addition to twenty-five denarii, half the usual subscription
until the attainment of puberty. The Iobacchoi shall meet on the ninth of
each month and on the anniversary of its foundation and on the festivals
of Bacchos and on any extraordinary feast of the god, and each member   45
shall take part in word or act or honorable deed, paying the fixed
monthly contribution for the wine. If he fail to pay, he shall be excluded
from the gathering and this exclusion shall be enforced by those whose
names are recorded in the decree, save in case of absence from home or   50
mourning or illness or if he who is to be admitted to the gathering was
under some strong compulsion, of which the priests are to judge. And if
the brother of an Iobacchos enter the Society after approval by vote, he
shall pay fifty denarii; but if any acolyte living outside pay the sums due   55
to the gods and to the Bacchic Society, he shall be an Iobacchos together
with his father, sharing with his father in a single libation. When anyone
has lodged his application and has been approved by vote, the priest
shall hand him a letter stating that he is an Iobacchos, but not until he   60
has first paid to the priest his entrance fee, and in the letter the priest
shall cause to be entered the sums paid under one head or another. No
one may either sing or create a disturbance or applaud at the gathering,
but each shall say and act his allotted part with all good order and quiet-   65
ness under the direction of the priest or the arch-bacchos. No Iobacchos
who has not paid his contributions for the monthly and anniversary
meetings shall enter the gathering until the priests have decided either   70
that he must pay or that he may be admitted. If anyone start a fight or be
found acting disorderly or occupying the seat of any other member or using insulting or abusive language to anyone, the person so abused or in-   75
sulted shall produce two of the Iobacchoi to state upon oath that they
heard him insulted or abused, and he who was guilty of the insult or
abuse shall pay to the Society twenty-five light drachmai, or he who was   80
responsible for the fight shall pay the same sum of twenty-five
drachmai, on pain of exclusion from the meetings of the Iobacchoi until
they make payment. And if anyone come to blows, he who has been
struck shall lodge a written statement with the priest or the vice-priest,   85
and he shall without fail convene a general meeting, and the Iobacchoi
shall decide the question by vote under the presidency of the priest, and
the penalty shall be exclusion for a period to be determined and a fine   90
not exceeding twenty-five silver denarii. And the same punishment shall

be imposed also on one who, having been struck, fails to seek redress with the priest or the arch-bacchos but has brought a charge before the public courts. And the same punishment shall be imposed upon the or-
95 derly officer if he failed to eject those who were fighting. And if any of the Iobacchoi, knowing that a general meeting ought to be convened for this purpose, fail to attend, he shall pay to the Society fifty light
100 drachmai, and if he fail to pay on demand, the treasurer shall have power to prevent him from entering the Bacchic Society until he pay. And if any of those who enter fail to pay the entrance-fee to the priest or
105 to the vice-priest, he shall be excluded from the banquet until he does pay, and the money shall be exacted in whatsoever way the priest may order. And no one shall deliver a speech without the leave of the priest
110 or of the vice-priest on pain of being liable to a fine of thirty light drachmai to the Society. The priest shall perform the customary services at the meeting and the anniversary in proper style, and shall set before
115 the meeting the drink-offering for the return of Bacchos and pronounce the sermon, which Nicomachus the ex-priest inaugurated as an act of public spirit. And the arch-bacchos shall offer the sacrifice to the god and
120 shall set forth the drink-offering on each tenth day of the month Elaphebolion. And when portions are distributed, let them be taken by the priest, vice-priest, arch-bacchos, treasurer, bucolic (*boukolikos*),
125 Dionysos, Kore, Palaimon, Aphrodite, and Proteurythmos; and let these names be apportioned by lot among all the members. And if any of the Iobacchoi receive any legacy or honor or appointment, he shall set before
130 the Iobacchoi a drink-offering corresponding to the appointment—marriage, birth, Choes, coming of age, citizen-status, the office of rodbearer, counselor, president of the games, Panhellene, elder, legislator (*thesmothetes*), or any magistracy whatsoever, the appointment as fellow
135 sacrificer or as justice of the peace, the title of victor in the games, or any other promotion attained by any Iobacchos. The orderly officer shall be chosen by lot or appointed by the priest, and he shall bear the thyrsus of the god to him who is disorderly or creates a disturbance. And anyone
140 beside whom the thyrsus is laid shall, with the approval of the priest or of the arch-bacchos, leave the banqueting-hall: but if he disobey, the "horses" who shall be appointed by the priests shall take him up and put
145 him outside the front door and he shall be liable to the punishment inflicted upon those who fight. The Iobacchoi shall elect a treasurer by ballot for a term of two years, and he shall take over all the property of the Bacchic Society in accordance with an inventory, and shall likewise hand
150 it over to his successor as treasurer. And he shall provide out of his own pocket the oil for the lights on each ninth day of the month and on the an-

niversary and at the assembly and on all the customary days of the god
and on those days when legacies or honors or appointments are cele-   155
brated. And he shall, if he wish, appoint a secretary at his own risk, and
he shall be allowed the treasurer's drink-offering and shall be free from
the payment of subscriptions for the two years. And if any Iobacchos
die, a wreath shall be provided in his honor not exceeding five denarii in   160
value, and a single jar of wine shall be set before those who have attended the funeral; but anyone who has not attended may not partake of
the wine.

PLATO, *REPUBLIC*, Book 2.6–7 (363C–365A)

In his *Republic* the Greek philosopher Plato discusses the figures of Orpheus and Mousaios (a famous mythical singer), together with their followers, the Orphics. To Plato certain of the teachings of Orphism (and
Pythagoreanism) clearly were attractive, and Plato's view of the immortal soul entrapped in the mortal body most likely was shaped by the
soma-sema doctrine of Orphism. Here in the second book of the *Republic*
Plato has the speaker Adeimantos tell Socrates of religious teachers who
belong to the Orphic movement. Adeimantos charges that some of these
followers of Orpheus ("mendicant prophets") cater to the superstitions
of the wealthy by performing acts of magic and sorcery—"at a small
cost." These teachers employ "a host of books written by Mousaios and
Orpheus" in order to offer sacrifices and sponsor mysteries for the expia-
tion of sin and the attainment of a good afterlife. They also teach that in
the afterlife, the righteous will receive the reward of an everlasting symposium, or drinking party, but the unrighteous will be punished appro-
priately. Since the unrighteous have not led lives of purity in this life, in
the next they will be compelled to dwell in mud, with only sieves available to carry the water for cleansing and purification.

The following excerpt from Plato is translated by B. Jowett, *Plato: The
Republic* (New York: Random House, Modern Library, n.d.).

Still grander are the gifts of heaven which Mousaios and his son vouch-   6
safe to the just; they take them down into the world below, where they
have the saints lying on couches at a feast (*symposion*), everlastingly
drunk, crowned with garlands; their idea seems to be that an immortality of drunkenness is the highest meed of virtue. Some extend their rewards yet further; the posterity, as they say, of the faithful and just shall
survive to the third and fourth generation. This is the style in which they
praise justice. But about the wicked there is another strain; they bury

them in a slough in Hades, and make them carry water in a sieve; also while they are yet living they bring them to infamy, and inflict upon them the punishments which Glaucon described as the portion of the just who are reputed to be unjust; nothing else does their invention supply. Such is their manner of praising the one and censuring the other.

7   Once more, Socrates, I will ask you to consider another way of speaking about justice and injustice, which is not confined to the poets, but is found in prose writers. The universal voice of mankind is always declaring that justice and virtue are honorable, but grievous and toilsome; and that the pleasures of vice and injustice are easy of attainment, and are only censured by law and opinion. They say also that honesty is for the most part less profitable than dishonesty; and they are quite ready to call wicked men happy, and to honor them both in public and private when they are rich or in any other way influential, while they despise and overlook those who may be weak and poor, even though acknowledging them to be better than the others. But most extraordinary of all is their mode of speaking about virtue and the gods: they say that the gods apportion calamity and misery to many good men, and good and happiness to the wicked. And mendicant prophets go to rich men's doors and persuade them that they have a power committed to them by the gods of making an atonement for a man's own or his ancestor's sins by sacrifices or charms, with rejoicings and feasts; and they promise to harm an enemy, whether just or unjust, at a small cost; with magic arts and incantations binding heaven, as they say, to execute their will. And the poets are the authorities to whom they appeal, now smoothing the path of vice with the words of Hesiod: "Vice may be had in abundance without trouble; the way is smooth and her dwelling-place is near. But before virtue the gods have set toil," and a tedious and uphill road: then citing Homer as a witness that the gods may be influenced by men; for he also says: "The gods, too, may be turned from their purpose; and men pray to them and avert their wrath by sacrifices and soothing entreaties, and by libations and the odor of fat, when they have sinned and transgressed." And they produce a host of books written by Mousaios and Orpheus, who were children of the Moon and the Muses—that is what they say—according to which they perform their ritual, and persuade not only individuals, but whole cities, that expiations and atonements for sin may be made by sacrifices and amusements which fill a vacant hour, and are equally at the service of the living and the dead; the latter sort they call mysteries, and they redeem us from the pains of hell, but if we neglect them no one knows what awaits us.

ORPHIC LAMELLA FROM THESSALY

Some sixteen gold sheets, or lamellae, have been discovered in connection with Hellenistic burials in Crete, southern Italy and Rome, and, as is the case with the lamella translated here, Thessaly. These lamellae illustrate Orphic interests and seem designed to aid deceased persons in their journey into the afterlife. The present lamella from Thessaly, currently housed in the J. Paul Getty Museum in Malibu, California, is composed of six lines of Greek inscribed onto a small, gold sheet, 22 by 37 mm. Its text opens with the lament of the thirsty soul of the deceased (in the Greek conception of the underworld, the plain of Lethe, or Oblivion, was a place of stifling heat). Yet the soul is enjoined to drink only of the spring on the right (presumably the spring of Mnemosyne, or Memory, as opposed to the water of Lethe). When asked about its identity and its origin, the soul replies with a self-predication ("I am" statement): the soul is of earth and of heaven, but its true home is heaven. This culminating statement conforms to the Orphic belief in the dual nature of a person. A person is composed of Titanic flesh (earth) and the divine nature of Dionysos (heaven), but it is the Dionysian soul that brings true life.

The translation of this gold lamella from Thessaly is by Marvin W. Meyer and is based on the published edition (with text and brief commentary) by Joseph Breslin, *A Greek Prayer* (Malibu: J. Paul Getty Museum, n.d.). See also Gilbert Murray, "Critical Appendix on the Orphic Tablets," in Jane Harrison, *Prolegomena to the Study of Greek Religion*, 3d ed. (New York: Meridian Books, 1959), 659–73, with several texts and translations of other lamellae.

> I am parched with thirst, and perishing.
> But drink of me, the ever-flowing spring on the
> right, (where) there is a fair cypress.
> Who are you? Where are you from?
> I am a child of Earth and of starry Heaven, but my
> race is of Heaven (alone).

ORPHIC HYMNS

The so-called Orphic hymns are a collection of eighty-seven hymns addressed to a wide variety of gods and goddesses. The date and place of authorship and the identity of the author or authors remain unknown. The hymns were probably composed during the Roman imperial period, though they include elements and ideas that may be considerably older. A leading scholar of Orphism, Otto Kern, has suggested that the hymns derive from Pergamum, but this suggestion too remains uncertain.

Orpheus and Mousaios were reputed to have been singers, so it is reasonable that poems and hymns might be composed and collected in their names. The marginally Orphic character of the Orphic Hymns is substantiated by such evidence as the numerous devout references to Dionysos; the phrase, so reminiscent of the Orphic lamellae, "child of earth and starry sky" ("To Kronos," hymn 13); the guarded mention of the Titanic origin of the human being ("To the Titans," hymn 37); and, of course, the opening poem allegedly written by Orpheus to Mousaios.

This selection illustrates the intensely syncretistic character of these hymns. The gods and goddesses of the Eleusinian mysteries, the Kouretes (Dioskouroi) of Samothrace, the Phrygian Mother and Sabazios, departed Adonis, Egyptian Isis—these and many other deities are invoked, along with Dionysos, by name and by epithet. The final hymn ("To Death," hymn 87) calls upon Death itself, which frees the *psyche* from the grip of the *soma*, to grant long life.

The selection of hymns here is translated by Apostolos N. Athanassakis, *The Orphic Hymns: Text, Translation and Notes*, Society of Biblical Literature Texts and Translations, no. 12 (Missoula, Mont.: Scholars, 1977).

A mystical association that made use of these hymns in its initiatory rites is briefly discussed in *The Orphic Hymns*, ix–x.

ORPHEUS TO MOUSAIOS

Friend, use it to good fortune.
1   Learn now, Mousaios, a rite mystic and most holy,
    a prayer which surely excels all others.
    Kind Zeus and Gaia, heavenly and pure flames
    of the Sun, sacred light of the Moon, and all the Stars;
5   Poseidon, too, dark-maned holder of the earth,
    pure Persephone and Demeter of the splendid fruit,
    Artemis, the arrow-pouring maiden, and you kindly Phoebus
    who dwell on the sacred ground of Delphi. And Dionysos,
    the dancer, whose honors among the blessed gods are the highest.
10 Strong-spirited Ares, holy and mighty Hephaistos,
    and the goddess foam-born to whose lot fell sublime gifts,
    and you, divinity excellent, who are king of the Underworld.
    I call upon Hebe, and Eileithyia, and the noble ardor of Heracles,

the great blessings of justice and piety,
the glorious Nymphs and Pan the greatest,   15
and upon Hera, buxom wife of aegis-bearing Zeus.
I also call upon lovely Mnemosyne and the holy Muses,
all nine, as well as upon the Graces, the Seasons, the Year,
fair-tressed Leto, divine and revered Dione,
the armed Kouretes, the Korybantes, the Kabeiroi,   20
great Saviors, Zeus's ageless scions,
the Idaian gods, and upon Hermes, messenger and herald
of those in heaven; upon Themis, too, diviner of men
I call and on Night, oldest of all, and light-bringing Day;
then upon Faith, Dike, blameless Thesmodoteira,   25
Rhea, Kronos, dark-veiled Tethys,
the great Ocean together with his daughters,
the might preeminent of Atlas and Aion,
Chronos the ever-flowing, the splendid water of the Styx,
all these gentle gods, and also Pronoia,   30
and the holy Daimon as well as the one baneful to mortals;
then upon divinities dwelling in heaven, air, water,
on earth, under the earth, and in the fiery element.
Ino, Leukothee, Palaimon giver of bliss,   35
sweet-speaking Nike, queenly Adresteia,
the great king Asklepios who grants soothing,
the battle-stirring maiden Pallas, all the Winds,
Thunder, and the parts of the four-pillared Cosmos.
And I invoke the Mother of the immortals, Attis and Men,   40
and the goddess Ouranie, immortal and holy Adonis,
Beginning and End, too, which to all is most important,
and ask them to come in a spirit of joyous mercy
to this holy rite and libation of reverence.

13. TO KRONOS,
incense—storax

Everlasting father of blessed gods and men,   1
resourceful, pure, mighty and powerful Titan,
you consume all things and replenish them, too.
Unbreakable is the hold you have on the boundless cosmos,
O Kronos, begetter of time, Kronos of contrasting discourse,   5
child of earth and starry sky.
In you there is birth and decline, august and prudent lord of Rhea,
who, as progenitor, dwell in every part of the world.

Hear my suppliant voice, O wily and brave one,
10 and bring an ever blameless end to a good life.

18. TO PLOUTON

1   Subterranean is your dwelling place, O strong-spirited one,
a meadow in Tartaros, thick-shaded and dark.
Chthonic Zeus, sceptered one, kindly accept this sacrifice,
Plouton, holder of the keys to the whole earth.
5   You give the wealth of the year's fruits to mankind,
and to your lot fell the third portion, earth, queen of all,
seat of the gods, mighty lap for mortals.
Your throne rests on a tenebrous realm,
the distant, untiring, windless and impassive Hades,
10 and on dark Acheron that encompasses the roots of the earth.
All-Receiver, with death at your command, you are master of mortals;
Euboulos, you once took pure Demeter's daughter as your bride
when you tore her away from the meadow and through the sea
upon your steeds you carried her to an Attic cave,
15 in the district of Eleusis, where the gates to Hades are.
You alone were born to judge deeds obscure and conspicuous;
holiest and illustrious ruler of all, frenzied god,
you delight in the worshiper's respect and reverence.
Come with favor and joy to the initiates. I summon you.

27. TO THE MOTHER OF THE GODS,
incense—et varia

1   Divine are your honors, O mother of the gods and nurturer of all.
Yoke your swift chariot drawn by bull-slaying lions
and, O mighty goddess who brings things to pass, join our prayers.
Many-named and reverend, you are queen of the sky,
5   for in the cosmos yours is the throne in the middle because
the earth is yours and you give gentle nourishment to mortals.
Gods and men were born of you,
and you hold sway over the rivers and all the sea.
Hestia is one of your names, and they call you giver of prosperity
10 because you bestow on men all manner of gifts.
Come to this rite, queen whom the drum delights,
all-taming, savior of Phrygia, consort of Kronos,
child of Ouranos, honored and frenzy-loving nurturer of life.
Joyously and graciously visit our deeds of piety.

29. HYMN TO PERSEPHONE

Persephone, blessed daughter of great Zeus, sole offspring   1
of Demeter, come and accept this gracious sacrifice.
Much honored spouse of Plouton, discreet and life-giving,
you command the gates of Hades in the bowels of the earth,
lovely-tressed Praxidike, pure bloom of Deo,   5
mother of the Furies, queen of the nether world,
whom Zeus sired in clandestine union.
Mother of loud-roaring and many-shaped Eubouleus,
radiant and luminous playmate of the Seasons,
august, almighty, maiden rich in fruits,   10
brilliant and horned, you alone are beloved of mortals.
In spring you rejoice in the meadow breezes
and you show your holy figure in shoots and green fruits.
You were made a kidnapper's bride in the fall,
and you alone are life and death to toiling mortals,   15
O Persephone, for you always nourish all and kill them, too.
Hearken, O blessed goddess, and send forth the earth's fruits.
You who blossom in peace, in soft-handed health,
and in a life of plenty that ferries old age in comfort
to your realm, O queen, and to that of mighty Plouton.   20

30. TO DIONYSOS,
incense—storax

I call upon loud-roaring and reveling Dionysos,   1
primeval, two-natured, thrice-born, Bacchic lord,
savage, ineffable, secretive, two-horned and two-shaped.
Ivy-covered, bull-faced, warlike, howling, pure,
you take raw flesh, you have triennial feasts, wrapt in foliage, decked   5
     with grape clusters.
Resourceful Eubouleus, immortal god sired by Zeus
when he mated with Persephone in unspeakable union.
Hearken to my voice, O blessed one, and with your fair-girdled nurses
breathe on me in a spirit of perfect kindness.

37. TO THE TITANS,
incense—frankincense

Titans, glorious children of Ouranos and Gaia,   1
forbears of our fathers, who dwell down below
in Tartarean homes, in the earth's bowels.

From you stem all toiling mortals,
5 the creatures of the sea and of the land, the birds,
and all generations of this world come from you,
and upon you I call to banish harsh anger,
if some earthly ancestor of mine stormed your homes.

38. TO THE KOURETES,
incense—frankincense

1 Bronze-beating Kouretes, with Ares' armament,
dwellers of heaven, earth and sea, thrice-blessed,
life-giving breezes, glorious saviors of the world,
who dwell in the sacred land of Samothrace
5 and who ward off dangers for mortals roaming the seas.
You were first to set up sacred rites for mortals,
O immortal Kouretes, with Ares' armament.
You rule Ocean, and likewise you rule the sea and the forests.
The earth resounds with the pounding of your nimble feet,
10 as you come in your gleaming armor. All wild beasts cringe
at your onrush, and the noise and shouts rise heavenward,
while the dust from your briskly marching feet
reaches the clouds. Then every flower is in bloom.
Immortal gods, you nurture, but you also destroy,
15 whenever angrily fretting over mankind,
you ruin livelihoóds, possessions, and men themselves.
   . . . the great, deep-eddying sea groans,
lofty trees are uprooted and fall upon the earth,
and the tumult from the leaves echoes in the sky.
20 Kouretes—Korybantes, mighty lords,
masters of Samothrace, veritable Dioskouroi,
airy, soul-nourishing and ever-blowing breezes,
you are called celestial twins on Olympus.
As gentle saviors who bring fair breezes and clear weather,
25 and as nurturers of seasons and of fruits, breathe upon us, O lords!

40. TO ELEUSINIAN DEMETER,
incense—storax

1 Deo, divine mother of all, goddess of many names,
august Demeter, nurturer of youths and giver of prosperity
and wealth. You nourish the ears of grain, O giver of all,
and you delight in peace and in toilsome labor.
5 Present at sowing, heaping, and threshing, O spirit of the unripe fruit,

you dwell in the sacred valley of Eleusis.
Charming and lovely, you give sustenance to all mortals,
and you were the first to yoke the ploughing ox
and to send up from below a rich and lovely harvest for mortals,
Through you there is growth and blooming, O illustrious companion of   **10**
  Bromios
and, torch-bearing and pure one (Hagne), you delight in the summer's
  yield.
From beneath the earth you appear and to all you are gentle,
O holy and youth-nurturing lover of children and of fair offspring.
You yoke your chariot to bridled dragons,
and round your throne you whirl and howl in ecstasy.   **15**
Only daughter with many children and many powers over mortals,
you manifest your myriad faces to the variety of flowers and sacred blossoms;
come, blessed and pure one, and laden with the fruits of summer,
bring peace together with the welcome rule of law,
riches, too, and prosperity, and health that governs all.   **20**

42. TO MISE,
incense—storax

I call upon law-giving (Thesmophoros) Dionysos who carries the fennel   **1**
  stalk—
unforgettable and many-named seed of Eubouleus—
and upon holy, sacred, and ineffable queen Mise,
whose twofold nature is male and female. As redeeming Iacchos,
I summon you, lord, whether you delight in your fragrant temple at   **5**
  Eleusis,
or with the Mother you partake of mystic rites in Phrygia,
or you rejoice in Cyprus with fair-wreathed Kythereia,
or yet you exult in hallowed wheat-bearing fields along
Egypt's river with your divine mother,
the august and black-robed Isis, and your train of nurses.   **10**
Lady, kind-heartedly come to those contesting for noble prizes.

44. TO SEMELE,
incense—storax

I call upon the daughter of Cadmus, queen of all,   **1**
fair Semele of the lovely tresses and the full bosom,
mother of thyrsus-bearing and joyous Dionysos.
She was driven to great pain by the blazing thunderbolt

5   which, through the counsels of immortal Kronian Zeus, burned her,
    and by noble Persephone she was granted honors
    among mortal men, honors given every third year.
    Then they reenact the travail for your son Bacchos,
    the sacred ritual of the table, and the holy mysteries.
10 Now, you, goddess, do I beseeech, daughter of Cadmus, queen,
    always to be gentle-minded toward the initiates.

45. HYMN TO DIONYSOS.
BASSAREUS AND TRIENNIAL

1   Come, blessed Dionysos, bull-faced god conceived in fire,
    Bassareus and Bacchos, many-named master of all.
    You delight in bloody swords and in the holy Maenads,
    as you howl throughout Olympus, O roaring and frenzied Bacchos.
5   Armed with thyrsus and wrathful in the extreme, you are honored
    by all the gods and by all the men who dwell upon the earth.
    Come, blessed and leaping god, and bring much joy to all.

46. TO LIKNITES,
incense—powdered frankincense

1   I summon to these prayers Dionysos Liknites,
    born at Nysa, blossoming, beloved and kindly Bacchos,
    nursling of the Nymphs and of fair-wreathed Aphrodite.
    The forests once felt your feet quiver in the dance
5   as frenzy drove you and the graceful Nymphs on and on,
    and the counsels of Zeus brought you to noble Persephone
    who reared you to be loved by the deathless gods.
    Kind-heartedly come, O blessed one, and accept the gift of this sacrifice.

48. TO SABAZIOS,
incense—aromatic herbs

1   Hear me, father Sabazios, son of Kronos, illustrious god.
    You sewed into your thigh Bacchic Dionysos, the roaring
    Eiraphiotes, that he might come whole
    to noble Tmolus, by the side of fair-cheeked Hipta.
5   But, O blessed ruler of Phrygia and supreme king of all,
    come kind-heartedly to the aid of the initiates.

56. TO ADONIS,
incense—aromatic herbs

1   Hear my prayer, O best and many-named god.

Fine-haired, solitary and full of lovely song;
Eubouleus, many-shaped and noble nurturer of all,
maiden and youth in one, . . . unwithering bloom, O Adonis,
you vanish and shine again in the fair seasons' turn.   5
Two-horned spirit of growth and blooming, much loved and wept for
you are, O fair and joyful hunter of the luxuriant mane.
Desire is in your mind, O sweet blossom and offshoot of Aphrodite and
    Eros,
child born on the bed of lovely-tressed Persephone.
Now you dwell beneath murky Tartaros   10
and now again toward Olympus you bring your full-grown body.

87. TO DEATH,
incense—powdered frankincense

Hear me you who steer the course of all mortals   1
and give holy time to all ahead of whom you lie.
Your sleep tears the soul free from the body's hold
when you undo nature's tenacious bonds,
bringing long and eternal slumber to the living.   5
Common to all, you are unjust to some
when you bring a swift end to youthful life at its peak.
In you alone is the verdict common to all executed,
for to prayers and entreaties you alone are deaf.
But, O blessed one, with sacrifices and pious vows   10
I beg you to grant long life,
that old age might be a noble prize among men.

5

The Anatolian Mysteries of the Great Mother and Her Lover, and the Syrian Goddess

5
The Anatolian Mysteries of the Great Mother and Her Lover, and the Syrian Goddess

In the highlands of central Anatolia lies the region of Phrygia, a mountainous region with fierce terrain as well as fierce religious traditions. Phrygia has produced or influenced the nature of such extraordinary deities as Dionysos, Sabazios, and, as we see in this chapter, the Great Mother (*Magna Mater*) and her lover Attis. Thus, we are not surprised that in this same area of Phrygia a Christian prophetic movement termed Montanism arose in the second century C.E. and celebrated the sort of religious enthusiasm and ecstasy, in Christian guise, for which Phrygia has long been famous.

Kybele (or Kybebe; Latin, Cybele), the Great Mother of Anatolia, was worshiped from ancient times in Phrygia (especially at Pessinus) and in Lydia. She was honored as a mother goddess of fertility, but her particular power was evidenced in the wilds of the untamed forests and mountains. In works of art she commonly was portrayed holding a *tympanon* (a tambourine—she inspired impassioned singing and dancing) and wearing a towered mural crown (she protected towns and castles), and she was accompanied by her lions, since she was the mistress of the wild animals. While the Great Mother was fairly well known within the Greek world, an occurrence in Rome at the very end of the third century B.C.E. proved to be a decisive event for the development of her religion in the Greco-Roman world. In 204 B.C.E. the goddess was formally welcomed into Rome and accepted into the Roman pantheon; thereafter, she was to function practically as a Roman national goddess. Later, during the period of the Roman Empire, the emperors increasingly favored her worship, beginning in the first century C.E. with Claudius, who opened the way for increased attention to be paid to the *Magna Mater* and now to Attis also. As a result, from the second century C.E. on, the Roman world became more and more familiar with the exotic festivals, the flamboyant Galli (eunuchs of the Great Mother) and Metragyrtai (mendicant priests of the Great Mother), and the gory *taurobolia* (ritual slaughter of bulls) within the celebrations of Kybele and Attis.

The most well-known Roman festival in honor of the Anatolian deities was celebrated in the spring, during March. Presumably this festival began to take shape by the first century C.E. Much of the evidence for specific components of the festival, however, dates from later centuries, so that the following schedule of events most accurately describes the festival as it was celebrated in the third or fourth century C.E. On March 15 the ceremonies opened, with the reed-bearers (*cannophori*) carrying their reeds into the sanctuary. The cut reeds may have been a symbolic representation of a feature of the story of Kybele and Attis: either the abandonment of baby Attis by the side of a river or his self-castration later in his life. The next several days of the spring festival were spent in fasting from bread, wine, and other food, as well as abstaining from sexual intercourse.

Then, on March 22 the tree-bearers (*dendrophori*) carried into the sanctuary a pine tree that was freshly cut and decorated with ornaments such as purple flowers or ribbons and an image of Attis. On that day and the day following, the worshipers mourned over the tree, for it commemorated the death of Attis. According to the sacred myth, Attis castrated himself and died under a pine tree and even could be identified with the tree. As the pine tree was cut down in death, so also was youthful Attis cut down.

March 24 was aptly named the Day of Blood (*Dies sanguinis*). On this day some of the fanatical celebrants flogged themselves until they bled and sprinkled their blood upon the image and the altars in the sanctuary, while others are said to have imitated Attis by castrating themselves. Such painful and dramatic acts allowed the worshipers to identify with the passion and death of Attis. The Hilaria on March 25 brought renewed joy and hope. There was feasting in honor of the Great Mother and good cheer. At least in some late fourth-century celebrations of the Hilaria, there also may have been affirmations of the resurrection of Attis. (Cp. the hints in Arnobius, *The Case Against the Pagans*, 5.7, and the denial of Attis's actual return to life. In Firmicus Maternus, *The Error of the Pagan Religions*, 3.1ff., explicit mention is made of the resurrection of Attis.) The spring festival came to a close with a much-needed day of rest (March 26) and a final day (March 27) on which the holy image of the Great Mother was bathed in the Almo River.

The precise nature of the actual mysteries of Kybele and Attis and their relationship to the ceremonies of the March festival are unknown. An interesting *symbolon* is cited, however, by Clement of Alexandria, and two other versions are offered by Firmicus Maternus. (See also Eusebius of Caesarea, *Preparation for the Gospel*, 2.3.18; scholiast on Plato, *Gorgias*, 497C, wrongly attributing the *symbolon* to the Eleusinian mysteries.) Clement's citation of the *symbolon* is as follows:

> "I have eaten from the drum (*tympanon*, tambourine);
> I have drunk from the cymbal (*kymbalon*);
> I have carried the sacred dish (i.e., the *kernos*);
> I have stolen into the inner chamber (*pastos*, shrine)."
> *(Exhortation to the Greeks, 2.15)*

Some scholars (such as G. W. Butterworth, Chapter 8) have taken *pastos* to mean "wedding chamber" and thus have concluded that a sacred marriage (*hieros gamos*) between the initiate and the Great Mother occurred in the mysteries, but such a conclusion is by no means certain. The fourth-century author Firmicus Maternus suggests two other readings for the final two lines of Clement's citation: "I have learned the secrets of religion" (in Latin), and "I have become an initiate (*mystes*) of Attis" (in Greek) (*The Error of the Pagan Religions*, 18.1). The tambourine and the cymbal are well known within the mysteries of Kybele and Attis, as is the *kernos*, or sacred vessel. The three options for the final statement are all vague, and deliberately so. After a ritual meal, Clement and Firmicus Maternus would have us believe, the initiate participated in the holiest ceremonies within a secret, inner chamber and thus became a true *mystes*.

For an exemplary study of the Great Mother and Attis, see Maarten J. Vermaseren, *Cybele and Attis: The Myth and the Cult* (New York and London: Thames and Hudson, 1977). Dated, but still cited, are Sir James G. Frazer, *Adonis, Attis, Osiris: Studies in the History of Oriental Religion*, part 4 of *The Golden Bough* (New York: University Books, 1961); and Hugo Hepding, *Attis, seine Mythen und sein Kult* (1903; reprint, Berlin: Töpelmann, 1967). See also Arthur Darby Nock, "Eunuchs in Ancient Religion," *Archiv für Religionswissenschaft* 23 (1925): 25–33, reprinted in *Essays on Religion and the Ancient World*, ed. Zeph Stewart (Cambridge: Harvard Univ. Press, 1972), 1.7–15. On the similar practices of those devoted to the Syrian Goddess, see Franz Cumont, *The Oriental Religions in*

Roman Paganism (1911; reprint, New York: Dover, 1956), 103–34; also Helmer Ringgren, *Religions of the Ancient Near East* (Philadelphia: Westminster, 1973), on Adonis, Astarte, Atargatis, and their divine predecessors (e.g. the Babylonian deities Tammuz and Ishtar, and the Sumerian deities Dumuzi and Inanna).

ARNOBIUS OF SICCA, *THE CASE AGAINST THE PAGANS, (ADVERSUS NATIONES)*, Book 5.5–7, 16–17

The sacred myth, or *hieros logos*, of the Anatolian Great Mother and her lover Attis is known from several ancient sources that present different versions (such as Herodotus, *History*, Book 1.34–35, on Atys; Ovid, *Fasti*, 4.221–46; Clement of Alexandria, *Exhortation to the Greeks*, 2.24). Arnobius of Sicca in book 5 of his tract *The Case Against the Pagans* provides one of the most significant versions.

Arnobius was a recent convert to Christianity who wrote *Against the Pagans* (seven books) at the very end of the third century C.E. or the first years of the fourth. Citing Timotheus as his authority, Arnobius recounts the following myth. From the rock of Mount Agdus emerges the Great Mother. The divine Father Jupiter loves the Mother, and although his advances are refused, she becomes pregnant (drops of semen apparently fall upon the rock). Agdistis (or Acdestis), a wild, androgynous child, is born as an alter ego of the Great Mother (Agdus). In consort with the other gods, Liber, god of wine, helps to get Agdistis drunk and casts a noose upon him, with the result that Agdistis inadvertently emasculates himself. From the blood spurting out of the wound, a pomegranate tree grows, and the fruit from the tree makes Nana, daughter of Sangarius, pregnant. As another figure representing the Great Mother, Nana gives birth to Attis, beloved of both the Great Mother and Agdistis. When Agdistis is about to be rejected by Attis, he (now, she) inspires madness within a gathering of people, and in a frenzy Attis castrates himself, with a flute, under a pine tree. Yet again, as with Agdistis, life comes from the blood: a violet-colored flower comes forth, the sacred pine tree is consecrated, and the promise of life is offered by the smallest hints of fecundity in the departed Attis. ("The very smallest of his fingers" may be a reference to the phallus of Attis; see section 7.)

The following selections from Arnobius are translated by George E. McCracken, *Arnobius of Sicca: The Case Against the Pagans* (New York: Paulist Press, Newman, 1949); sections 5–7 of book 5 recount the myth, and sections 16–17 are also included because of the observations concerning the rituals practiced within the mysteries of the Great Mother and the implications of a close link between the myth and the rites.

In Timotheus, a man not unknown among theologians, and among oth-   5
ers, too, equally learned, the following story is told concerning the origin
of the Great Mother of the Gods and concerning her sacrifices as dug up
out of the obscure books of antiquities and from the most esoteric mysteries, as he himself writes and implies.

In the territory of Phrygia there is, he says, a rock of an unheard-of
desolation throughout, the name of which is Agdus, so called by the natives of that region. Stones taken from it, as Themis had enjoined by an
oracle, were thrown on the earth, empty of mortals, by Deucalion and
Pyrrha; and from these, along with the others, this Great Mother, as she
is called, was shaped and given divine breath. Her, resting and sleeping
on the very crest of the rock, Jupiter craved for himself with incestuous
desires. But in spite of his continued efforts, he failed to accomplish
what he had proposed to himself and was defeated. Then the rock conceived and, with many groans going before, in the tenth month,
Acdestis is born, so called from his mother's name. In him there was in-
superable strength and uncontrollable ferocity of disposition, a lust mad
and furious and stimulated by both sexes. Violently he plundered, laid
waste, wherever his monstrous spirit led him. He cared not for the gods
nor men, nor did he think anything more powerful than himself; he despised earth, heaven, and the stars.

When in the councils of the gods the question was brought up again   6
and again how his insolence could be either tamed or suppressed, Liber,
the rest holding back, takes the task upon himself. With most potent
wine he fortifies a spring which that fellow knew well and where he had
been wont to slake his burning thirst roused by sport and hunting. On
an occasion when he felt the need of it, Acdestis runs hither to drink. He
gulps down an immoderate draught into his eager veins. Overcome by
this unaccustomed experience, he sinks into a most profound sleep.
Liber lurks nearby in ambush. Over his foot he casts the end of a noose
woven cunningly of hairs. When the power of the wine had been slept
off, he jumps up violently and, straining hard on the knots he himself,
by his own strength, robs himself of that by which he had been ⟨a man⟩.
There is an immense flow of blood; this is snatched up and swallowed by
the earth; thence suddenly is born a pomegranate tree with apples.
Nana, daughter of the king or river Sangarius, gazing in astonishment at
the beauty of this fruit, plucks and takes some to her bosom. By this she

becomes pregnant. As if she had been ravished, her father shuts her up and tries to have her die of starvation. With apples and other food she is supported by the Mother of the Gods. She labors and is delivered of a child, but Sangarius orders it to be exposed. Somebody finds it and takes it, nourishes it on he-goat's milk, and because Lydia calls people who are handsome thus, or because the Phrygians in their dialect name goats *attagi*, it happened that the boy's name Attis was thus derived. Him the Mother of the Gods loved as none other because he was most superb of countenance. Acdestis ⟨loved⟩ him also, his doting companion in his adolescence and who in the only way remaining bound him to himself by his improper attentions, taking him through the wooded glades and giving him many gifts of wild beasts. These the boy Attis at first boasted were the fruit of his own toil and labor; later, under the influence of wine, he admits that he is loved by Acdestis and from him receives woodland gifts as rewards. For this reason it is forbidden for those polluted with wine to enter the sanctuary because it betrayed his silence.

7   Then the king of Pessinus, Midas, desiring to win the boy away from so disgraceful an association, plans to give him his daughter in marriage, and so that no one of sinister omen might break in upon their marriage joys, he caused the town to be closed. But the Mother of the Gods, knowing the youth's fate, and that he would be safe among human beings so long as he was free of a matrimonial alliance, to prevent anything untoward from happening, enters the closed city, having lifted its walls with her head, which began to have towers because of this. As for Acdestis, bursting with anger at having the boy torn from him and brought to have interest in a wife, he inspires all the guests with fury and madness. Terror-stricken, the Phrygians cry out "Adore, adore"; the daughter of the concubine of Gallus cuts off her breasts ⟨in emulation of the self-mutilator⟩. Attis snatches the flute which the one who was goading them to fury was carrying, and being himself full of frenzy, and roving about, hurls himself down at last, and under a pine tree mutilates himself.

With the stream of blood his life flits away. From the blood which flowed, a flower springs up, the violet, and entwines the tree. Thence was derived and arose the custom that even now the sacred pines are veiled and garlanded. The maiden who had been the bride, whom Valerius the pontifex writes was named Ia, covers the breast of the lifeless one with soft wool, sheds tears with Acdestis, and slays herself. When she dies, her blood is changed into purple violets. The Mother of the Gods digs under these, from which an almond grows, signifying the bitterness of burial. She then bears away the pine tree under which Attis had robbed himself of his manhood, to her cave, and about the trunk of the motionless tree, joining in lamentations with Acdestis, she beats and wounds her breast. Jupiter refuses Acdestis's request that Attis might come back to life. But what is possible by concession of fate, this he grants without objecting: that his body should not decay, that his hair should ever grow, that the very smallest of his fingers should live and alone react by continued motion. Satisfied with these favors, Acdestis, it is said, consecrated the body in Pessinus, and honored it with annual rites and with a sacred ministry.

And for all that, how can you assert that representation not to be true **16** when the very rites you continue to practice at each returning anniversary are evidence that you believe it to be true and consider that it has been verified and found worthy of credence? What, for example, does that pine mean which you always introduce on appointed days into the sanctuary of the Mother of the Gods? Is it not symbolic of that tree under which the mad and unhappy youth laid hands on himself and which the parent of the gods consecrated as a solacè for her grief? What is the meaning of the fleeces of wool with which you bind and surround the trunk of the tree? Is it not a recollection of the woolens with which Ia covered him who was expiring and believed that she could procure some warmth for his limbs as they grew cold? What is the meaning of the little branches of the tree decked and girt round with garlands of violets? Do they not signify how the Mother adorned the pine with the earliest blossoms, as a memorial and testimony of her sad misfortune? What is the meaning of the Galli with hair dishevelled, beating their breasts with their hands? Do they not commemorate the sorrow with which the tower-bearing Mother, together with the tearful Acdestis, lamented the boy? What is the meaning of the fasting from bread to which you have given the term *castus*? Is it not an imitation of the time when in the poignancy of her grief the divinity abstained from Ceres' fruit?

Or if what we say is not so, speak out, tell us yourselves: those eu- **17** nuchs and effeminates we see in your midst in the services for that divinity—what is their business there, what their concern, their charge? And why do they like mourners beat their arms and breasts and represent the misfortune of those who experience a woeful lot? What is the meaning of those garlands, those violets, those swathings and coverings of soft wool? Why, finally, is the pine itself, a little while before swaying in the thickets—an utterly inert piece of wood—next set up in the quarters of the Mother of the Gods like some present and most august divinity? Well, either this is the cause—the one we have found in your writings

and treatises, and it is clear that you do not practice divine rites but that
you are giving a representation of sad events; or, if there is another reason which the obscurity of the mystery has withheld from us, it, too,
must be involved in the infamy of some disgrace. Indeed, who is there
that would believe that there is anything noble in what those worthless
Galli put their hands to, what effeminate debauchees perform?

LIVY, *HISTORY OF ROME,* Book 29.10–14

In 204 B.C.E. the worship of the Great Mother Kybele (Cybele) came
to Rome. At the time of the Second Punic War, Livy writes, the Roman
troops were suffering, and the Roman populace grew ever more superstitious. The Sibylline Books were consulted, as was the oracle at Delphi,
and the prophetic message was clear: the fortunes of Rome would im-
prove if the Mother of Gods were brought to Rome. Livy offers an account of the political and military climate of the day, the events that led
to the transportation of the sacred stone of the Great Mother to Rome,
and the welcome accorded her by the leading Roman women. Livy
closes with a reference to the establishment of the Roman festival, celebrated in April, called the Megalesia (or Megalensia).

Livy's account is translated by Aubrey de Sélincourt, *Livy: The War
with Hannibal* (New York: Penguin, 1965).

For a more detailed account of the reception of the Mother of the
Gods in Rome, see Ovid, *Fasti,* 4.247–348. Ovid recounts a wonder that
took place at the Tiber River. When the boat on which the sacred image
was loaded became stuck in the shallow water of the river, it was noble
Claudia Quinta, with the aid of the goddess, who redeemed her reputation by freeing the boat from its position. According to rumors, Claudia
did not live a pure and chaste life, but the Great Mother answered
Claudia's prayer and vindicated her innocence by enabling her to lead
the image of the goddess to the city of Rome.

10   The time for the elections was already approaching, when a dispatch
reached Rome from the consul Licinius, reporting that he and his army
were in the grip of a severe epidemic, and that they could not have held
out had not the enemy been attacked by a disease equally serious, or
worse. Accordingly, since he could not himself attend, he proposed,
with the Senate's approval, to name Quintus Caecilius Metellus as dictator to preside at the elections. It would be, he added, in the public interest to disband Metellus's army, since at the moment his troops were of
no use. Hannibal had withdrawn into winter quarters and so serious an

epidemic had found its way into Metellus's own camp that, unless the men were quickly disbanded, not one of them, it seemed, would be left alive. Licinius received permission from the Senate to do what he thought consistent with his duty and the public interest.

About this time a sudden wave of superstition swept over Rome. The Sibylline Books had been consulted because it had rained stones that year more often than usual, and in the Books a prophecy was found that if ever a foreign enemy should invade Italy, he could be defeated and driven out if Cybele, the Idaean Mother of the Gods, were brought from Pessinus to Rome. The effect upon the Senate of the discovery of this prophecy by the decemvirs was all the greater because the envoys who had taken the offering to Delphi declared that all the omens had been favorable when they sacrificed to the Pythian Apollo, and also that they had been granted a response by the oracle to the effect that a much greater victory was awaiting the Roman people than the one from the spoils of which they were bringing their offering. In support of these hopes the Senate was also inclined to adduce the sanguine temper of Scipio who, in that he demanded the right to operate in Africa, seemed to be confidently anticipating the end of the war. So they began seriously to consider the best means of transferring the image of the Goddess to Rome, in order to enjoy as soon as possible the victory which so many omens and oracles portended—from Delphi, from the Sibylline Books, and from the inexplicable confidence of Scipio.

Rome had not as yet any allies amongst the Asiatic states. But the Romans remembered that once upon a time the aid of Aesculapius the Healer had been called in to deal with an epidemic while there was still no treaty of alliance with Greece, and also that at the present juncture they were on friendly terms with King Attalus because of their common quarrel with Philip. In the belief, therefore, that Attalus would do what he could for them, they decided to send him a deputation. The envoys selected were Marcus Valerius Laevinus, who had been twice consul and had seen active service in Greece, the ex-praetor Marcus Caecilius Metellus, the ex-aedile Servius Sulpicius Galba, and two former quaestors, Gnaeus Tremelius Flaccus and Marcus Valerius Falto. Five quinqueremes were assigned to the deputation so that in a manner worthy of the dignity of Rome it might approach lands where it was desirable that the Roman name should win for itself the highest respect. The envoys on their way to Asia went up to Delphi, where they consulted the oracle, inquiring what hope it foresaw for them and the Roman people of bringing their mission to a successful conclusion. The answer, so it is said, was that they would get what they wanted by the help of King

Attalus, and that when they had brought the Goddess to Rome it would be necessary for them to make sure that she was hospitably welcomed by the best man in the City.

The envoys then visited Attalus in Pergamum. He received them courteously, escorted them to Pessinus in Phrygia, gave them the sacred stone supposed by the natives to represent the Mother of the Gods, and told them to take it back to Rome. Falto was sent in advance by the other envoys to announce that the Goddess was on the way and to tell people that the best man in the State must be sought out to give her due welcome.

Quintus Caecilius Metellus was named dictator by the consul in Bruttium to preside at the elections, and his army was disbanded. Lucius Veturius Philo was appointed his master of Horse. The elections were duly held; Marcus Cornelius Cethegus and Publius Sempronius Tuditanus were returned as consuls, the latter in his absence, as he was serving in Greece. The new praetors were Tiberius Claudius Nero, Marcus Marcius Ralla, Lucius Scribonius Libo, and Marcus Pomponius Matho. After the elections the dictator resigned from office.

The Roman Games were repeated on three, the Plebeian Games on seven days. The curule aediles were Gnaeus and Lucius Cornelius Lentulus; the latter was serving at the time in Spain, so he was not present either at his election or during his tenure of that office. The plebeian aediles were Tiberius Claudius Asellus and Marcus Junius Pennus. Marcellus dedicated this year the temple of Valor at the Porta Capena; it was sixteen years since it had been vowed by his father, in his first consulship, at Clastidium in Gaul. This year also saw the death of Marcus Aemilius Regillus, the priest of Mars.

12   For the past two years little attention had been paid to the situation in Greece. Philip, in consequence, compelled the Aetolians, abandoned as they were by the Romans, who had been their sole defense, to ask for peace and accept a settlement on his own terms. Had he not used every effort to bring this about promptly, he would have been surprised while still at war by the proconsul Sempronius, who had been sent out to relieve Sulpicius with a force of ten thousand infantry, one thousand cavalry, and thirty-five warships—aid to Rome's allies of no negligible weight. Hardly had peace been made when Philip received the news that the Romans were at Dyrrachium, that the Parthini and other neighboring peoples were up in arms in hope of a revolution, and that Dimallum was under siege. The Roman force had been sent to help the Aetolians, but had been diverted to Dimallum out of resentment against them for having made peace contrary to the treaty and without Roman consent. Philip, on receiving the news, was anxious to prevent a more serious rising amongst neighboring tribes and peoples; so he hurried to Apollonia on the track of Sempronius, who had gone there after sending his lieutenant Laetorius into Aetolia with a part of his forces and fifteen ships, to study the situation and upset the peace if he could. Philip devastated the outlying farms at Apollonia, marched up to the town and offered the Roman commander battle; but finding that Sempronius made no move, but contented himself with the defense of the walls, Philip, since he lacked confidence in his ability to storm the town and wanted peace with the Romans if he could get it, as well as with the Aetolians, or, failing peace, at least an armistice, withdrew to his own kingdom without further embittering relations with Rome by a fresh conflict.

About this time the Epirotes, sick of the long and tedious war, first assured themselves of Roman sympathy and then sent envoys to Philip to propose negotiating a general peace and to express their confidence that it would be agreed upon if he entered into personal talks with the Roman commander Sempronius. Philip, being by no means adverse to peace, was easily persuaded to go to Epirus; at the town of Phoenice he held preliminary talks with the Epirote officials Aeropus, Derdas, and Philippus, and afterwards met Sempronius. Present at the conversation between the two leaders were Amynander, King of the Athamanians, and other high officials of the Epirotes and Acarnanians. The first to speak was the Epirote magistrate Philippus, who made a joint request to the king and the Roman commander to do his people the favor of stopping hostilities. Sempronius then laid down as the conditions of peace the cession to Rome of the Parthini, Dimallum, Bargullum, and Eugenium, and the annexation of Atintania to Macedon, provided that Philip sent envoys to Rome and obtained the Senate's permission. These terms being agreed upon, Prusias King of Bithynia, the Achaeans, Boeotians, Thessalians, Acarnanians, and Epirotes were written into the treaty as on Philip's side, with the Ilii, King Attalus, Pleuratus, Nabis tyrant of Lacedaemon, the Eleans, Messenians, and Athenians on the Roman. The treaty was put in writing and signed, and a two months' armistice was agreed upon, to allow envoys to be sent to Rome in order to obtain the people's sanction for the peace terms. All the tribes gave their consent, as now that the war looked like shifting to Africa, they wanted to be relieved for the time being of all military commitments elsewhere. Sempronius, when the settlement had been made, left for Rome to enter upon his consulship.

It was now the fifteenth year of the Carthaginian war; new consuls, 13
Cornelius Cethegus and Sempronius Tuditanus, by decree of the Senate

were given command respectively of Etruria, with the old army, and of Bruttium, with orders to raise fresh troops. The City praetorship fell by lot to Marcius; the "Foreign" together with responsibility for Gaul to Libo; Sicily to Matho, and Sardinia to Nero. Scipio's command, together with the sea and land forces already under his control, was prolonged for a further year; the same was done in the case of Publius Licinius, who was to hold Bruttium with two legions for as long as the consul judged it expedient that he should remain there with full military powers. Livius and Lucretius also had their commands extended, each with the two legions with which they had defended Gaul against Mago, and Octavius's was extended with orders to hand over Sardinia and his legion to Nero, the new praetor, and with a fleet of forty ships to protect the coast within limits to be defined by the Senate. To Matho, the new praetor in Sicily, were assigned the two legions of the army of Cannae. Titus Quinctius and Gaius Hostilius Tubulus, as pro-praetors, were to hold respectively Tarentum and Capua, as in the previous year and in each case with the old garrison. As to the command in Spain, the people were formally consulted about which two men they wished to be sent there with proconsular powers, and the tribes were unanimous in naming for that duty the same two men as in the previous year, Cornelius Lentulus and Manius Acidinus. The consuls then began the task of raising fresh troops, both for the new legions which were to serve in Bruttium and also, according to the Senate's instructions, to reinforce the other armies.

14   The Senate had never yet openly decreed that Roman armies were to operate in Africa; they were keeping the project dark, I fancy, in order to prevent the Carthaginians from getting wind of their intentions. Nevertheless all Rome was confidently expecting that there would be fighting that year in Africa and that the end of the war was at hand. This sense of an impending crisis had produced a wave of superstition, and there was general readiness both to report and to believe stories of unnatural phenomena. A great many such stories were consequently in circulation: two suns, for instance, had been seen; daylight had appeared during the night; at Setia a meteor was seen to cross the sky from east to west; at Tarracina a gate had been struck by lightning, and at Anagnia both a gate and also the wall in a number of places; a strange noise, accompanied by a frightful crash, had been heard in the temple of Juno Sospita at Lanuvium. A day of prayer was ordered as an act of propitiation, and to deal with the rain of stones a further nine days' religious ceremony was held. In addition to all this there were deliberations about the reception in Rome of the Idaean Mother; Marcus Valerius, one of the envoys, had

hurried home in advance of the others to report that at any moment she would be in Italy, and another, more recent, message had arrived stating that she had already reached Tarracina. It was no easy question which the Senate had to decide—who, namely, was the best man in the State; and anyone would certainly have valued a clear victory in that contest above any high command or civil magistracy which might be offered him by the votes of Senate or people. The man whom the senate judged to be the best of good men in the whole community was Publius Scipio, son of the Gnaeus Scipio who was killed in Spain and therefore cousin of the Scipio who was soon to lead his army into Africa, and a young man not yet old enough to hold the office of quaestor. What particular virtues led them to this judgment I should gladly pass on to posterity if only contemporary chroniclers had told us what they were; but I do not propose to put forward any views of my own, which could only be guesswork in a matter so remote in time and consequently so obscure. This young Scipio, then, was ordered to meet the Goddess at Ostia, accompanied by the married women of Rome; he was to receive her out of the ship, carry her ashore, and deliver her into the matrons' hands. When his ship, according to instructions, reached the mouth of the Tiber, he sailed on out to sea, received the Goddess from the priests, and took her ashore. The leading women of Rome, of whom one distinguished name is that of Claudia Quinta, then took her from him—Claudia, whose previously dubious reputation, the story goes, has made her virtue all the more famous in after times as a result of this solemn service in the cause of religion. The women then passed the Goddess from hand to hand, one to another in succession, while all the population came thronging to meet her; censers were placed before the doorways on her route with burning incense, and many prayers were offered that she might enter the city of Rome with kindly purpose and benignant thoughts. So the procession moved on, till they brought her to the temple of Victory on the Palatine. It was the day before the Ides of April, and that day was held sacred. People crowded to the Palatine with gifts to the Goddess, and there was a Strewing of Couches and Games, called the Megalesia.

CATULLUS, *POEM 63*

During the first century B.C.E., the Latin poet Catullus (b. ca. 84–d. ca. 54) composed a poem about a person called Attis and his castration. Attis, in the madness of ecstasy, emasculates himself with a sharp flint, and becomes *notha mulier*, "counterfeit woman." After the frenzy of the

music and dance, Attis awakens the next morning to recall the bloody
deed of the night before, and "she" bemoans her fate. "Ego mulier, ego
adolescens, ego ephebus, ego puer . . . ego Maenas" ("A woman now, I
have been man, youth, and boy. . . . I, a Maenad"). Thus Attis becomes
a slave of the Great Mother and lives her life with Cybele. At the close of
the poem, Catullus prays that the fate of this Attis, and all those Galli
who thus emulate the mythic Attis, may not befall him. "Alios age
incitatos, alios age rabidos."

This translation (somewhat improved) is by C. H. Sisson, *The Poetry
of Catullus* (New York: Orion, 1967).

1 Carried in a fast ship over profound seas
   Attis, eager and hurried, reached the Phrygian grove,
   The goddess's dark places, crowned with woodland.
   And there, exalted by amorous rage, his mind gone,
5 He cut off his testicles with a sharp flint.
   She then, aware of her limbs without the man,
   While the ground was still spotted with fresh blood
   Quickly took in her snowy hands a tambourine
   Such as serves your initiates, Cybele, instead of a trumpet,
10 And shaking the hollow calf-hide with delicate fingers,
   Quivering, she began to sing to the troop this:
   "Go together, votaresses, to the high groves of Cybele.
   Go together, wandering herd of the lady of Dindymus.
   Quick into exile, you looked for foreign places
15 And, following me and the rule I had adopted,
   You bore with the salt tide and the violence of the high sea
   And emasculated your bodies from too much hatred of Venus:
   Delight the lady's mind with your errant haste.
   Overcome your reluctance: together
20 Go to the Phrygian shrine of Cybele, to her groves
   Where the voice of cymbals sounds, the tambourines rattle,
   Where the Phrygian piper sings with the deep curved pipe,
   Where Maenads wearing ivy throw back their heads,
   Where they practice the sacred rites with sharp yells.
25 Where they flutter around the goddess's cohort:
   It is there we must go with our rapid dances."
   As Attis, the counterfeit woman, sang this to her companions,
   The choir howled suddenly with tumultuous tongues.
   The tambourine bellows, the cymbals clash again;

The swift troop moves off to Ida with hurrying feet.   30
Crazy, panting, drifting, at her last gasp,
Attis with her tambourine leads them through the opaque groves
Like an unbroken heifer refusing the yoke:
The swift votaresses follow their swift-footed leader.
When they reach Cybele's shrine, feeble and worn,   35
From too much toil they take their rest without bread (Ceres).
Sleep covers their eyes with a heavy blanket;
Their rabid madness subsides to a girlish quiet.
But when the golden sun with his streaming eyes
Purified the white sky, hard land, wild sea,   40
And drove away the shadows of night with his thundering horses,
Attis was aroused and Sleep went quickly from her
Back to the trembling arms of the goddess Pasithea.
Then from her girlish quiet, with no hurrying madness,
Attis remembered what she had done   45
And saw in her lucid mind what was missing and where she was.
Tempestuously she turned back to the shore.
There, looking at the open sea with tearful eyes,
With grief in her voice she addressed her native land:
"Land which begot me, land which brought me forth,   50
I am abject to abandon you like a runaway slave.
My feet have carried me to the groves of Ida
To be among snow in the cold lairs of wild beasts;
I shall visit their violent haunts.
Where, O my land, can I imagine you are?   55
My eye desires you and narrows as it turns towards you
In this short interval when my mind is unfrenzied.
Shall I be carried to the forests, from my far-off home?
Away from country, goods, friends, family?
From the Forum, palaestra, racecourse, and gymnasium?   60
There is nothing for me but misery.
What shape is there that I have not had?
A woman now, I have been man, youth, and boy;
I was athlete, the wrestler.
There were crowds round my door, my fans slept on the doorstep;   65
There were flowers all over the house
When I left my bed at sunrise.
Shall I be a waiting maid to the gods, the slave of Cybele?
I a Maenad, I a part of myself, I impotent?

70   Shall I live above the snow line on green Ida?
     Shall I pass my life under the rocky peaks of Phrygia
     Where the doe runs in the woods, where the boar mooches in the glade?
     I regret now, now, what I have done, I repent of it, now!"
     As these words hurried away from her pink lips,
75   Bringing a new message to the ears of the gods,
     Cybele, letting her lions off the leash
     And urging forward the beast on the left hand,
     Said, "Get on, be fierce, see that he's driven mad;
     Make him insane enough to return to the forest;
80   He has had the impertinence to want to be out of my power.
     Come on, lash around with your tail till you hurt yourself:
     Make the whole neighborhood ring with your bellowing roar.
     Be fierce, shake the red mane on your muscular neck."
     Thus the threatening Cybele, and she wound the leash round her hand.
85   The beast stirs up his courage and rouses himself to fury.
     He is off, he roars, he breaks up the undergrowth.
     When he came to the wet sand on the whitening shore
     And saw tender Attis by the waters of the sea,
     He charged: Attis, mad, flew into the wild woods:
90   There, for the rest of her life, she lived as a slave.

     Great Goddess, Goddess Cybele, Goddess lady of Dindymus,
     May all your fury be far from my house.
     Incite the others, go. Drive other men mad.

PRUDENTIUS, *ON THE MARTYRS' CROWNS (PERISTEPHANON),*
10.1011–50

The Christian Latin poet Prudentius (b. 348–d. after 405) wrote with
obvious disgust about a ritual that was practiced, with various modifica-
tions, in the worship of the Great Mother and Attis especially in the second, third, and fourth centuries C.E. As Prudentius describes it, the
taurobolium (the ritual slaughter of a bull; compare to the similar
criobolium, the ritual slaughter of a ram) consisted of the sacrifice of an
animal above a pit into which a devotee descended, in order to be
drenched with the blood for the sake of spiritual purification. At times
certain "powers" of the sacrificial bull (most likely the genitals; cp. Clement of Alexandria, *Exhortation to the Greeks*, 2.15, on Zeus and the testicles
of a ram) were offered to the Mother of the Gods, and eventually, by the
time of Prudentius, the *taurobolium* functioned as a bloody baptism, con-

ferring rebirth upon the one so bathed. Sometimes the *taurobolium* could be repeated, and it seems to have been usual for a period of twenty years to elapse before the ceremony would be reenacted. One late inscription (376 c.e.) suggests that a person who submitted to the bath of blood was *in aeternum renatus*, "reborn for eternity."

This translation is from Maarten J. Vermaseren, *Cybele and Attis: The Myth and the Cult* (New York and London: Thames and Hudson, 1977), 102–03. For a good study on the *taurobolium*, see Robert Duthoy, *The Taurobolium: Its Evolution and Terminology*, EPRO, tome 10 (Leiden: Brill, 1969); cp. Vermaseren, 101–106.

Deep down into the pit the priest descends,
His temples with elaborate ribbons bound
And crowned with gold; his sacerdotal robe
Is made of silk, and in old Roman style
Tight round his waist traditionally girt.   1015
Across the pit is laid a board of planks
Too loosely joined in careless workmanship
And in its surface holes are cut and drilled;
The wood is riddled through, and everywhere
The eye discovers crevices and cracks.   1020
The formidable bull with lowering brow
Whose horns and withers are with garlands decked
Is presently escorted to the spot;
His forehead glitters with the trembling gold
And little golden discs flash on his flanks.   1025
The victim is thus quite rigged up to die
And with the sacred spear they penetrate its chest;
The wound gapes wide and pours in mighty waves
A stream of gushing blood over the wood,
An all-pervading odor spoils the air.   1030
Through thousand fissures now the shower drips
Of sordid fluid down the dismal pit
And on his head the priest catches the drops
With utmost care, his vestment soiled with blood
And all his body dabbled with the gore,   1035
Nay, bending backwards he presents his face,
His mouth and cheeks now to the scarlet flood;
His eyes he washes in the gory flow.
He moistens then his palate and his tongue

1040   And sucks and sips and gulps the somber blood.
       The bloodless rigid body of the beast
       Is dragged away now from its wooden bed;
       The priest, a gruesome sight, emerges from the pit
       And shows his head, his soggy bloody beard,
1045   His ribbons and his robe, drenched with the blood.
       Defiled by the atrocious sacrifice,
       Polluted by his recent horrid bath
       He is respectfully, but from afar, saluted
       Because the crowd has seen how in his tomb
1050   A bull's inferior blood has washed him clean.

LUCIAN OF SAMOSATA(?), THE SYRIAN GODDESS (DE DEA SYRIA), 1–16; 30–60

The tract *De Dea Syria*, attributed to Lucian of Samosata (second century C.E.), is a significant source of information on Syrian religion during the Roman period. The text begins with a rapid tour of several sacred sites in Phoenicia, including the great sanctuary of Aphrodite (cp. the Canaanite goddess Astarte) at Byblos, where the rites of Adonis, who was killed by a boar, were observed. (The author's comments about Osiris at Byblos [*The Syrian Goddess*, section 7] may be compared with Plutarch, *On Isis and Osiris*, 15–17.) The locale of particular interest to the author, however, is Hierapolis, "Holy City" (Bambyce, modern Mambij). There the deities worshiped are given Greek names by the author, who intimates that the gods and goddesses are not so named by the local worshipers (*The Syrian Goddess*, 31).

The temple and the rituals are dedicated to Zeus, Hera, and a bearded Apollo. Since the worship of the Syrian gods and goddesses was Semitic in character, these deities with Greek names may very well be the familiar Canaanite god El, the bearded patriarch of the gods, along with Baal or Hadad, and Atargatis. The Syrian goddess "Hera" is commonly called Atargatis or Derketo and is so closely linked to fish that at times she is portrayed as half woman and half fish (cp. *The Syrian Goddess*, 14). Her daughter is Semiramis, whose worship is linked to the dove.

As the text shows, the cult of the Syrian goddess was similar in some respects to that of the Great Mother of Phrygia (here named Rhea).

This translation is by Harold W. Attridge and Robert A. Oden, *The Syrian Goddess (De Dea Syria)*, Society of Biblical Literature Texts and

Translations, no. 9 (Missoula, Mont.: Scholars, 1976). The portion omitted (17–29) tells the story of Combabus's act of self-castration as the possible prototype of the similar acts of the Galli. For another text on the
Galli of the Syrian goddess, see Apuleius, *The Golden Ass*, book 8, in this
chapter.

In Syria there is a city not far from the Euphrates River. It is called   1
"Hire" (Holy) and it is the Holy City of the Assyrian Hera. I think that
this was not the name of the city when it was founded, and the ancient
name was different. Later, when their rites became important, the name
was changed to the present one. Concerning this city I am going to describe whatever is in it. I will tell of the customs which they observe in
connection with the rites, the festivals which they hold and the sacrifices
which they perform. I will also relate whatever stories they tell about
those who founded the sanctuary and about how the temple came into
being. I write as an Assyrian, and some of the things I relate I learned
firsthand, but what happened before my time I have learned from the
priests.

Now then, the Egyptians are supposedly the first men who formed a   2
conception of gods, established sanctuaries and sacred precincts, and in-
stituted festivals. They were also the first to conceive of holy names and
to tell sacred tales. Not long afterwards, the Assyrians heard an account
about gods from the Egyptians, and they established sanctuaries and
temples in which they placed images and set up statues.—In antiquity,   3
however, temples among the Egyptians were without a sanctuary.—In
Syria, too, there are sanctuaries almost as old as the Egyptian ones. Most
of these I have seen, in particular the one of Heracles at Tyre. This is not
the Heracles whom the Greeks celebrate in song. The one I mean is
much older and is a Tyrian hero.

There is another great sanctuary in Phoenicia, which the Sidonians   4
possess. According to them, it belongs to Astarte, but I think that
Astarte is Selene. One of the priests, however, told me that it is a sanctuary of Europa, the sister of Cadmus; that she was the daughter of
Agenor the king, and when she disappeared, the Phoenicians honored
her with a temple and told a holy tale about her, namely that Zeus desired her since she was beautiful, that he assumed the form of a bull,
seized her, and carried the girl off with him to Crete. I heard the same
tale from the other Phoenicians as well, and the coinage which the
Sidonians use depicts Europa sitting on the bull, which is Zeus, but they
do not agree that the temple is that of Europa.

5   The Phoenicians have yet another sanctuary, not Assyrian but Egyptian, which came to Phoenicia from Heliopolis. I have not seen it, but it is both large and ancient.

6   I did see, however, in Byblos a great sanctuary of Aphrodite of Byblos in which they perform the rites of Adonis, and I learned about the rites. They say, at any rate, that what the boar did to Adonis occurred in their territory. As a memorial of his suffering each year they beat their breasts, mourn, and celebrate the rites. Throughout the land they perform solemn lamentations. When they cease their breast-beating and weeping, they first sacrifice to Adonis as if to a dead person, but then, on the next day, they proclaim that he lives and send him into the air. They also shave their heads, as do the Egyptians when Apis dies. The women who refuse to shave pay this penalty: For a single day they stand offering their beauty for sale. The market, however, is open to foreigners only and the payment becomes an offering to Aphrodite.

7   There are some inhabitants of Byblos who say that the Egyptian Osiris is buried among them and that all the laments and the rites are performed not for Adonis but for Osiris. I will also tell you on what grounds they consider this account to be reliable. Each year a head comes from Egypt to Byblos, making the voyage in seven days, and the winds carry it by divine guidance. It does not turn aside in any direction, but comes only to Byblos. This is quite miraculous. It occurs every year; indeed, it happened while I was present in Byblos and I saw the "Byblian" head.

8   There is also another marvel in the land of Byblos. A river from Mount Lebanon empties into the sea. Adonis is the name given to the river. Each year the river becomes blood red and, having changed its color, flows into the sea and reddens a large part of it, giving a signal for lamentations to the inhabitants of Byblos. They tell the story that on these days Adonis is being wounded up on Mt. Lebanon and his blood, as it goes into the water, alters the river and gives the stream its name. This is the general version, but a certain man of Byblos, who seemed to me to be telling the truth, recounted another reason for the phenomenon. This is his account: "The River Adonis, stranger, comes through the Lebanon and Mt. Lebanon has a quite ruddy soil. Then strong winds come up on these days and deposit the earth, which is quite red, in the river, and the soil makes it blood red. The cause of this phenomenon is not the blood, as people say, but it is the land." This is the account which the man of Byblos gave me, but even if his version is correct, I consider the chance intervention of the wind quite divine.

9   Then I went up onto the Lebanon, a day's journey from Byblos, upon learning that an ancient sanctuary of Aphrodite, which Cinyras

founded, was there. I saw the sanctuary, and it is an ancient one. These then are the ancient and great sanctuaries in Syria.

But even if they are like this, it seems to me that none of them is 10 greater than those in the Holy City, nor could any other temple be more sacred nor any other region more holy. In the temple are many expensive artifacts and ancient offerings, many marvelous things and statues befitting the gods. Moreover, gods are readily manifest to the inhabitants. For the statues among them sweat and move about and give oracles, and a shouting often occurs in the temple when the sanctuary is locked, and many have heard it. Certainly in regards to wealth it is foremost among the places which I know about. For many treasures come to them from Arabia, Phoenicia, and Babylonia and still more from Cappadocia. The Assyrians as well as the Cilicians bring some.—I saw also what is secretly stored in the temple, much clothing and other items separated into silver or gold.—For in the matter of feasts and festivals, among no other people have so many been designated.

When I enquired about the age of the temple and whom they con- 11 sider its goddess to be, I heard many accounts. Some of them were sacred, some profane, some quite fabulous. Some were barbarian, and some agree with what the Greeks tell. I will tell them all, but in no way do I accept them.

Well then, the majority say that Deucalion, called Sisythes, founded 12 the sanctuary. This is the Deucalion in whose lifetime the flood occurred. About Deucalion I have heard an account among the Greeks, which the Greeks tell about him. The story goes as follows:

This race, the men of the present time, was not the first. As for the previous race, all in it perished. These current men are of the second race, which multiplied again from Deucalion. Concerning those earlier men they say the following. They were extremely violent and committed lawless deeds, for they neither kept oaths nor welcomed strangers nor spared suppliants. As punishment for these offenses the great disaster came upon them. Suddenly the earth poured forth a flood of water. Heavy rains fell, rivers rushed down in torrents, and the sea rose on high, until everything became water, and all the people perished. Deucalion alone among men was left for the second race because of his prudence and piety. This was the manner of his salvation: He embarked his children and his wives into a great ark which he possessed and he himself went in. As he boarded, pigs and horses, species of lions, snakes and every kind of creature that grazes on earth came to him, all of them in pairs. He welcomed all, and none harmed him. Instead, from some divine source, there was great friendship among them, and in a single ark

all sailed as long as the flood prevailed. This, then, is the story which
Greeks tell about Deucalion.

13   What happened after this, however, is the subject of a story told by
the inhabitants of the Holy City, and we may rightly be amazed at it.
They say that in their land a great chasm was formed and it took in all
the water. When this happened, Deucalion set up altars and built over
the chasm a temple sacred to Hera. I myself saw the chasm. It is beneath
the temple and quite small. Whether it was large of old, and now such a
size as it is, I do not know. In any case, the one that I saw is small.

As a symbol of this story they do this: Twice each year water from the
sea is carried to the temple. Not only priests, but the whole of Syria
and Arabia brings it and from beyond the Euphrates many men come
to the sea and all bring water. First they pour it out in the temple. Afterwards it goes down into the chasm, and the chasm, though small,
takes in a great deal of water. In doing these things they claim that
Deucalion established this custom in the sanctuary as a memorial both
of the disaster and of the divine favor. Such is their traditional account
about the sanctuary.

14   Others, however, think that Semiramis the Babylonian, whose deeds
in Asia are many, also founded this site and that she founded it not for
Hera, but for her own mother, whose name was Derketo. I saw a likeness of Derketo in Phoenicia, a strange sight! It is a woman for half its
length, but from the thighs to the tips of the feet a fish's tail stretches
out. The Derketo in the Holy City, however, is entirely a woman, and
the grounds for their account are not very clear. They consider fish something sacred and they never touch one. They eat all other birds, apart
from the dove. For them this is sacred. They think that these customs
came about on account of Derketo and Semiramis, the first because
Derketo has the form of a fish, and the second because Semiramis ultimately became a dove. Well, perhaps I accept the temple as a work of
Semiramis, but I certainly cannot believe that the sanctuary belongs to
Derketo. For among the Egyptians, some people do not eat fish, and
they do not do this to honor Derketo.

15   There is another sacred account, which I heard from a wise man, that
the goddess is Rhea, and the sanctuary is a creation of Attis. Attis was a
Lydian by birth, and he first taught rites pertaining to Rhea. All the rites
which Phrygians, Lydians, and inhabitants of Samothrace perform, they
learned from Attis. When Rhea castrated him, he ceased his male life
style. He took on instead a feminine form and donned female clothing.
He went out into every land, performed the rites, related his sufferings
and sang the praises of Rhea. On these journeys he came to Syria. Since

the men beyond the Euphrates accepted neither him nor the rites, he established the sanctuary in this place. Here is the proof: The goddess is similar in many ways to Rhea, for lions carry her, she holds a tympanum and wears a tower on her head, just as the Lydians depict Rhea. The wise man also said about the Galli who are in the temple, that Galli never castrate themselves for Hera, but they do for Rhea and they also imitate Attis. This explanation seems plausible to me but untrue, since I heard another reason for the castration which is much more believable.

I like what they say concerning the sanctuary, since they agree in **16** most respects with the Greeks in considering the goddess Hera and the construction a creation of Dionysos, son of Semele. For Dionysos came to Syria on that journey which he made to Ethiopia, and in the temple there are many indications that Dionysos is the founder. Among them are the foreign clothes and the Indian gems and the tusks of elephants, which Dionysos brought from Ethiopia. In addition, two quite large phalli stand at the gateway. On them is an inscription: "These phalli I, Dionysos, dedicated to Hera, my stepmother." As far as I am concerned, this is sufficient proof, but I will tell of another holy object of Dionysos which is in the temple. Greeks erect phalli to Dionysos on which they have something of this sort: small wooden men with large genitals. These are called puppets. This, too, is in the sanctuary. In the right part of the temple sits a small man of bronze with a large penis.

The temple faces the rising sun. In its form and structure, it is like the **30** temples which they build in Ionia. A large platform rises above the ground to a height of twelve feet and on this the temple rests. A ramp up to it is made out of stone and is not very long. When one has ascended, the front hall of the temple presents a marvelous sight, for it is furnished with doors of gold. From within, the temple gleams with a great quantity of gold and the roof is all gold. An ambrosial fragrance comes from it, such as they say comes from the land of Arabia. And as you approach even from a distance it sends forth a scent that is very pleasant. And as you depart, it does not leave you. Your clothes retain the scent for a long time, and you remember it forever.

In the interior, the temple is not a single unit, for a second chamber **31** has been made in it. The entry ramp to it is also short. It is not furnished with doors, but on the front it is completely open. All enter the large part of the temple, but into the chamber only priests go, and not even all the priests, but only those who are particularly close to the gods and to whom the overall service of the temple is entrusted. In this chamber are set statues of gods. One is Hera and the other is Zeus, whom, however, they call by another name. Both are of gold and both are seated, but lions support Hera, while the god sits on bulls.

The statue of Zeus certainly looks like Zeus in every respect: his head, clothes, throne. Nor will you, even if you want to, liken him to

32 anyone else. As one looks at Hera, however, she presents many different forms. On the whole, she is certainly Hera, but she also has something of Athena, Aphrodite, Selene, Rhea, Artemis, Nemesis, and the Fates. In one hand she holds a scepter, in the other a spindle. On her head she bears rays and a tower and she wears a girdle with which they adorn only celestial Aphrodite. On the surface of the statue is an overlay of gold and very costly gems, some of which are white, some the color of water, many have the hue of wine, and many are fiery. There are also many sardonyxes and sapphires and emeralds, which the Egyptians, Indians, Ethiopians, Medes, Armenians, and Babylonians bring.

I will tell what is worthy of a longer discussion. Hera bears a stone on her head. It is called a ruby light, and its name conforms with its function. A great light shines from this by night, and the whole temple is illumined by it as if by lamps. By day its glow is weak, although the gem still has a very fiery quality. There is also another wondrous feature in the statue. If you stand opposite and look directly at it, it looks back at you and as you move its glance follows. If someone else looks at it from another side, it does the same things for him.

33 Between the two statues stands another golden image, not at all like the other statues. It does not have its own particular character, but it bears the qualities of the other gods. It is called "Sign" by the Assyrians themselves, and they have not given it any particular name, nor do they speak of its origin or form. Some attribute it to Dionysos, others to Deucalion, still others to Semiramis. Indeed, on its head stands a golden dove. For this reason, then, they say that this "Sign" belongs to Semiramis. Twice each year the statue journeys to the sea to fetch the water which I mentioned previously.

34 In the temple itself, on the left of those entering, there is placed first the throne of Helios, but his image is not on it. For only of Helios and Selene do they not display statues. The reason for this custom I also discovered. They say it is right to make images for the other gods, for their forms are not visible to everyone, but Helios and Selene are completely visible and all see them. So, what reason is there to make statues of those gods who appear in the open air?

35 Behind this throne stands a statue of Apollo, but not as it is usually made. For all others think of Apollo as young and show him in the prime of youth. Only these people display a statue of a bearded Apollo. In act-

ing in this way they commend themselves and accuse the Greeks and anyone else who worships Apollo as a youth. They reason like this. They think it utter stupidity to make the forms of the gods imperfect, and they consider youth an imperfect state. They make yet another innovation in their Apollo, for they alone adorn Apollo with clothing.

About his deeds I could say a great deal, but I will describe only what **36** is especially remarkable. I will first mention the oracle. There are many oracles among the Greeks, many among the Egyptians, some in Libya, and many in Asia. None of the others, however, speaks without priests or prophets. This god takes the initiative himself and completes the oracle of his own accord. This is his method. Whenever he wishes to deliver an oracle, he first moves on his throne, and the priests immediately lift him up. If they do not lift him, he begins to sweat and moves still more. When they put him on their shoulders and carry him, he leads them in every direction as he spins around and leaps from one place to another. Finally the chief priest meets him face to face and asks him about all sorts of things. If the god does not want something done, he moves backwards. If he approves of something, like a charioteer he leads forward those who are carrying him. In this manner they collect the divine utterances, and without this ritual they conduct no religious or personal business. The god also speaks of the year and of all its seasons, even when they do not ask. He also talks about the "Sign," when it must make the journey which I have mentioned. I will tell something else which he did **37** while I was present. The priests were lifting him up and beginning to carry him, but he left them below on the ground and went off alone into the air. Behind the statue of Apollo is one of Atlas, and behind that is **38** one of Hermes and one of Eileithyia.

The objects within the temple are arrayed in the way we have de- **39** scribed. Outside stands a large bronze altar. Also there are myriads of other bronze statues of kings and priests. I will enumerate the especially memorable ones. On the left of the temple stands a statue of Semiramis indicating the temple on her right. She was set up for this reason: She established a law for the inhabitants of Syria that they should worship her as a goddess and that they should ignore the other deities, even Hera herself, and this they did. Later, when the diseases, disasters, and sorrows sent by the gods came upon them, she ceased from her madness, admitted her mortality, and ordered her subjects to turn once again to Hera. Therefore she still stands like this, demonstrating to those who come that they should worship Hera, and confessing that she is no longer a goddess but that the other is.

I also saw there statues of Helen, Hecabe, Andromache, Paris, Hec- **40** tor, and Achilles. I also saw an image of Nereus, son of Aglaie, and of Philomele and Procne, when they were still women, and of Tereus himself as a bird and another statue of Semiramis and the one of Combabus which I have described, and a very beautiful image of Stratonice, and one of Alexander very much like him. Next to him stood Sardanapallus in an unusual form and with unusual clothing.

41 In the courtyard large bulls, horses, eagles, bears, and lions graze at will. They do not harm men at all. Rather, all are sacred and tame.

42 Many priests have been appointed for the inhabitants, some of whom slaughter the sacrificial beasts, and some bear the libations. Others are called "Fire-bearers" and others "Altar Attendants." While I was there more than three hundred attended the sacrifice. Their robes are entirely white, and they wear a pilos on their head. A different high priest takes office each year. He alone wears purple and is crowned with a

43 golden tiara. There is also another group of holy men, flute players, pipers, and Galli, as well as women, who are frenzied and deranged.

44 Sacrifice is performed twice each day, and everyone comes to it. They sacrifice to Zeus in silence, neither singing nor playing the flute, but when they begin the ceremony to Hera, they sing and play flutes and shake rattles. They were unable to give me a clear explanation about this custom.

45 There is also a lake there, not far from the sanctuary. In it many sacred fish of different kinds are raised. Some of them become quite large. These fish have names and come when they are summoned. When I was there, there was one among them wearing gold. On its fin rests a golden artifact. I often saw the fish, and it always had the object.

46 The depth of the lake is great. I did not test it, but they say that it is more than 1,200 feet deep. In its middle stands an altar of stone. At first glance you might think it is adrift and floating on the water and many actually believe that it is, but I think that a great pile stands beneath it and supports the altar. It is always garlanded and has incense, and each day many people, to fulfill a vow, swim out carrying garlands.

47 At that spot great festivals also take place, and they are called "Descents to the Lake," because on these occasions all the sacred objects go down to the lake. Among them Hera goes first, for the sake of the fish, for fear Zeus see them first. For if this happens, they say that all the fish perish. He does come to have a look, but she stands in front of him, holds him off, and with many entreaties sends him away.

48 Their greatest festivals are those customarily observed by the sea. About these I have no reliable information to give, for I did not attend the festival myself, nor did I attempt this pilgrimage. I did see what they

do when they have returned and will describe it. Each person brings a vessel filled with water and these are sealed with wax. They themselves do not break the seal and pour out the water. Instead, there is a sacred cock, which lives by the lake. He receives the vessels from them, inspects the seal, and, when he receives a fee, breaks the bond and takes away the wax. Much money is collected by the cock as a result of this activity. Then they carry the water into the temple, pour libations and once they have sacrificed, they return home.

Of all the festivals I have known about, however, the greatest is the **49** one they hold at the beginning of spring. Some call it "Fire-Festival," others "Lamp Festival." During the festival they sacrifice like this: They chop down large trees and stand them in the courtyard. Then they drive in goats, sheep, and other livestock and hang them alive from the trees. In the trees are also birds, clothes, and gold and silver artifacts. When they have made everything ready, they carry the sacred objects around the trees and throw fire in, and everything is immediately burnt. Many men come to this feast from Syria and all the surrounding lands. Each group brings its own holy objects and each has a "Sign" made in imitation of the one here.

On appointed days, the crowd assembles at the sanctuary while **50** many Galli and the holy men whom I have mentioned perform the rites. They cut their arms and beat one another on the back. Many stand about them playing flutes, while many others beat drums. Still others sing inspired and sacred songs. This ceremony takes place outside the temple and none of those who performs it enters the temple.

On those days, too, men become Galli. For while the rest are playing **51** flutes and performing the rites, frenzy comes upon many, and many who have come simply to watch subsequently perform this act. I will describe what they do. The youth for whom these things lie in store throws off his clothes, rushes to the center with a great shout and takes up a sword, which I believe has stood there for this purpose for many years. He grabs it and immediately castrates himself. Then he rushes through the city holding in his hands the parts he has cut off. He takes female clothing and women's adornment from whatever house he throws these parts into. This is what they do at the Castration.

At death Galli do not receive a burial like other men. Instead, when- **52** ever a Gallus dies, his companions lift him up and carry him to the outskirts of the city. They set him down along with the bier with which they carried him. Then they pile up stones upon him and after completing this task they return home. They observe a period of seven days, then enter the sanctuary. If they enter before this time, they commit a sacrilege. **53**

In such matters they abide by the following customs: If anyone of them sees a corpse, he does not enter the sanctuary that day. On the following day, after purifying himself, he enters. When the corpse is that of a relative, they observe thirty days, shave their heads and then enter the temple. It is sacrilegious for them to enter sooner.

54 They sacrifice bulls and cows as well as goats and sheep. Swine alone they consider polluted, neither sacrificing nor eating them. Other people consider them holy, not polluted. Among birds they believe the dove to be something most holy and they do not think it right even to touch one. Indeed, if they touch one inadvertently, they are under a curse for that day. Consequently, doves are their associates. They come into their homes and often feed on the floor.

55 Now I will tell what each of the pilgrims does. Whenever someone is about to come to the Holy City, he shaves his head and his eyebrows. Then after sacrificing a sheep, he carves it and dines on the other parts. The fleece, however, he lays on the ground and kneels upon it, and the feet and the head of the animal he puts on his own head. When he prays, he asks that the present sacrifice be accepted and promises a larger one for the next time. After finishing these activities he puts a garland on his own head and those of everyone making the same pilgrimage. Then he sets out from his own country and makes the journey, using cold water both for bathing as well as drinking, and he always sleeps on the ground, for it is a sacrilege for him to touch a bed before he completes the journey

56 and returns to his own country. In the Holy City a host whom he does not know receives him, for there are specified hosts there for each city and they inherit this family duty. These men are called by the Assyrians "Instructors," because they explain everything to the pilgrims.

57 People do not sacrifice in the sanctuary itself, but when each has brought a sacrificial animal to the altar and has made a libation, he leads it off again alive to his own dwelling. Once there, he sacrifices it and prays by himself.

58 There is another form of sacrifice here. After putting a garland on the sacrificial animals they hurl them down alive from the gateway and the animals die from the fall. Some even throw their children off the place, but not in the same manner as the animals. Instead, having laid them in a pallet, they lower them down by hand. At the same time they mock them and say that they are oxen, not children.

59 All people are marked, some on their wrists and some on their necks. For this reason all Assyrians carry a mark.

60 Another thing they do resembles a custom which occurs among the Greeks only at Troezen. I will tell what these Greeks do. The people of

Troezen have a custom for their virgins and young men that they do not marry at all until they cut their locks in honor of Hippolytus, and this they do. This occurs also in the Holy City. The young men make an offering of their beards, while the young women let their "sacred locks" grow from birth and when they finally come to the temple, they cut them. When they have placed them in containers, some of silver and many of gold, they nail them up to the temple, and they depart after each inscribes his name. When I was still a youth I, too, performed this ceremony and even now my locks and name are in the sanctuary.

APULEIUS OF MADAUROS, *THE GOLDEN ASS* (*METAMORPHOSES*), Book 8.23–31

In the hilarious Latin novel *Metamorphoses* (or *The Golden Ass*), the second century c.e. author Apuleius of Madauros (in North Africa) gives his own description of the Galli or begging priests of the Syrian Goddess. The hero of the novel, Lucius, wants to explore the potent realm of magic and by mistake turns himself into an ass. The adventures of the ass-man Lucius constitute the balance of the novel. (On the salvific intervention of Isis and the initiation of Lucius into the Egyptian mysteries, see Chapter 6.)

In book 8 of *The Golden Ass*, poor Lucius encounters a "wicked old eunuch" named Philebus, who purchases the donkey as a beast of burden to carry the image of the goddess. Hardly a tale sympathetic to the practices of the Galli, the story of Lucius and the eunuchs nonetheless delights the reader and communicates the popular impression that the eunuch priests made upon many of the more skeptical Romans.

The following passage from Apuleius is translated by Jack Lindsay, *Apuleius: The Golden Ass* (Bloomington: Indiana Univ. Press, 1962).

Quitting this ill-omened house where the farm-hands were still upset **23** by this episode, we continued our march. Traveling all day across a plain we came tired-out on a proud and well-populated city. Here our men determined to set up their permanent hearth and home—partly because they could find no more dependable place in which to hide from any belated pursuers, partly because they knew the district to be plentifully blessed with provisions. They gave me and the other beasts three days in which to get fit and make ourselves more saleable; and then they led us out to the market. The crier roared out the price of each of us; and all the horses and the other asses were quickly purchased by well-to-do gentlemen. Me, however, the buyers either disregarded or regarded insultingly.

After a while I lost my patience at their way of poking me about and looking at my teeth to compute my age; and at last, when one man with a particularly offensive hand refused to leave off jabbing his dirty fingers into my gums, I snapped at him and nearly maimed him for life. This earned me the name of being a vicious brute, and further deterred the buyers.

Then the crier, lifting up his raucous voice till his throat almost split, pelted me in my misfortune with rotten jokes:

"Why do we stand here trying to sell this caricature of an ass, that's as old as the hills? His hooves are out-of-date, and his carcass is scraggy. He's idle except when backsliding, and his sole use in the world is to have sieves made out of hide. Let's make a free present of him to any man that won't grudge him a handful of hay."

24   In this manner the crier had all the market-folk rolling with laughter; but my cruel Fortune—which, far as I had fled, I had been unable to outdistance—which, deeply as I had paid, I had been unable to placate—once more squinted her blind eyes upon me and selected a buyer—yes, somebody bought me—the man most likely to give me a worse time. A eunuch bought me, wicked old eunuch, bald on the top and grizzledcurly over the ears, one of the lowest of the low among the charlatans that turn the Syrian Goddess into a beggar-wench, huckstering her about the highways and the towns, and jingling on cymbals and castanets. This man, taking a fancy to buy me, asked the crier what was the country of my origin.

"Cappadocian," answered the crier, "and strong as they make 'em."

The eunuch next inquired my age.

The crier cracked another joke. "The astrologer who calculated his nativity," he said, "told me five years; but probably the ass can best inform you out of his own mouth what is the registered number. For I certainly wouldn't like to bring the law down upon me for selling you a true-born Roman citizen as a slave. But if you take the risk and buy him, you'll have a good honest servant ready to do your pleasure at home or abroad."

This odious buyer then went on with question after question till he came anxiously to the subject of my disposition.

25   "Gentle?" exclaimed the crier. "He'll do anything you ask of him. Why, that's not an ass you're looking at; it's a lamb. He's not a biter, nor is he a kicker. He's such a model of an ass that you'd think he was a godfearing man hiding under an ass's skin. Prove it for yourself. Just put

your face between his hind legs, and you'll see in a twinkle how patient he is."

Thus the crier exerted his wit on the old gipsy, who, seeing through the mockery, exploded in rage. "Here you deaf and dumb fossil!" he shrilled. "You cracked crier! may the all-potent and all-procreant Syrian Goddess, and holy Sabazius, and Bellona, and the Idaean Mother, and Our Lady Venus with her dear Adonis, strike you blind for the scurrilous scoffs you've been slinging at me all this while! Do you think, you lout, that I'd put the Goddess on the back of a buck-jumping beast? That I'd let him give the Divine Image a spill? That I'd let him send me running about with my hair loose in the wind to find a doctor for my Goddess sprawling in the mud?"

When I heard this speech I considered going mad and curveting into the air as a sample of my intractable spirit and a warning against the purchase. But the man, keen to own me, planked down the money, seventeen pence, which my master promptly snatched up, as overjoyed as I was worried. Philebus—so my new owner was named—took immediate possession. He caught hold of the straw-bridle round my neck and led his new serving-beast straight towards home.

As soon as he reached the threshold, he cried out, "Girlies, troop up 26 and spy the darling slavelet I've brought you."

The girls, however, turned out to be a band of eunuchs, who at once began squeaking for delight in their splintering harsh womanish voices, thinking that it was really a man brought home trussed to do them good service. When they saw their mistake—not a stag as proxy for a virgin, but an ass for a man—they turned up their noses and sneered at their chief, saying that this wasn't a servant for them but a husband for himself. "But mind," they ended, "don't keep the pretty chickabud all to yourself. Don't forget that your dovie-wovies want a look-in sometimes."

Thus prattling, they took and fastened me to a manger. There was also among them a portly young fellow, well-versed on the flute, bought at market out of their collection-box. When they went out to carry the Syrian Goddess in processional, he walked in front, blowing tunes; and when they came indoors, he acted as rooster for the set of hens. My arrival was witnessed by this man with an expression of pleasure. He heaped the manger high with fodder and rapturously welcomed me. "You come in good time to take over the wear-and-tear of my job. Long life and good service to you, my ass! and what a chance to get my breath back for myself!"

27   These remarks made me brood over the troubles in store for me; but
next day the priesthood went out in a body, gowned in all the colors under the sun and hideously bedizened. Their faces were ruddied with cos-
metics and their eyes ringed darkly; they wore little turbans; their linen
was saffron-hued; and they were surpliced with silk. Some had donned
white tunics covered with purple stripes pointing out every way spear-
wise; and the whole mob displayed girdles and yellow shoes. They
dressed the Goddess in a silk-vestment, and placed her upon my back.
Then swinging oversized swords and axes, with their arms bared shoul-
der-high, they frolicked and bounded in maddened ritual-dance to the in-
citing flute-accompaniment.

    After performing before several cottages, they arrived at a rich man's
villa; and screeching their tuneless threnes from the moment they saw
the gates, they rushed frantically inside. Bending their heads, they
twisted, writhed, and rolled their necks to and fro, while their long hair
swung round in circles. Every now and then they dug their teeth into
their own flesh; and as a finishing effect each man slashed his arms with
the two-edged sword that he flourished. There was one of them preeminently ravished with religious ecstasy. Panting out deep sighs from his
heaving breast as if filled to bursting with the divine breath, he acted the
part of a raving lunatic—as though the presence of gods did not raise

28   man above himself but depressed him into disease and disorder. However, you will see that heavenly providence had the last word in sending
these rascallions their deserts. With a babbling parade of inspiration the
fellow began testifying against himself, pouring out a deal of idiocies
about the way in which he had sinned the Inexpiable Sin, and calling
upon his own hands to take vengeance upon him. He thereupon
snatched up one of the scourges which figure among the properties of
these half-men, and which have several long lashes of twisted wool
strung with sheeps-knucklebones; and with this knotty contraption he
flogged himself cruelly, bearing the pain of the blows with astonishing
fortitude. You could see the ground thickly sprinkled with the epicene
blood that gushed from the sword-cuts and the whip-weals. This spectacle of blood spouting from wounds on every side made me feel very
queasy lest the Goddess's belly might crave for ass's blood, as some
men's for ass's milk.

    When they wearied at last, or felt that they had flagellated their sins
sufficiently, they desisted from this shambles-show. Then the audience
vied with one another in showering coins, not only copper but silver
also, into the opened folds of the performers' gowns; and they heaped
up winecasks, milk, cheeses, barley, and wheaten meal—not to mention

barley for myself the depository of the Goddess. All these presents the priests greedily smuggled at once into bags kept ready for such alms; and the bags were festooned about my back—so that, doubly burdened, I was simultaneously walking Temple and Barn.

One day, feeling cheerful at the amount of the booty which a certain **29** town had forked-out, the priests decided to have a jovial supper party. They wheedled a very meaty ram from a farmer by means of some fortune-telling roguery, telling him that they would sacrifice it as supper for the hungry Goddess. When all the preparations were concluded, they went off to the Baths and returned later with a lusty young rustic, obviously chosen for his goodly proportions; and before the first course of a few herb-dishes had been fully dispatched, they lewdly fetched out in front of the table all the bawdy apparatus for the perfect perpetration of privy perversions. Gathering round the young fellow, naked and variously supine they turned upon him a stream of horrid solicitations.

Unable to bear such a sorry sight a moment longer, I did my best to shout "Help here!" but finding myself deprived of articulation, I could manage to produce no more than "Hee . . . haw . . ." That much was clear, resounding and appropriate to an ass, however unfortunate in the circumstances. For a crowd of young men of the neighborhood, who were in search of an ass stolen the night before, chanced to be prying and snooping into all the inns roundabouts. They heard my penetrating bray and thought that I was their ass concealed inside the house. Marshalling their ranks, they burst through the doors precipitately into the room and took the priests in flagrant filth. They at once called in everybody within hearing; and with a wealth of ironical compliments belauding priestly chastity, they disclosed the wicked scene that they had interrupted.

Dismayed at this exposure, which was rapidly rumored round and **30** which aroused the people's dislike and contempt, the priests collected their belongings and made a sneaking exit from the town about midnight. A fair distance was covered before the first sparkle of day; and we arrived shortly after sunrise in a deserted region where my owners held a long murmuring together and then girded themselves for my slaughter. They removed the Goddess from my back and laid her on the soil; they took off all my trappings and fastened me to a tree; and then they swung their whips tasselled with sheeps-knuckles and beat me till I was on the brink of passing-out. One of them threatened to cut my hamstrings with his hatchet, because I had infamously brayed his snow-white chastity away; but the others voted that I should be spared—out of consideration for the Goddess, not for me.

They therefore restored the load to my back; and cursing me on with blows from the flat of their swords, they proceeded till they reached a fine city. One of its chief citizens, a very religious man with a partiality for the Goddess, heard the clash of the cymbals, the thumping of the timbrels, and the mollifying drone of the Phrygian music. He hurried out to meet us and to offer his pious protection to the Goddess; and lodging us within the walls of his magnificent mansion, he courted divine favor with humble homage and sacrifice-de-luxe.

31   Here, however, I endured the greatest of all the dangers that I can remember. A certain farmer had sent to our host, his landlord, a fat thigh of a full-grown stag as a toll on his hunting. The venison had been negligently hung rather low behind the kitchen-door; and a dog, intruding for a sniff, pulled it down and made off with it in glee. The cook, on noticing his loss, blamed himself with a wailing waste of unavailing tears and at length, when the master asked for supper to be served, the cook, devastated with grief and terror, gave a farewell-kiss to his small son, picked up a cord, and prepared to hang himself in place of the meat. But his loving wife got wind of her husband's sad fix and arrived in time to seize the fatal noose with both her hands.

"What's this?" she cried. "Has an accident terrified your senses away? Don't you behold the lucky substitute that the gods' providence has provided? If this whirlwind of fate hasn't dizzied you out of your wits, rouse yourself and lend an ear. Take this new arrival of an ass to some lonely spot and cut his throat. Hack from his carcass a haunch like the lost one, cook it and baste it in the most piquant savory sauces you can invent, and then serve ass up to your master disguised as stag."

The heartless jailbird grinned at the notion of saving himself at my cost; and verbosely praising his better-half's shrewdness, he began whetting his knives for a proposed butchery.

HIPPOLYTUS OF ROME, REFUTATION OF ALL HERESIES (REFUTATIO OMNIUM HAERESIUM), 5.7.1–24; 8.31–9.11

The mysteries of the Great Mother and Attis were exciting and entertaining, but for many thoughtful people they were simply too bizarre to be experienced directly. Some thinkers, such as the fourth-century emperor Julian (called "the Apostate"), studied the mysteries of the Mother of the Gods with great care and then drew philosophical or ethical conclusions. In his *Orations* Julian tries to show, for instance, that the real lesson to be learned from the account of the cutting of the pine tree in the myth of the Great Mother and Attis is that one should harvest the best crop possible, namely virtue and piety, and strive upward like a tree toward the goddess above (*Hymn to the Mother of the Gods,* 169). The philosopher Sallustius, in *Concerning the Gods and the Universe* (*De deis et mundo*), likewise interprets the myth of Cybele and Attis allegorically, according to the tenets of Neoplatonism (see particularly section 4 of his treatise).

In his *Refutation of All Heresies,* the Christian heresiologist Hippolytus (b. ca. 170–d. ca. 236) reports on certain Christian Gnostics, the Naassenes (from the Hebrew for "serpent"), who also reinterpreted the mysteries of the Great Mother and Attis to suit their own religious purposes. The Naassenes, like so many other Gnostics, were intensely eclectic and sought religious truth from a variety of sources—particularly sources within the mysteries. Hippolytus's account of the Naassenes refers to themes from the mysteries of Adonis, Demeter and Persephone (or Kore), and Isis and Osiris, but the statements about the mysteries of the Great Mother and Attis are most important for our purposes.

The Naassene Gnostics attended the celebrations of the mysteries of the Great Mother so that they might thereby come to a better understanding of "the universal mystery." Because they claimed that "everything is spiritual," the Naassenes did not become Galli physically but rather spiritually: "they only perform the functions of those who are castrated" by abstaining from sexual intercourse (*Refutation of All Heresies,* 5.9.10). The myth of the castration of Attis led the Naassenes to conclude that the image of emasculation was a symbol of salvation. The masculine power (that is, the heavenly portion) of the soul is severed from the earth, so that it can ascend to the divine realm above (ibid., 5.7.13–15; cp. 8.44).

This translation from Hippolytus is by Werner Foerster, *Gnosis: A Selection of Gnostic Texts,* vol. 1 (Oxford: Clarendon, 1972). Incorporated into the passages on the Naassenes are two remarkable hymns to Attis (ibid., 5.9.8–9), both of which are syncretistic in character. The second hymn advocates a domestication of the wilder side of Attis: Attis is praised in harmony with "the muse of Phoebus's (Apollo's) lyre."

Two excellent studies of the Naassenes are available: R. Scott Birdsall, "The Naassene Sermon and the Allegorical Tradition: Allegorical Interpretation, Syncretism, and Textual Authority" (Ph.D. dissertation, Claremont Graduate School, 1984); and Josef Frickel, *Hellenistische Erlösung in christlicher Deutung: Die Naassenerschrift,* Nag Hammadi Studies, vol. 19 (Leiden: Brill, 1984).

T hese are the principal points out of a great number of discourses 7.1
which James the Lord's brother is said to have delivered to

2 Mariamne. . . . The basis of their system is the Man Adamas, and they
  say that he is the subject of the text, "His generation, who shall declare
3 it?" . . . The earth it was, according to the Greeks, that first produced
  man, bearing a noble gift; for she desired to be the mother, not of senseless plants nor of brute beasts but of a tractable and God-loving creature.
4 But it is hard to discover, he says, whether with the Boeotians beyond
  Lake Cephisis Alalcomeneus appeared as the first of mankind, or
  whether it was the Kouretes of Mount Ida, that divine race, or the
  Phrygian Korybantes, whom first the sun beheld springing up like trees;
  or did Arcadia (see) Pelasgus, a man older than the moon, or Eleusis
  (see) Diaulus who dwelt in Raria; or did Lemnos engender the fair child
  Kabiros in an unspeakable ecstasy, or Pellene the Phlegraean Alcyoneus,
5 the eldest of the giants? But the Libyans say that Garamas was the first-
  born, who arose from the desert lands, and began upon the sweet acorn
  of Zeus. And in Egypt the Nile enriching her silt to this very day, he
  says, brings to life (creatures) clothed in flesh by her moist warmth and
6 bears living beings. The Assyrians say that Oannes the fish-eater came
  from them, the Chaldaeans speak (likewise) of Adam. And they say that
  he was the man whom the earth produced by herself; and he lay without
  breath, without motion, without a tremor, like a statue, being an image
  of that celestial being praised in song, the Man Adamas; and he was
  made by the many powers, who are severally described at length.
7   Now in order that the great Man from on high should be completely
  held fast, "from whom," as they say, "every family that is named on
  earth and in heaven" originates, there was given to him also a soul, so
  that through his soul suffering and punishment in slavery might come
  upon the creation of that great and most noble and perfect Man; for
8 that is what they call him. So they inquire again, what is the soul, and
  whence comes it, and what is its nature, that by coming into man and
  quickening him it should enslave and punish the creation of the perfect
  Man; and they make this inquiry, not from the scriptures, but once
  again from the secret writings. And they say that the soul is most hard
  to discover and hard to conceive, for it does not remain in the same
  form or shape all the time, or in one condition, so that one could de-
9 scribe its character or conceive its substance. These manifold alterations
  they have set down in the Gospel entitled "According to the Egyptians." And they wonder, like all the other Gentiles, whether it comes
  from the Pre-existent or from the Self-originate or from the outpoured
  chaos.
      And first, since they envisage the threefold division of mankind, they
  take refuge in the rites of the Assyrians. For the Assyrians are the first

who have held that the soul is divided in three, (yet) also one. For, they **10**
say, every species seeks after soul, but in different ways. For the soul is
the cause of everything that comes into being; for, he says, everything
that takes nourishment and grows requires a soul. For nothing, he says,
is able to obtain either nourishment or growth if a soul is not present.
Even the stones, he says, have souls; for they possess the power of
growth. And growth could never take place without nourishment; for
the things that grow, grow by adding (to themselves); and the addition
is the nourishment of the thing that takes nourishment. So every spe- **11**
cies, he says, "of things in heaven and things on earth and things under
the earth" seeks after soul. And the Assyrians call this Adonis or
Endymion. And when it is called Adonis, he says, then Aphrodite loves
and desires the soul of this name; and Aphrodite for them means generation. But when Persephone, who is also called Kore, loves Adonis, then, **12**
he says, the soul is something mortal, separated from the generation
that belongs to Aphrodite. And if Selene comes to desire of Endymion
and to love of form (or: formation), the higher creation, he says, also requires soul. But if, he says, the mother of the gods castrates Attis, **13**
though she too is in love with him, then, he says, the sublime and
blessed nature of the supercelestial and eternal (realities) recalls the masculine power of the soul to herself.

For Man, they say, is bisexual. So in accordance with this thought of **14**
theirs, the intercourse of woman with man is in their teaching shown to
be most wicked and prohibited.

For, he says, Attis was castrated, that is, (cut off) from the earthly **15**
parts of the creation (here) below, and has gone over to the eternal substance above where, he says, there is neither female nor male, but a new
creature, "a new man," who is bisexual. . . .

And, they say, their thought is confirmed not only by Rhea alone, **16**
but by practically the whole creation. And, they explain, this is what is
meant by the text, "For his invisible things have been discerned since the
creation of the world, being known through his works, namely his eternal power and glory, so that those men have no excuse; because although they knew God they did not glorify him as God nor render him
thanks, but their senseless heart was made futile. For though they said **17**
they were wise, they became fools, and exchanged the glory of the incorruptible God for likenesses of the form of corruptible man and of birds,
beasts, and creeping things. Therefore God has given them over to
shameful passions; for their women have exchanged natural intercourse
for unnatural"—and what natural intercourse is in their view we shall de- **18**
scribe in due course—" and likewise the men, giving up natural inter-

course with women, have been inflamed with passion for one another;
men behaving shamelessly with men"—and shamelessness for them is
(lack of form, the) primal, blessed, formless substance, which is the
cause of all forms in the things that are formed—"and receiving in them-
19 selves the due reward for their error." For these words spoken by Paul,
they say, contain the whole secret and unspeakable mystery of blessed
enjoyment. For the promise of the washing (in baptism) is, they say,
nothing less than the introduction into unfading enjoyment of him who
in their fashion is washed in living water and anointed with unutterable
anointing.

20   And not only the mysteries of the Assyrians and Phrygians but also
those of the Egyptians, they say, confirm their thought about the blessed
nature, concealed and yet disclosed, of what has come to pass and
comes to pass and will come to pass, which he says is the kingdom of
heaven within man which is sought after, concerning which they clearly
deliver (their teaching) in the Gospel entitled "According to Thomas," in
these words, "He who seeks will find me in children from seven years
onwards; for there I am found, who am hidden, in the fourteenth age
21 (Aion)." . . . Hence they locate the generative nature of the universe in
the generative seed and say . . . that a child of seven years is half a father, that he reveals himself at fourteen years, according to Thomas.
This is the unutterable and mystical doctrine that they hold.

22   They say indeed that the Egyptians, who next to the Phrygians are
the oldest (race) of all mankind, and admittedly were the first to teach all
other men after them the rites and orgies of all the gods and their forms
and activities, possess the holy and venerable mysteries of Isis that must
23 not be disclosed to the uninitiate. And these are nothing else than that
which was stolen and was sought by the lady of the seven robes and the
sable clothing, the "shame" (i.e., genital part) of Osiris. Now Osiris is
their name for water. And nature has seven robes, since it wears and is
robed in seven ethereal robes—for thus they refer to the planets by their
allegory, and call them ethereal; and through these, they say, the process of change is displayed by the ineffable, unimaginable, inconceiv-
24 able, formless being, transforming creation. And this is what is meant by
the text, "Seven times the righteous one shall fall and shall arise"; for
these "falls," they say, are the changing positions of the stars as they are
moved by him who moves all things.

8.31   This same being is also called "the unfruitful" by the Phrygians. For
he is unfruitful when he is carnal and executes "the desire of the flesh."
This, he says, is the saying, "Every tree that does not bear good fruit is

cut down and cast into the fire." For these fruits, he says, are nothing but the rational, the living men, those who enter through the third gate. So they say, "If you ate dead things and made them living, what will you do if you eat living things?" By "living" they mean reasons and minds and men, the pearls belonging to that uncharacterized being that are thrown down into the molded creature. This is the saying, "Do not throw what is holy to the dogs, nor pearls to the pigs," for they say that this is pigs' and dogs' business, the intercourse of women with men.

This same being, he says, the Phrygians call Aipolos (the Goatherd), not, he says, because he pastured goats and kids, as the psychic (unenlightened) men name him, but, he says, because he is *aeipolos*, that is, he who "always pulls" round and turns and rotates the whole universe in a circle. For "pulling" means turning and altering things. For this reason, he says, the two centers of the heavens are always called "poles." And the poet says, "Here turneth in (*poleitai*) a sage old merman, the immortal Proteus of Egypt"; he does not mean that he is on sale (*poleitai*) but that he turns in his place and as it were goes round. And the cities in which we live are called cities (*poleis*) because we turn around and circulate (*poloumen*) in them. So, he says, the Phrygians call him Aipolos, who always everywhere turns all things round and changes them to his own.

And, he says, the Phrygians also call him "the Fruitful one," because, he says, "the deserted wife has more children than she that keeps her husband," that is, many are those who are reborn, who are immortal and last for ever, even if those who are born are few; what is carnal, he says, is always corruptible, even if there are very many who are born. For this reason, he says, "Rachel wept for her children, and would not be comforted as she wept over them; for she knew," he says, "that they are not." And Jeremiah also laments for the earthly Jerusalem, (meaning) not the city in Phoenicia, but the corruptible earthly generation; for, he says, Jeremiah knew the perfect man who is regenerated "by water and the spirit," not the carnal one. Indeed Jeremiah himself said, "He is a man, and who shall know him?" This (shows), he says, how very deep and incomprehensible is the knowledge of the perfect man: for, he says, the beginning of perfection is the knowledge of man, but complete perfection is the knowledge of God.

But the Phrygians, he says, also call him "the green ear that is harvested," and the Athenians also, following the Phrygians, when they make the initiations of Eleusis and display to the beholders that great and wondrous and most perfect mystery which is to be beheld there is silence, a harvested ear. Now this ear is for the Athenians too the great and perfect Illuminator coming from the uncharacterized one; likewise the hierophant himself, who is not indeed castrated, like Attis, but is made a eunuch with hemlock and is separated from all carnal generation, when he celebrates the great and unutterable mysteries by night at Eleusis under a brilliant light, calls out and proclaims these words: "A holy child is born to the Lady Brimo, Brimos"—that is, to the Strong one,

41 the Strong. Lady, he says, means the spiritual birth, the heavenly, higher (birth); and strong is the man who is born in this fashion. And the mystery aforesaid is called Eleusis and Anactoreum; Eleusis, he says, because we have come, we who are spiritual, flowing down from above, from Adamas—for *eleusesthai*, he says, means "to come"—and

42 Anactoreum because of our ascent on high (*ano*). This, he says, is what the devotees of the Eleusinian cult call the great mysteries; for it is the custom that those who have been initiated into the lesser should again be initiated into the great ones; for "greater dooms gain greater desti-

43 nies." For the lesser mysteries, he says, are those of Persephone here below; and of these mysteries and the road that leads there, which is "broad and wide" and leads those who are perishing to Persephone, the poet also says: "But beneath it is an awesome pathway, cavernous and clayey; but this is the best that leads to the pleasant grove of glorious

44 Aphrodite." This means, he says, the lesser mysteries of birth in the flesh; and when men have been initiated into these they must wait a little before they are initiated into the great, heavenly ones. For those who are allotted those dooms, he says, receive greater destinies. For this, he says, is "the gate of heaven," and this is "the house of God," where the good God dwells alone, where no unclean person, he says, shall enter, no psychic (unspiritual), no carnal man, but it is reserved for the spiritual alone; and when men come there they must lay down their clothing and all become bridegrooms, being rendered wholly male through the

45 virgin spirit. For she is the virgin who is with child and conceives and bears a son, who is not psychic, not bodily, but a blessed Aion of Aions. Concerning this, he says, the Savior has said clearly that "straight and narrow is the way that leads to life, and few there are that enter upon it; but wide and broad is the way that leads to destruction, and many there are who pass over it."

9.1   The Phrygians also say that the Father of the universe is Amygdalus, an almond (tree); it is not a tree that is amygdalus, he says, but it is that preexistent being, who having within himself the perfect fruit, which was so to say stirring and moving deep within him, opened his heart and begot that invisible, unnameable, and unutterable Son of his, of

2 whom we are speaking. For (the word) *amyxai* means to break and cut open, as in the case of bodies which are inflamed, he says, and have in

them a sort of gathering such as doctors call *amychai* when they cut them open. So, he says, the Phrygians call the preexistent being Amygdalus, from whom there came forth and was begotten the invisible one through whom "all things were made and without him nothing was made." And **3** the Phrygians call that offspring of his a "flute-player," because that offspring is a spirit in harmony. For "God is a spirit," he says, "and therefore it is neither in this mountain nor in Jerusalem that the true worshipers offer worship, but in the spirit." For the worship of the perfect, he **4** says, is spiritual, not carnal. And the spirit, he says, is there wherever the Father is named together with the Son who was begotten there from this same Father. This, he says, is the being with many names, the thousand-eyed, the incomprehensible, after whom every nature strives in its own fashion.

This, he says, is the word of God, namely the word of the Exposition **5** (*Apophasis*) of the Great Power; "hence it shall be sealed and covered and veiled, stored up in the dwelling-place where the root of all things has its foundation"—(the root) of Aions, powers, conceptions, of gods, angels, and courier spirits, of (all) that are and that are not, originate and unoriginate, incomprehensible and comprehensible, of years, months, days, and hours, of the indivisible point from which the smallest thing gradually begins to grow; for the indivisible point, he says, which is nothing and consists of nothing, will by its conception of itself become an inconceivable magnitude. This, he says, is the kingdom of heaven, the **6** mustard-seed, the indivisible point existing in the body which, he says, no man knows but the spiritual only. This, he says, is what is written, "There are no words nor speeches, whose voices are not heard." So they **7** ramble on, adapting everything that was said or done by anyone to their own theory, saying that everything is spiritual. Hence they say that even the performers in the theater do not speak or act without providence. Therefore, he says, when the community assembles in the theater and there enters one clothed in a peculiar dress carrying a lyre and singing to it, then in his hymn he declares the great mysteries without knowing what he says:

Be it the race of Kronos, or the blessed child of Zeus or of great Rhea, **8**
Hail to thee, Attis, sad message of Rhea;
Assyrians call thee thrice-desired Adonis, all Egypt, Osiris,
The wisdom of the Greeks, the heavenly crescent moon,
The Samothracians, venerable Adamas,
The men of Haemus, Korybas,
The Phrygians, sometimes Papas, or again the Dead, or God,

Or the Unfruitful, the Goatherd, or the green Ear that is harvested,
Or the Man, the Flute-player, born of the fruitful Almond.

9 This being, he says, is the many-formed Attis, whom they describe as follows in their hymns:

I will sing of Attis, the son of Rhea,
Not with the clang of bells nor with the flute or with the bellowing of the
    Kouretes of Ida,
But I will tune it to the muse of Phoebus's lyre.
All hail! All hail!—as Pan, as Bacchos,
    as shepherd of the shining stars

10 Because of these words, and others like them, they attend the so-called mysteries of the Great Mother, thinking that through those (sacred) actions they will best understand the universal mystery. For these men have nothing (to offer) beyond what is done there, except that they are not castrated, they only perform the functions of those who

11 are castrated. For they urge most severely and carefully that one should abstain, as those men do, from intercourse with women; their behavior otherwise, as we have fully explained, is like that of the castrated.

6
The Egyptian
Mysteries of Isis
and Osiris

6
The Egyptian Mysteries of Isis and Osiris

Of the hundreds of gods and goddesses worshiped in ancient Egypt, Isis, Osiris, and the members of their divine family were among the most influential. Isis, a mother goddess of remarkable magical powers, is closely identified with the royal throne of the pharaoh. In hieroglyphic characters her name (Seat) is the throne, and her role in Egyptian myth guarantees an orderly succession on the throne of Egypt from one pharaoh to another. Osiris is the brother and husband of Isis, and he possesses generative powers that enable the Egyptian land watered by the Nile to be fertile and productive of crops. Politically, Osiris is the prototype of the pharaoh, specifically the deceased pharaoh who vacates the throne in the upper world and functions as ruler of the underworld. For this reason Egyptian artists portray Osiris as a mummy in linen wrappings, with a crown upon his head and emblems of sovereignty, such as the crook and flail, in his hands.

In Egyptian mythology the brother and rival of Osiris, Set, kills him, but Horus, the son of Isis and Osiris, defeats Set. Thus Horus, as the mythological counterpart of the living pharaoh, succeeds his dead father and ensures the triumph of continuity and order in Egyptian life. Isis, meanwhile, along with Thoth, Horus, Anubis, and Nephthys, employs her magical powers to mummify Osiris and thereby to restore him from death to life.

Already in ancient Egypt, at Abydos and other locales, there were "mysteries" of Isis and Osiris, but they were different from the Greco-Roman mysteries that have been discussed. Egyptologists write about such a "mystery" as the mystery play of succession, which made use of elaborate rites to dramatize, mythologically, the death of one pharaoh and the accession of another, who still is related to and united with the dead king. Another "mystery" in ancient Egypt, related to the mystery play of succession, was the funerary ritual of mummification and burial. The Egyptians believed that one who experienced the appropriate funerary rites would live again by being joined, mystically, to Osiris. Initially, those rites were reserved for royalty, but eventually nobles and even ordinary people could have hope for spiritual resurrection.

By the Hellenistic period the worship of Isis and Osiris had become established in one form or another among the Greeks, and a bit later it was also common among the Romans. Often the worship took the form of the Greco-Roman mysteries of these Egyptian deities. Fortunately, book 11 of the *Metamorphoses* of Apuleius tells us much about the mysteries of Isis and Osiris. (A translation of book 11 is given in this chapter.) In addition to furnishing a full account of the public ceremonies that precede the initiation itself, Apuleius offers a guarded description of what happened during the evening of the secret initiation of Lucius (the "I" of the text) within the Holy of Holies in the temple of Isis:

> I approached the confines of death. I trod the threshold of Proserpine; and borne through the elements I returned. At midnight I saw the Sun shining in all his glory. I approached the gods below and the gods above, and I stood beside them, and I worshiped them. (*Metamorphoses*, 11.23)

This brief account recalls the depiction in the Egyptian *Book of the Dead* of the deceased person encountering Osiris, Re the Sun god, and the other deities in the next life. In Apuleius, too, the experience of initiation is taken to be an experience of death. That is obvious not only from the present passage, but also from a previous reference in the same book to "the act of initiation" as "a voluntary death" (*Metamorphoses*, 11.21). The comment about Lucius being "borne through the elements" is similar to the statement at the opening of the *Mithras Liturgy* (see Chapter 7) about the transformation and glorification of the elements in the body of an initiate. Furthermore, within the realm of death, Lucius sees the Sun. The experience of beholding the light in the darkness may very well have been prompted by priests manipulating torches at key points in the ritual, but the interpretation of the experience as one of seeing the Sun is thoroughly in keeping with ancient descriptions of the realm of death, particularly Egyptian descriptions. The Egyptians believed that the Sun traveled through the underworld during the night, so that a person who entered the underworld could greet the Sun, as well as the other deities of the underworld, and worship them there.

In Apuleius's account, on the morning after the solemn initiation, Lucius appears as the rising sun. It is not unlikely that the initiated Lucius is thought to have been reborn; Apuleius himself uses the Latin term *renatus*, "reborn" or "born again," elsewhere in book 11. Lucius emerges from the Holy of Holies wearing twelve stoles (probably symbolic either of having passed the twelve hours of the night in the underworld or of the twelve signs of the zodiac), a glorious vestment of embroidered linen, and a crown decorated with palm leaves that look like the sun's rays. This day is a day of feasting and celebration, a birthday of sorts.

Two *symbola* quoted by the fourth-century Christian author Firmicus Maternus may shed additional light upon the mysteries of Isis and Osiris in Roman antiquity. According to Firmicus Maternus, on a certain holy occasion the devotees of Isis and Osiris cry out, *heurekamen, synchairomen,* "We have found! We rejoice together!" (*The Error of the Pagan Religions,* 2.9). The occasion for this exultant cry is the celebration observed in November in Rome, called the Inventio Osiridis, the "finding of Osiris." During this celebration the worshipers share the grief and the joy of Isis, who sought for the body of Osiris and finally found and embalmed him (cp. Plutarch, *On Isis and Osiris,* 27). Firmicus Maternus also quotes a second *symbolon* that probably derives from the mysteries of Isis and Osiris (according to some scholars, it may come from the mysteries of Attis). Even though Firmicus Maternus does not specify its source, it corresponds well with the joyful perspective of the previous *symbolon.* After the worshipers have mourned over a prone statue, a light is carried into the place, and a priest anoints the throats of the mourners and whispers, "Be of good cheer, O initiates (*mystai*), for the god is saved, and we shall have salvation from our woes" (*The Error of the Pagan Religions,* 22.1).

Given the popularity of the Egyptian goddess Isis in the Roman world, we are not surprised to observe that the worship of Isis shaped the veneration of the Virgin Mary in Christian circles. Isis and Mary both are blessed Mothers who were acclaimed queen of heaven (*regina caeli*), were linked to the moon, and were often portrayed with their sons (Horus or Jesus) sitting formally on their laps.

On the ancient Egyptian worship of Isis and Osiris see E. A. Wallis Budge, *The Gods of the Egyptians: Studies in Egyptian Mythology,* 2 vols. (1904; reprint, New York: Dover, 1969); idem, *Osiris,* 2 vols. (1911; reprint, New York: Dover, 1961); Henri Frankfort, *Ancient Egyptian Religion: An Interpretation* (New York: Harper & Row, 1948); idem, *Kingship and the Gods: A Study of Ancient Near Eastern Religion as the Integration of Society and Nature* (Chicago: Univ. of Chicago Press, 1948), esp. Chapter 11, "The Mystery Play of the Succession," 123–39; Siegfried Morenz, *Egyptian Religion* (Ithaca, N.Y.: Cornell Univ. Press, 1973); Georges Nagel,

"The 'Mysteries' of Osiris in Ancient Egypt," in *The Mysteries*, ed. Joseph Campbell, Bollingen Series, no. 30, Papers from the Eranos Yearbooks (Princeton: Princeton Univ. Press, 1978), 119–34. Special attention may be given to the *Book of the Dead* (or *Chapters of Going Forth by Day*), in which the deceased is described as united with Osiris and renewed to live in the sunlight of Re; cp.Thomas George Allen, trans., *The Book of the Dead, or Going Forth by Day* (Chicago: Univ. of Chicago Press, 1974); readily available but outdated is the translation by E. A. Wallis Budge, *The Book of the Dead: The Papyrus of Ani* (1895; reprint, New York: Dover, 1967). On the worship of Isis and Osiris in the later periods, see H. Idris Bell, *Cults and Creeds in Graeco-Roman Egypt* (Chicago: Ares, 1975); Friedrich Solmsen, *Isis Among the Greeks and Romans*, Martin Classical Lectures, vol. 25 (Cambridge: Harvard Univ. Press, 1979); Ladislav Vidman, *Sylloge inscriptionum religionis Isiacae et Sarapiacae* (Berlin: De Gruyter, 1969); R. E. Witt, *Isis in the Graeco-Roman World* (Ithaca, N.Y.: Cornell Univ. Press, 1971).

PLUTARCH OF CHAERONEA, *ON ISIS AND OSIRIS* (*DE ISIDE ET OSIRIDE*), 12–19; 27–29; 32–36; 52–55 (355D–358E; 361D–362E; 364A–365C; 372E–373E)

Plutarch's treatise *On Isis and Osiris* is indispensable for the study of Egyptian religion during Greco-Roman antiquity. Dedicated to Clea, a priestess at Delphi, the treatise discusses the *hieros logos* (sacred myth) of Isis and Osiris and interprets the stories and customs of Egyptian religion allegorically, in accordance with Greek philosophical wisdom.

Plutarch's version of the myth of Isis and Osiris connects the various episodes, many of which can be documented from Egyptian sources, into a single, running narrative (*On Isis and Osiris*, 12–19). The story begins with Kronos (Geb, the Egyptian earth god) and Rhea (Nut, the Egyptian sky goddess) overcoming the curse of Helios (Re, the sun god) with the help of Hermes (Thoth, the Egyptian moon god) by producing five children on five intercalary days: Osiris, Horus, Typhon (Set), Isis, and Nephthys. As pharaoh of Egypt Osiris brings civilization to that country and to the whole world. Typhon, however, gathers conspirators and plots to kill Osiris. First he imprisons Osiris within a coffin and throws it into the Nile River, and later he dismembers the body of Osiris and scatters the pieces all around Egypt. One piece, the penis, is lost forever in the Nile River. In both episodes the reproductive power of Osiris is submerged in the Nile. (Isis grieving and searching for Osiris and burning away the mortality of the infant prince of Byblos can be compared with the actions of Demeter in the *Homeric Hymn to Demeter;* Osiris becoming encased within the tree trunk at Byblos can be compared with the identification of Attis with the pine tree.) Horus, the son of Isis and Osiris, then takes up the struggle against Typhon, to avenge the evil done to his father and mother. He ultimately prevails.

By way of interpretation, Plutarch asserts that Osiris, like Dionysos, is the god of vivifying moisture, whereas Typhon is the god of deadly drought; and Isis, impregnated by Osiris, is the good mother goddess, "the female principle of Nature" (*On Isis and Osiris,* 53).

Regarding Sarapis or Osiris-Apis (Osiris joined with the Apis bull), who was a popular god in his own right, compare Plutarch's treatment in *On Isis and Osiris* (27–29) with Aelius Aristides, *Oration* 8, in praise of Sarapis. (A portion of this oration is translated by Edwyn R. Bevan, *Later Greek Religion* [New York: AMS, 1927], 71–76; Bevan also presents a translation of a dinner invitation to a sacred feast of the Lord Sarapis [71]; see also the Oxyrhynchus Papyri 110 and 523.) See also Helmut Engelmann, *The Delian Aretalogy of Sarapis,* EPRO, tome 44 (Leiden: Brill, 1975); E. A. Wallis Budge, *The Gods of the Egyptians: Studies in Egyptian Mythology* (1904; reprint, New York: Dover, 1969), 2.195–201; John E. Stambaugh, *Sarapis under the Early Ptolemies,* EPRO, tome 25 (Leiden: Brill, 1972).

The following translation is by Frederick Cole Babbitt, *Plutarch's Moralia: V* (Loeb Classical Library, 1969). For a very helpful study of the treatise, see J. Gwyn Griffiths, *Plutarch: De Iside et Osiride* (Cambridge: Univ. of Wales, 1970).

Here follows the story related in the briefest possible words with the 12 omission of everything that is merely unprofitable or superfluous:

They say that the Sun, when he became aware of Rhea's intercourse with Kronos, invoked a curse upon her that she should not give birth to a child in any month or any year; but Hermes, being enamored of the goddess, consorted with her. Later, playing at draughts with the moon, he won from her the seventieth part of each of her periods of illumination, and from all the winnings he composed five days, and intercalated them as an addition to the three hundred and sixty days. The Egyptians even now call these five days intercalated and celebrate them as the birthdays of the gods. They relate that on the first of these days Osiris was born, and at the hour of his birth a voice issued forth saying, "The Lord of All advances to the light." But some relate that a certain Pamyles, while he was drawing water in Thebes, heard a voice issuing from the shrine of Zeus, which bade him proclaim with a loud voice that a mighty

and beneficent king, Osiris, had been born; and for this Kronos entrusted to him the child Osiris, which he brought up. It is in his honor
that the festival of Pamylia is celebrated, a festival which resembles the
phallic processions. On the second of these days Aroueris was born
whom they call Apollo, and some call him also the elder Horus. On the
third day Typhon was born, but not in due season or manner, but with a
blow he broke through his mother's side and leapt forth. On the fourth
day Isis was born in the regions that are ever moist; and on the fifth
Nephthys, to whom they give the name of Finality and the name of Aphrodite, and some also the name of Victory. There is also a tradition that
Osiris and Aroueris were sprung from the Sun, Isis from Hermes, and
Typhon and Nephthys from Kronos. For this reason the kings considered the third of the intercalated days as inauspicious, and transacted no
business on that day, nor did they give any attention to their bodies until
nightfall. They relate, moreover, that Nephthys became the wife of
Typhon; but Isis and Osiris were enamored of each other and consorted
together in the darkness of the womb before their birth. Some say that
Aroueris came from this union and was called the elder Horus by the
Egyptians, but Apollo by the Greeks.

13   One of the first acts related of Osiris in his reign was to deliver the
Egyptians from their destitute and brutish manner of living. This he did
by showing them the fruits of cultivation, by giving them laws, and by
teaching them to honor the gods. Later he traveled over the whole earth,
civilizing it without the slightest need of arms, but most of the peoples
he won over to his way by the charm of his persuasive discourse combined with song and all manner of music. Hence the Greeks came to
identify him with Dionysos.

During his absence the tradition is that Typhon attempted nothing
revolutionary because Isis, who was in control, was vigilant and alert;
but when he returned home Typhon contrived a treacherous plot against
him and formed a group of conspirators seventy-two in number. He had
also the cooperation of a queen from Ethiopia who was there at the time
and whose name they report as Aso. Typhon, having secretly measured
Osiris's body and having made ready a beautiful chest of corresponding
size artistically ornamented, caused it to be brought into the room where
the festivity was in progress. The company was much pleased at the
sight of it and admired it greatly, whereupon Typhon jestingly promised
to present it to the man who should find the chest to be exactly his
length when he lay down in it. They all tried it in turn, but no one fitted
it; then Osiris got into it and lay down, and those who were in the plot
ran to it and slammed down the lid, which they fastened by nails from

the outside and also by using molten lead. Then they carried the chest to the river and sent it on its way to the sea through the Tanitic Mouth. Wherefore the Egyptians even to this day name this mouth the hateful and execrable. Such is the tradition. They say also that the date on which this deed was done was the seventeenth day of Athyr, when the sun passes through Scorpion, and in the twenty-eighth year of the reign of Osiris; but some say that these are the years of his life and not of his reign.

The first to learn of the deed and to bring to men's knowledge an ac- **14** count of what had been done were the Pans and Satyrs who lived in the region around Chemmis, and so, even to this day, the sudden confusion and consternation of a crowd is called a panic. Isis, when the tidings reached her, at once cut off one of her tresses and put on a garment of mourning in a place where the city still bears the name of Kopto. Others think that the name means deprivation, for they also express "deprive" by means of *koptein*. But Isis wandered everywhere at her wits' end; no one whom she approached did she fail to address, and even when she met some little children she asked them about the chest. As it happened, they had seen it, and they told her the mouth of the river through which the friends of Typhon had launched the coffin into the sea. Wherefore the Egyptians think that little children possess the power of prophecy, and they try to divine the future from the portents which they find in children's words, especially when children are playing about in holy places and crying out whatever chances to come into their minds.

They relate also that Isis, learning that Osiris in his love had con- sorted with her sister through ignorance, in the belief that she was Isis, and seeing the proof of this in the garland of melilote which he had left with Nephthys, sought to find the child; for the mother, immediately af- ter its birth, had exposed it because of her fear of Typhon. And when the child had been found, after great toil and trouble, with the help of dogs which led Isis to it, it was brought up and became her guardian and atten- dant, receiving the name of Anubis, and it is said to protect the gods just as dogs protect men.

Thereafter Isis, as they relate, learned that the chest had been cast up **15** by the sea near the land of Byblos and that the waves had gently set it down in the midst of a clump of heather. The heather in a short time ran up into a very beautiful and massive stock, and enfolded and embraced the chest with its growth and concealed it within its trunk. The king of the country admired the great size of the plant, and cut off the portion that enfolded the chest, which was now hidden from sight, and used it as a pillar to support the roof of his house. These facts, they say, Isis ascertained by the divine inspiration of Rumor, and came to Byblos and sat down by a spring, all dejection and tears; she exchanged no word with anybody, save only that she welcomed the queen's maidservants and treated them with great amiability, plaiting their hair for them and imparting to their persons a wondrous fragrance from her own body. But when the queen observed her maidservants, a longing came upon her for the unknown woman and for such hairdressing and for a body fragrant with ambrosia. Thus it happened that Isis was sent for and became so intimate with the queen that the queen made her the nurse of her baby. They say that the king's name was Malcander; the queen's name some say was Astarte, others Saosis, and still others Nemanus, which the Greeks would call Athenais.

16   They relate that Isis nursed the child by giving it her finger to suck instead of her breast, and in the night she would burn away the mortal portions of its body. She herself would turn into a swallow and flit about the pillar with a wailing lament, until the queen who had been watching, when she saw her babe on fire, gave forth a loud cry and thus deprived it of immortality. Then the goddess disclosed herself and asked for the pillar which served to support the roof. She removed it with the greatest ease and cut away the wood of the heather which surrounded the chest; then, when she had wrapped up the wood in a linen cloth and had poured perfume upon it, she entrusted it to the care of the kings; and even to this day the people of Byblos venerate this wood which is preserved in the shrine of Isis. Then the goddess threw herself down upon the coffin with such a dreadful wailing that the younger of the king's sons expired on the spot. The elder son she kept with her, and, having placed the coffin on board a boat, she put out from land. Since the Phaedrus river toward the early morning fostered a rather boisterous wind, the goddess grew angry and dried up its stream.

17   In the first place where she found seclusion, when she was quite by herself, they relate that she opened the chest and laid her face upon the face within and caressed it and wept. The child came quietly up behind her and saw what was there, and when the goddess became aware of his presence, she turned about and gave him one awful look of anger. The child could not endure the fright, and died. Others will have it so, but assert that he fell overboard into the sea from the boat that was mentioned above. He also is the recipient of honors because of the goddess; for they say that the Maneros of whom the Egyptians sing at their convivial gatherings is this very child. Some say, however, that his name was Palaestinus or Pelusius, and that the city founded by the goddess was named in his honor. They also recount that this Maneros who is the

theme of their songs was the first to invent music. But some say that the word is not the name of any person, but an expression belonging to the vocabulary of drinking and feasting: "Good luck be ours in things like this!" and that this is really the idea expressed by the exclamation "maneros" whenever the Egyptians use it. In the same way we may be sure that the likeness of a corpse which, as it is exhibited to them, is carried around in a chest, is not a reminder of what happened to Osiris, as some assume; but it is to urge them, as they contemplate it, to use and to enjoy the present, since all very soon must be what it is now and this is their purpose in introducing it into the midst of merry-making.

As they relate, Isis proceeded to her son Horus, who was being **18** reared in Buto, and bestowed the chest in a place well out of the way; but Typhon, who was hunting by night in the light of the moon, happened upon it. Recognizing the body he divided it into fourteen parts and scattered them, each in a different place. Isis learned of this and sought for them again, sailing through the swamps in a boat of papyrus. This is the reason why people sailing in such boats are not harmed by the crocodiles, since these creatures in their own way show either their fear or their reverence for the goddess.

The traditional result of Osiris's dismemberment is that there are many so-called tombs of Osiris in Egypt; for Isis held a funeral for each part when she had found it. Others deny this and assert that she caused effigies of him to be made and these she distributed among the several cities, pretending that she was giving them his body, in order that he might receive divine honors in a greater number of cities, and also that, if Typhon should succeed in overpowering Horus, he might despair of ever finding the true tomb when so many were pointed out to him, all of them called the tomb of Osiris.

Of the parts of Osiris's body the only one which Isis did not find was the male member, for the reason that this had been at once tossed into the river, and the lepidotus, the sea-bream, and the pike had fed upon it; and it is from these very fishes the Egyptians are most scrupulous in abstaining. But Isis made a replica of the member to take its place, and consecrated the phallus, in honor of which the Egyptians even at the present day celebrate a festival.

Later, as they relate, Osiris came to Horus from the other world and **19** exercised and trained him for the battle. After a time Osiris asked Horus what he held to be the most noble of all things. When Horus replied, "To avenge one's father and mother for evil done to them," Osiris then asked him what animal he considered the most useful for them who go forth to battle; and when Horus said, "A horse," Osiris was surprised and raised the question why it was that he had not rather said a lion than a horse. Horus answered that a lion was a useful thing for a man in need of assistance, but that a horse served best for cutting off the flight of an enemy and annihilating him. When Osiris heard this he was much pleased, since he felt that Horus had now an adequate preparation. It is said that, as many were continually transferring their allegiance to Horus, Typhon's concubine, Thoueris, also came over to him; and a serpent which pursued her was cut to pieces by Horus's men, and now, in memory of this, the people throw down a rope in their midst and chop it up.

Now the battle, as they relate, lasted many days and Horus prevailed. Isis, however, to whom Typhon was delivered in chains, did not cause him to be put to death, but released him and let him go. Horus could not endure this with equanimity, but laid hands upon his mother and wrested the royal diadem from her head; but Hermes put upon her a helmet like unto the head of a cow.

Typhon formally accused Horus of being an illegitimate child, but with the help of Hermes to plead his cause it was decided by the gods that he also was legitimate. Typhon was then overcome in two other battles. Osiris consorted with Isis after his death, and she became the mother of Harpocrates, untimely born and weak in his lower limbs.

27   Stories akin to these and to others like them they say are related about Typhon; how that, prompted by jealousy and hostility, he wrought terrible deeds and, by bringing utter confusion upon all things, filled the whole Earth, and the ocean as well, with ills, and later paid the penalty therefor. But the avenger, the sister and wife of Osiris, after she had quenched and suppressed the madness and fury of Typhon, was not indifferent to the contests and struggles which she had endured, nor to her own wanderings nor to her manifold deeds of wisdom and many feats of bravery, nor would she accept oblivion and silence for them, but she intermingled in the most holy rites portrayals and suggestions and representations of her experiences at that time, and sanctified them, both as a lesson in godliness and an encouragement for men and women who find themselves in the clutch of like calamities. She herself and Osiris, translated for their virtues from good demigods (*daimones*) into gods, as were Heracles and Dionysos later, not incongruously enjoy double honors, both those of gods and those of demigods, and their powers extend everywhere, but are greatest in the regions above the earth and beneath the earth. In fact, men assert that Plouton is none other than Sarapis and that Persephone is Isis, even as Archemachus of Euboea has

said, and also Heracleides Ponticus who holds the oracle in Canopus to be an oracle of Plouton.

Ptolemy Soter saw in a dream the colossal statue of Plouton in **28** Sinope, not knowing nor having ever seen how it looked, and in his dream the statue bade him convey it with all speed to Alexandria. He had no information and no means of knowing where the statue was situated, but as he related the vision to his friends there was discovered for him a much traveled man by the name of Sosibius, who said that he had seen in Sinope just such a great statue as the king thought he saw. Ptolemy, therefore, sent Soteles and Dionysius, who, after a considerable time and with great difficulty, and not without the help of divine providence, succeeded in stealing the statue and bringing it away. When it had been conveyed to Egypt and exposed to view, Timotheus, the expositor of sacred law, and Manetho of Sebennytus, and their associates, conjectured that it was the statue of Plouton, basing their conjecture on the Cerberus and the serpent with it, and they convinced Ptolemy that it was the statue of none other of the gods but Sarapis. It certainly did not bear this name when it came from Sinope, but, after it had been conveyed to Alexandria, it took to itself the name which Plouton bears among the Egyptians, that of Sarapis. Moreover, since Heracleitus the physical philosopher says, "The same are Hades and Dionysos, to honor whom they rage and rave," people are inclined to come to this opinion. In fact, those who insist that the body is called Hades, since the soul is, as it were, deranged and inebriate when it is in the body, are too frivolous in their use of allegory. It is better to identify Osiris with Dionysos and Sarapis with Osiris, who received this appellation at the time when he changed his nature. For this reason Sarapis is a god of all peoples in common, even as Osiris is; and this they who have participated in the holy rites well know.

It is not worthwhile to pay any attention to the Phrygian writings, in **29** which it is said that Sarapis was the son of Heracles, and Isis was his daughter, and Typhon was the son of Alcaeus, who also was a son of Heracles; nor must we fail to contemn Phylarchus, who writes that Dionysos was the first to bring from India into Egypt two bulls, and that the name of one was Apis and of the other Osiris. But Sarapis is the name of him who sets the universe in order, and it is derived from "sweep" (*sairein*), which some say means "to beautify" and "to put in order." As a matter of fact, these statements of Phylarchus are absurd, but even more absurd are those put forth by those who say that Sarapis is no god at all, but the name of the coffin of Apis; and that there are in Memphis certain bronze gates called the Gates of Oblivion and Lamentation, which are opened when the burial of Apis takes place, and they give out a deep and harsh sound; and it is because of this that we lay hand upon anything of bronze that gives out a sound. More moderate is the statement of those who say that the derivation is from "shoot" (seuesthai) or "scoot" (sousthai), meaning the general movement of the universe. Most of the priests say that Osiris and Apis are conjoined into one, thus explaining to us and informing us that we must regard Apis as the bodily image of the soul of Osiris. But it is my opinion that, if the name Sarapis is Egyptian, it denotes cheerfulness and rejoicing, and I base this opinion on the fact that the Egyptians call their festival of rejoicing sairei. In fact, Plato says that Hades is so named because he is a beneficent and gentle god towards those who have come to abide with him. Moreover, among the Egyptians many others of the proper names are real words; for example, that place beneath the earth, to which they believe that souls depart after the end of life, they call Amenthes, the name signifying "the one who receives and gives." Whether this is one of those words which came from Greece in very ancient times and were brought back again we will consider later, but for the present let us go on to disuss the remainder of the views now before us.

33   Let this, then, be stated incidentally, as a matter of record that is common knowledge. But the wiser of the priests call not only the Nile Osiris and the sea Typhon, but they simply give the name of Osiris to the whole source and faculty creative of moisture, believing this to be the cause of generation and the substance of life-producing seed; and the name of Typhon they give to all that is dry, fiery, and arid, in general, and antagonistic to moisture. Therefore, because they believe that he was personally of a reddish sallow color, they are not eager to meet men of such complexion, nor do they like to associate with them.

Osiris, on the other hand, according to their legendary tradition, was dark, because water darkens everything, earth and clothes and clouds, when it comes into contact with them. In young people the presence of moisture renders their hair black, while greyness, like a paleness as it were, is induced by dryness in those who are passing their prime. Also the spring-time is vigorous, prolific, and agreeable; but the autumn, since it lacks moisture, is inimical to plants and unhealthful for living creatures.

The bull kept at Heliopolis which they call Mneuis and which is sacred to Osiris—some hold it to be the sire of Apis— is black and has honors second only to Apis. Egypt, moveover, which has the blackest of soils, they call by the same name as the black portion of the eye, "Chemia," and compare it to a heart; for it is warm and moist and is enclosed by the southern portions of the inhabited world and adjoins them, like the heart in a man's left side.

They say that the sun and moon do not use chariots, but boats in **34** which to sail round in their courses; and by this they intimate that the nourishment and origin of these heavenly bodies is from moisture. They think also that Homer, like Thales, had gained his knowledge from the Egyptians, when he postulated water as the source and origin of all things; for, according to them, Ocean is Osiris, and Tethys is Isis, since she is the kindly nurse and provider for all things. In fact, the Greeks call emission *apousia* and coition *synousia*, and the son (*hyios*) from water (*hydor*) and rain (*hysai*); Dionysos also they call Hyes since he is lord of the nature of moisture; and he is no other than Osiris. In fact, Hellanicus seems to have heard Osiris pronounced Hysiris by the priests, for he regularly spells the name in this way, deriving it, in all probability, from the nature of Osiris and the ceremony of finding him.

That Osiris is identical with Dionysos who could more fittingly know **35** than yourself, Clea? For you are at the head of the inspired maidens of Delphi, and have been consecrated by your father and mother in the holy rites of Osiris. If, however, for the benefit of others it is needful to adduce proofs of this identity, let us leave undisturbed what may not be told, but the public ceremonies which the priests perform in the burial of the Apis, when they convey his body on an improvised bier, do not in any way come short of a Bacchic procession; for they fasten skins of fawns about themselves, and carry Bacchic wands (thyrsi) and indulge in shoutings and movements exactly as do those who are under the spell of the Dionysiac ecstasies. For the same reason many of the Greeks make statues of Dionysos in the form of a bull; and the women of Elis invoke him, praying that the god may come with the hoof of a bull; and the epithet applied to Dionysos among the Argives is "Son of the Bull." They call him up out of the water by the sound of trumpets, at the same time casting into the depths a lamb as an offering to the Keeper of the Gate. The trumpets they conceal in Bacchic wands, as Socrates has stated in his treatise on *The Holy Ones*. Furthermore, the tales regarding the Titans and the rites celebrated by night agree with the accounts of the dismemberment of Osiris and his revivification and regenesis. Similar agreement is found too in the tales about their sepulchers. The Egyptians, as has already been stated, point out tombs of Osiris in many places, and the people of Delphi believe that the remains of Dionysos rest with them close beside the oracle; and the Holy Ones offer a secret sacrifice in the shrine of Apollo whenever the devotees of Dionysos wake the God of the Mystic Basket (Liknites). To show that the Greeks regard Dionysos as the lord and master not only of wine, but of the nature of every sort of moisture, it is enough that Pindar be our witness, when he says,

> May gladsome Dionysos swell the fruit upon the trees,
> The hallowed splendor of harvest-time.

For this reason all who reverence Osiris are prohibited from destroying a cultivated tree or blocking up a spring of water.

36   Not only the Nile, but every form of moisture they call simply the effusion of Osiris; and in their holy rites the water jar in honor of the god heads the procession. And by the picture of a rush they represent a king and the southern region of the world, and the rush is interpreted to mean the watering and fructifying of all things, and in its nature it seems to bear some resemblance to the generative member. Moreover, when they celebrate the festival of the Pamylia which, as has been said, is of a phallic nature, they expose and carry about a statue of which the male member is triple; for the god is the Source, and every source, by its fecundity, multiplies what proceeds from it; and for "many times" we have a habit of saying "thrice," as, for example, "thrice happy," and

> Bonds, even thrice as many, unnumbered,

unless, indeed, the word "triple" is used by the early writers in its strict meaning; for the nature of moisture, being the source and origin of all things, created out of itself three primal material substances, Earth, Air, and Fire. In fact, the tale that is annexed to the legend to the effect that Typhon cast the male member of Osiris into the river, and Isis could not find it, but constructed and shaped a replica of it, and ordained that it should be honored and borne in processions, plainly comes round to this doctrine, that the creative and germinal power of the god, at the very first, acquired moisture as its substance, and through moisture combined with whatever was by nature capable of participating in generation.

53   But let us now take up again the proper subject of our discussion. Isis is, in fact, the female principle of Nature, and is receptive of every form of generation, in accord with which she is called by Plato the gentle nurse and the all-receptive, and by most people has been called by countless names, since, because of the force of Reason, she turns herself to this thing or that and is receptive of all manner of shapes and forms. She has an innate love for the first and most dominant of all things, which is identical with the good, and this she yearns for and pursues; but the portion which comes from evil she tries to avoid and

to reject, for she serves them both as place and means of growth, but inclines always towards the better and offers to it opportunity to create from her and to impregnate her with effluxes and likenesses in which she rejoices and is glad that she is made pregnant and teeming with these creations. For creation is the image of being in matter, and the thing created is a picture of reality.

It is not, therefore, out of keeping that they have a legend that the **54** soul of Osiris is everlasting and imperishable, but that his body Typhon oftentimes dismembers and causes to disappear, and that Isis wanders hither and yon in her search for it, and fits it together again; for that which really is and is perceptible and good is superior to destruction and change. The images from it with which the sensible and corporeal is impressed, and the relations, forms, and likenesses which this takes upon itself, like impressions of seals in wax, are not permanently lasting, but disorder and disturbance overtakes them, being driven hither from the upper reaches, and fighting against Horus, whom Isis brings forth, beholden of all, as the image of the perceptible world. Therefore it is said that he is brought to trial by Typhon on the charge of illegitimacy, as not being pure nor uncontaminated like his father, reason unalloyed and unaffected of itself, but contaminated in his substance because of the corporeal element. He prevails, however, and wins the case when Hermes, that is to say Reason, testifies and points out that Nature, by undergoing changes of form with reference to the perceptible, duly brings about the creation of the world. The birth of Apollo from Isis and Osiris, while these gods were still in the womb of Rhea, has the allegorical meaning that before this world was made visible and its rough material was completely formed by Reason, it was put to the test by Nature and brought forth of itself the first creation imperfect. This is the reason why they say that this god was born in the darkness a cripple, and they call him the elder Horus; for there was then no world, but only an image and outline of a world to be.

But this Horus is himself perfected and complete; but he has not **55** done away completely with Typhon, but has taken away his activity and strength. Hence they say that at Kopto the statue of Horus holds in one hand the privy members of Typhon, and they relate a legend that Hermes cut out the sinews of Typhon, and used them as strings for his lyre, thereby instructing us that Reason adjusts the Universe and creates concord out of discordant elements, and that it does not destroy but only cripples the destructive force. Hence this is weak and inactive here, and combines with the susceptible and changeable elements and attaches itself to them, becoming the artificer of quakes and tremblings in the

earth, and of droughts and tempestuous winds in the air, and of light-
ning-flashes and thunderbolts. Moreover, it taints waters and winds
with pestilence, and it runs forth wanton even as far as the moon, oftentimes confounding and darkening the moon's brightness; according to
the belief and account of the Egyptians, Typhon at one time smites the
eye of Horus, and at another time snatches it out and swallows it, and
then later gives it back again to the Sun. By the smiting, they refer allegorically to the monthly waning of the moon, and by the crippling, to its
eclipse, which the Sun heals by shining straight upon it as soon as it has
escaped the shadow of the earth.

ISIS ARETALOGY FROM CYME

In antiquity claims about the virtues and the powers of a god or goddess were often presented in the form of self-predications, or "I am"
statements, which are lists of the deity's mighty deeds (in Greek,
"aretalogies"). Several aretalogies of Isis are known, including those
from Andros, Ios, Nysa (according to Diodorus Siculus), and the one
from Cyme that is translated here. (Compare this also with the self-reve-
lation of Isis as narrated near the beginning of book 11 of Apuleius's
Metamorphoses in this chapter.) This Isis aretalogy from Cyme in Asia
Minor may be dated to the second century C.E. and is said to have been
copied from a stele in Memphis, Egypt. Most notable for our purposes
are the claims that Isis reveals mysteries (*myeseis*, "initiations"), creates
the walls of cities (compare Kybele and her mural crown), and is called
Thesmophoros, "Lawgiver" (Thesmophoros is also a familiar epithet of
Demeter; compare with the Thesmophoria). The aretalogy concludes
with two parallel lines proclaiming that Isis's powers can overcome
even inexorable Fate (*to heirmarmenon*).

The following translation is by Frederick C. Grant, *Hellenistic Religions: The Age of Syncretism* (Indianapolis: Bobbs-Merrill, Liberal Arts
Press, 1953), 131–33. See also Jan Bergman, *Ich bin Isis* (Uppsala: Alm-
qvist and Wiksell, 1968); Dieter Müller, *Ägypten und die griechischen Isis-
Aretalogien* (Berlin: Akademie-Verlag, 1961); Werner Peek, *Der Isishymnus
von Andros und verwandte Texte* (Berlin: Weidmann, 1930).

1   Demetrius, son of Artemidorus, and Thraseas, the Magnesian from
the Maeander, crave the blessing of Isis. The following was copied from
the stele which is in Memphis, where it stands before the temple of
Hephaistos:

I am Isis, the mistress of every land, and I was taught by Hermes,and with Hermes I devised letters, both the sacred (hieroglyphs) and the demotic, that all things might not be written with the same (letters).

I gave and ordained laws for men, which no one is able to change.
I am eldest daughter of Kronos.   5
I am wife and sister of King Osiris.
I am she who findeth fruit for men.
I am mother of King Horus.
I am she that riseth in the Dog Star.
I am she that is called goddess by women.   10
For me was the city of Bubastis built.
I divided the earth from the heaven.
I showed the paths of the stars.
I ordered the course of the sun and the moon.
I devised business in the sea.   15
I made strong the right.
I brought together woman and man.
I appointed to women to bring their infants to birth in the tenth month.
I ordained that parents should be loved by children.
I laid punishment upon those disposed without natural affection toward 20
    their parents.
I made with my brother Osiris an end to the eating of men.
I revealed mysteries unto men.
I taught (men) to honor images of the gods.
I consecrated the precincts of the gods.
I broke down the governments of tyrants.   25
I made an end to murders.
I compelled women to be loved by men.
I made the right to be stronger than gold and silver.
I ordained that the true should be thought good.
I devised marriage contracts.   30
I assigned to Greeks and barbarians their languages.
I made the beautiful and the shameful to be distinguished by nature.
I ordained that nothing should be more feared than an oath.
I have delivered the plotter of evil against other men into the hands of
    the one he plotted against.
I established penalties for those who practice injustice.   35
I decreed mercy to suppliants.
I protect (or: honor) righteous guards.

With me the right prevails.
I am the Queen of rivers and winds and sea.
40 No one is held in honor without my knowing it.
I am the Queen of war.
I am the Queen of the thunderbolt.
I stir up the sea and I calm it.
I am in the rays of the sun.
45 I inspect the courses of the sun.
Whatever I please, this too shall come to an end.
With me everything is reasonable.
I set free those in bonds.
I am the Queen of seamanship.
50 I make the navigable unnavigable when it pleases me.
I created walls of cities.
I am called the Lawgiver (Thesmophoros).
I brought up islands out of the depths into the light.
I am Lord of rainstorms.
55 I overcome Fate.
Fate harkens to me.
Hail, O Egypt, that nourished me!

ISIS LOVE SPELL FROM THE GREAT MAGICAL PAPYRUS OF PARIS (BIBLIOTHÈQUE NATIONALE, PAPYRUS 574), lines 94–153

A codex sometimes called "the Great Magical Papyrus of Paris" contains a love spell to be used for obtaining a lover. The spell is given in Coptic (late Egyptian), except for two brief sets of instructions given in Greek. The text may be divided into two sections, the first section recounting the story of Osiris's adultery with Nephthys and Isis's subsequent use of magic to make Osiris come back to her, and the second section offering magical spells for attracting a love. The story of Osiris's adultery is also in Plutarch, *On Isis and Osiris*, 14 (in this chapter), but in Plutarch the infidelity of Osiris and the grief of Isis are minimized.

The translation of the love spell is by Marvin W. Meyer, in *The Greek Magical Papyri in Translation*, ed. Hans Dieter Betz (Chicago: Univ. of Chicago Press, 1986). The translation is based upon the Coptic and Greek text published in *Papyri Graecae Magicae: Die griechischen Zauberpapyri*, ed. Karl Preisendanz, 2d ed., ed. Albert Henrichs (Stuttgart: Teubner, 1973). For further analysis of the spell, see Marvin W. Meyer, "The Love Spell of *PGM IV*. 94–153: Introduction and Structure," in *Acts of the Second International Congress of Coptic Studies*, eds. Tito Orlandi and Frederik Wisse

(Rome: C.I.M., 1985), 193–201. On the Greek magical papyri in general, see Arthur Darby Nock, "Greek Magical Papyri," *The Journal of Egyptian Archaeology* 15 (1929): 219–35, reprinted in *Essays on Religion and the Ancient Word*, ed. Zeph Stewart (Cambridge: Harvard Univ. Press, 1972), 1.176–94.

The portion of the love spell that is translated from the Coptic is printed in italics.

Isis is the one who comes from the mountain at midday in summer, the dusty maiden; her eyes are full of tears and her heart is full of sighs. Her father Thoth **95**
the great came in unto her and asked her, "O my daughter Isis, dusty maiden, why are your eyes full of tears, your heart full of sighs, and [the   ] of your garment soiled? (Away with) the tears of your eyes!" She said [to him], "He is not with me, O my father, Ape Thoth, Ape [Thoth], my father. I have been betrayed **100**
by my female companion. I have discovered [a] secret: yes, Nephthys is having intercourse with Osiris [   ] my brother, my own mother's son." He said to her, "Behold, this is adultery against you, O my daughter Isis." She [said] to him, "It is adultery against you, O my father, [Ape] Thoth, Ape Thoth, my father; it is **105**
pregnancy proper for me myself." He said to her, "Arise, O my daughter Isis, and [go] to the south to Thebes, to the north to Abydos. There are [   ] those who trample (?) there. Take for yourself Belf son of Belf, [the one whose] foot is of **110**
bronze and whose heels are of iron, [that] he forge for you a double iron nail with a [   ] head, a thin base, a strong point, and light iron. Bring it before me, dip it in the blood of Osiris, and hand it over; we [   ] this mysterious (?) flame to me."

"Every flaming, every cooking, every heating, every steaming, and every **115**
sweating that you (masc.) will cause in this flaming stove, you (will) cause in the heart, in the liver, (in) the area of the navel, and in the belly of NN whom NN has borne, until I bring her to the house of NN whom NN has borne and she puts what is in her hand into my hand, what is in her mouth into my mouth, what is **120**
in her belly onto my belly, what is in her female parts onto my male parts— quickly, quickly! immediately, immediately! Rise up to the kings of Alchah, speak the truth (?) in Oupoke, arouse god (after) NN whom NN has borne, and I shall send her to be with NN whom NN has borne. For I am To son of To; I am the **125**
Great son of the Great; I am Anubis, who bears the glorious crown of Re and puts it upon King Osiris, King Osiris Onnophris, . . . who rouses the whole earth, that you may arouse the heart of NN whom NN has borne, that I may know what **130**
is in her heart for me, for NN whom NN has borne, on this day."

If a large amount of saliva forms in your mouth as you speak, understand that she is distressed and wants to talk with you; if you yawn frequently, she wants to come to you. But if you sneeze two times or more, **135**

she is in good health and is returning to where she lives; if you have a
headache and are crying, she is distressed or even dying.

140 *"Rise up to heaven, and arouse the High One (masc.) after the Noble One
(fem.). Rise up to the abyss, and arouse Thoth after Nabin; arouse the heart of
these two bulls, Hapi and Mneuis; arouse the heart of Osiris after Isis; arouse Re
after the light; arouse the heart of NN whom NN has borne, after NN whom NN
has borne."*

(Say) these things on behalf of women. But when (you are speaking)
145 about women, then speak, conversely, so as to arouse the females after
the males:

*"When she drinks, when she eats, when she has intercourse with someone
else, I will bewitch her heart, I will bewitch the heart of her, I will bewitch her
150 breath, I will bewitch her 365 members, I will bewitch her inner part . . . wherever I desire, until she comes to me and I know what is in her heart, (what) she
does, and of what she thinks—quickly, quickly! immediately, immediately!"*

APULEIUS OF MADAUROS, *THE GOLDEN ASS* (*METAMORPHOSES*), Book 11

In book 11 of his *Metamorphoses*, the second century C.E. Latin novel-
ist Apuleius describes how Lucius, whose curiosity about magic had
made him into an ass, finally regains his human form through the intervention of the goddess Isis. At the time of the full moon (a most propi-
tious time to invoke a goddess with lunar powers), Lucius purifies himself in the sea near Corinth seven times and prays fervently to the queen
of heaven, who is known by many names. The goddess reveals herself
to Lucius in his sleep and describes her various cult names, and concludes by saying that those who know her best call her by her true name,
Queen Isis. Isis promises Lucius that he will be saved from his asinine
condition and delivered from the clutches of Fate, if he follows the instructions of the goddess. He is to watch the procession in honor of Isis
on the occasion of the Ploiaphesia (or Navigium Isidis), a March festival
that celebrates the new season of navigation. In this procession the
priest of Isis will carry a wreath of roses and Lucius is to eat of them. He
does so and is transformed. Thus saved, he determines to be initiated
into the holy mysteries of Isis. Apuleius's description of the initiation of
Lucius includes not only an account of the preliminary ritual, but also a
necessarily vague but still helpful statement about the initiation ceremony itself: it is an experience of entering the realm of darkness and
death and emerging the next morning as the sun, reborn for a new day.
The book closes with more abbreviated accounts of Lucius also being ini-

tiated into the mysteries of Osiris and the Roman mysteries of Isis. After this Lucius becomes a member of the College of Pastophori (those who carry the sacred shrines) and proudly displays the shaved head that characterizes Egyptian priests.

This translation is by Jack Lindsay, *Apuleius: The Golden Ass* (Bloomington: Indiana Univ. Press, 1962). For an excellent study of book 11, see J. Gwyn Griffiths, *Apuleius of Madauros, The Isis-Book (Metamorphoses, Book XI): Introduction, Translation and Commentary*, EPRO, tome 39 (Leiden: Brill, 1975).

About the first watch of the night I was aroused by sudden panic. Look- 1
ing up I saw the full orb of the Moon shining with peculiar luster and that very moment emerging from the waves of the sea. Then the thought came to me that this was the hour of silence and loneliness when my prayers might avail. For I knew that the Moon was the primal Goddess of supreme sway; that all human beings are the creatures of her providence; that not only cattle and wild beasts but even inorganic objects are vitalized by the divine influence of her light; that all the bodies which are on earth, or in the heavens, or in the sea, increase when she waxes, and decline when she wanes. Considering this, therefore, and feeling that Fate was now satiated with my endless miseries and at last licensed a hope of salvation, I determined to implore the august image of the risen Goddess.

So, shaking off my tiredness, I scrambled to my feet and walked straight into the sea in order to purify myself. I immersed my head seven times because, according to the divine Pythagoras, that number is specially suited for all ritual acts; and then, speaking with lively joy, I lifted my tear-wet face in supplication to the irresistible Goddess:

"Queen of Heaven (*regina caeli*), whether you are fostering Ceres the 2
motherly nurse of all growth, who, gladdened at the discovery of your lost daughter, abolished the brutish nutriment of the primitive acorn and pointed the way to gentler food, as is yet shown in the tilling of the fields of Eleusis; or whether you are celestial Venus who in the first moment of Creation mingled the opposing sexes in the generation of mutual desires, and who, after sowing in humanity the seeds of indestructible continuing life, are now worshiped in the wave-washed shrine of Paphos; or whether you are the sister of Phoebus, who by relieving the pangs of childbirth travail with soothing remedies have brought safe into the world lives innumerable, and who are now venerated in the thronged sanctuary of Ephesus; or whether you are Proserpine, terrible with the howls of midnight, whose triple face has

power to ward off all the assaults of ghosts and to close the cracks in the
earth, and who wander through many a grove, propitiated in divers
manners, illuminating the walls of all cities with beams of female light,
nurturing the glad seeds in the earth with your damp heat, and dispens-
ing abroad your dim radiance when the sun has abandoned us—O by
whatever name, and by whatever rites, and in whatever form, it is permitted to invoke you, come now and succour me in the hour of my calamity. Support my broken life, and give me rest and peace after the tribulations of my lot. Let there be an end to the toils that weary me, and an
end to the snares that beset me. Remove from me the hateful shape of a
beast, and restore me to the sight of those that love me. Restore me to Lucius, my lost self. But if an offended god pursues me implacably, then
grant me death at least since life is denied me."

3   Having thus poured forth my prayer and given an account of my bitter sufferings, I drowsed and fell asleep on the same sand-couch as before. But scarcely had I closed my eyes before a god-like face emerged
from the midst of the sea with lineaments that gods themselves would re-
vere. Then gradually I saw the whole body, resplendent image that it
was, rise out of the scattered deep and stand beside me.

I shall now be so brave as to attempt a description of this marvelous
form, if the poverty of human language will not altogether distort what I
have to say, or if the divinity herself will deign to lend me a rich enough
stock of eloquent phrase. First, then, she had an abundance of hair that
fell gently in dispersed ringlets upon the divine neck. A crown of inter-
laced wreaths and varying flowers rested upon her head; and in its
midst, just over the brow, there hung a plain circlet resembling a mirror
or rather a miniature moon—for it emitted a soft clear light. This orna-
ment was supported on either side by vipers that rose from the furrows
of the earth; and above it blades of grain were disposed. Her garment,
dyed many colors, was woven of fine flax. One part was gleaming white;
another was yellow as the crocus; another was flamboyant with the red
of roses. But what obsessed my gazing eyes by far the most was her
pitch-black cloak that shone with a dark glow. It was wrapped round
her, passing from under the right arm over the left shoulder and fastened with a knot like the boss of a shield. Part of it fell down in pleated

4   folds and swayed gracefully with a knotted fringe along the hem. Upon
the embroidered edges and over the whole surface sprinkled stars were
burning; and in the center a mid-month moon breathed forth her floating beams. Lastly, a garland wholly composed of every kind of fruit and
flower clung of its own accord to the fluttering border of that splendid
robe.

Many strange things were among her accoutrements. In her right hand she held a brazen sistrum, a flat piece of metal curved like a girdle, through which there passed some little rods—and when with her arm she vibrated these triple chords they produced a shrill sharp cry. In her left hand she bore an oblong golden vessel shaped like a boat, on the handle of which, set at the most conspicuous angle, there coiled an asp raising its head and puffing out its throat. The shoes that covered her ambrosial feet were plaited from the palm, emblem of victory.

Such was the goddess as breathing forth the spices of pleasant Arabia she condescended with her divine voice to address me.

"Behold, Lucius," she said, "moved by your prayer I come to you—I, **5** the natural mother of all life, the mistress of the elements, the first child of time, the supreme divinity, the queen of those in hell, the first among those in heaven, the uniform manifestation of all gods and goddesses— I, who govern by my nod the crests of light in the sky, the purifying wafts of the ocean, and the lamentable silences of hell—I, whose single godhead is venerated all over the earth under manifold forms, varying rites, and changing names. Thus, the Phrygians that are the oldest human stock call me Pessinuntia, Mother of the Gods. The aboriginal races of Attica call me Cecropian Minerva. The Cyprians in their island-home call me Paphian Venus. The archer Cretans call me Diana Dictynna. The three-tongued Sicilians call me Stygian Proserpine. The Eleusinians call me the ancient goddess Ceres. Some call me Juno. Some call me Bellona. Some call me Hecate. Some call me Rhamnusia. But those who are enlightened by the earliest rays of that divinity the sun, the Ethiopians, the Arii, and the Egyptians who excel in antique lore, all worship me with their ancestral ceremonies and call me by my true name, Queen Isis.

"Behold, I am come to you in your calamity. I am come with solace and aid. Away then with tears. Cease to moan. Send sorrow packing. Soon through my providence shall the sun of your salvation arise. Hearken therefore with care unto what I bid. Eternal religion has dedicated to me the day which will be born from the womb of this present darkness. Tomorrow my priests will offer to me the first fruits of the year's navigation. They will consecrate in my name a new-built ship. For now the tempests of the winter are lulled; the roaring waves of the sea are quieted; and the waters are again navigable. You must await this ceremony, without anxiety and without wandering thoughts. For the priest at my sug- **6** gestion will carry in the procession a crown of roses attached to the sistrum in his right hand; and you must unhesitatingly push your way through the crowd, join the procession, and trust in my good will. Approach close to the priest as if you meant to kiss his hand, and gently crop the roses. Instantly you will slough the hide of this beast on which I have long looked with abhorrence.

"Fear for no detail of the work to which I once put my hand. Even at this moment of time in which I appear before you, I am also in another place instructing my priest in a vision what is to be brought to pass. By my command the crush of people will open to give you way; and despite all the gay rites and ferial revelries not one of my worshipers will feel disgust because of the unseemly shape in which you are incarcerated. Neither will any one of them misinterpret your sudden metamorphosis or rancorously use it against you.

"Only remember, and keep the remembrance fast in your heart's deep core, that all the remaining days of your life must be dedicated to me, and that nothing can release you from this service but death. Neither is it aught but just that you should devote your life to her who redeems you back into humanity. You shall live blessed. You shall live glorious under my guidance; and when you have traveled your full length of time and you go down into death, there also, on that hidden side of earth, you shall dwell in the Elysian Fields and frequently adore me for my favors. For you will see me shining on amid the darkness of Acheron and reigning in the Stygian depths.

"More, if you are found to merit my love by your dedicated obedience, religious devotion, and constant chastity, you will discover that it is within my power to prolong your life beyond the limit set to it by Fate."

7   At last the end of this venerable oracle was reached, and the invincible Goddess ebbed back into her own essence. No time was lost. Immediately snapping the threads of sleep, and wrung with a sweat of joy and terror, I wakened. Wondering deeply at so direct a manifestation of the Goddess's power, I sprinkled myself with salt water; and eager to obey her in every particular, I repeated over to myself the exact words in which she had framed her instructions. Soon the sun of gold arose and sent the clouds of thick night flying; and lo, a crowd of people replenished the streets, filing in triumphal religious procession. It seemed to me that the whole world, independent of my own high spirits, was happy. Cattle of every kind, the houses, the very day, all seemed to lift serene faces brimful with jollity. For sunny and placid weather had suddenly come upon us after a frosty yesterday; and the tuneful birdlets, coaxed out by the warmths of the Spring, were softly singing sweet hymns of blandishment to the Mother of the Stars, the Producer of the Seasons, the Mistress of the Universe. The trees also, both those that blossomed into fruit and those that were content to yield only sterile

shade, were loosed by the southerly breezes; and glistening gaily with their budded leaves, they swished their branches gently in sibilant sighs. The crash of storm was over; and the waves, no longer mountainous with swirling foam, lapped quietly upon the shore. The dusky clouds were routed; and the heavens shone with clear sheer splendor of their native light.

By this time the forerunners of the main procession were gradually 8 appearing, every man richly decked as his votive fancy suggested. One fellow was girded about the middle like a soldier; another was scarfed like a huntsman with hunting-knife and shoes; another, wearing gilt sandals, silken gown, and costly ornaments, walked with a woman's mincing gait; another with his leg-harness, targe, helm, and sword, looked as if he had come straight from gladiatorial games. Then, sure enough, there passed by a man assuming the magistrate with fasces and purple robe, and a man playing the philosopher with cloak, staff, wooden clogs, and goat's beard; a fowler with bird-lime elbowing a fisherman with hooks. I saw also a tame she-bear dressed as a matron and carried in a sedan-chair; an ape with bonnet of plaited straw and saffron-hued garment, holding in his hand a golden cup and representing Phrygian Ganymede the shepherd; and lastly, an ass with wings glued on his back ambling after an old man—so that you could at once have exclaimed that one was Pegasus and the other Bellerophon, and would have laughed at the pair in the same breath.

Into this playful masquerade of the overflowing populace the procession proper now marched its way. Women glowing in their white vestments moved with symbolic gestures of delight. Blossomy with the chaplets of the Spring, they scattered flowerets out of the aprons of their dresses all along the course of the holy pageant. Others, who bore polished mirrors on their backs, walked before the Goddess and reflected all the people coming after as if they were advancing towards the Image. Others, again, carrying combs of ivory, went through the various caressive motions of combing and dressing the queenly tresses of their Lady; or they sprinkled the street with drops of unguent and genial balm.

There was a further host of men and women who followed with lanterns, torches, waxtapers, and every other kind of illumination in honor of Her who was begotten of the Stars of Heaven. Next came the musicians, interweaving in sweetest measures the notes of pipe and flute; and then a supple choir of chosen youths, clad in snow-white holiday tunics, came singing a delightful song which an expert poet, by grace of the Muses, had composed for music, and which explained the antique origins of this day of worship. Pipers also, consecrated to mighty Sarapis, played the tunes annexed to the god's cult on pipes with transverse-mouthpieces and reeds held sidelong towards the right ear; and a number of officials kept calling out, "Make way for the Goddess!"

10   Then there came walking a great band of men and women of all classes and ages, who had been initiated into the Mysteries of the Goddess and who were all clad in linen garments of the purest white. The women had their hair anointed and hooded in limpid silk; but the men had shaven shining polls. Terrene stars of mighty deity were these men and women; and they kept up a shrill continuous tingle upon sistra of brass and silver and even gold. The chief ministers of the ceremony, dressed in surplices of white linen tightly drawn across the breast and hanging loose to the feet, bore the relics of the mighty gods exposed to view. The first priest held on high a blazing lamp—not at all like the lamps that illumine our evening suppers; for its long bowl was gold, and it thrust up from an aperture in the middle a fat flame. The second priest was similarly vestured, but he carried in both hands model altars to which the auxiliary love of the supreme Goddess has given the fitting title of Auxilia. The third priest grasped a palm-tree with all its leaves subtly wrought in gold, and the wand of Mercury. The fourth priest displayed the Symbol of Equity; a left hand molded with open palm, since the left hand seemed to be more adapted to administer equity than the busier, craftier right hand. The same man also bore a vessel of gold rounded into the shape of a woman's breast, from which he let milk trickle to the ground. The fifth priest had a winnowing-fan constructed with thickset sprigs of gold; and the sixth priest had an amphora.

11   After these came the Gods themselves, deigning to walk before our eyes on the feet of men. First we saw the dreadful messenger of the gods of heaven and hell, Anubis, with his face blackened on one side and painted gold on the other, lifting on high his dog's head and bearing his rod in his left hand. Close upon his heels followed a Cow, emblem of the Goddess that is fruitful mother of all, sitting upright upon the proud shoulders of her blessed worshiper. Another man carried the chest that contained the Secret Things of her unutterable mystery. Another bore in his beatified bosom a venerable effigy of Supreme Deity, which showed no likeness to any bird or beast, wild or tame, or even to man, but which was worthy of reverence because of its exquisite invention and originality: a symbol inexpressible of the true religion that should be veiled in Deep Silence. This effigy was of burnished gold, made as follows: a small urn was delicately hollowed out with a round bottom; the strange hieroglyphs of the Egyptians covered its outside; the spout was shaped

rather low but jutting out like a funnel; the handle on the other side pro-
jected with a wide sweep; and on this stood an asp, stretching up his
scaly, wrinkled, swollen throat and twining round the whole length.

At last the glorious moment which the presiding Goddess had prom- **12**
ised me was at hand. For the priest, adorned exactly as she had described, neared with the instrument of my salvation. In his right hand he
carried the Goddess's sistrum and a crown of roses. Ah, by Hercules, a
crown indeed it was for me, since by the providence of the overmaster-
ing gods, after so many toils of experience, I was now to find my efforts
crowned with victory over Fortune, my cruel foe.

However, though shaken with up-bubbling joy, I did not dash immediately forwards; for I did not want the peaceful order of the holy procession to be disturbed by an unruly beast. Instead, I nosed through the
crowd with a polite all-but-human tread and a sidelong twist of my
body; and, as the people, clearly by the Goddess's dispensation,
disparted to let me through, I slowly approached the flowers. But the **13**
priest, as was obvious to me, recollected his admonitory vision of the
night. He at once stopped stock-still; and spontaneously raising his right
hand, he held the bunch up to my mouth. Trembling, with a thudding
heart, I seized the crown in which some fine rose blooms were brightly
woven; and greedily I masticated the whole lot.

Nor did the heavenly promise fail. At once my ugly and beastly form
left me. My rugged hair thinned and fell; my huge belly sank in; my
hooves separated out into fingers and toes; my hands ceased to be feet
and adapted themselves to the offices of my erected state; my long neck
telescoped itself; my face and head became round; my flapping ears
shrank to their old size; my stony molars waned into human teeth; and
my tail, the worst cross of my ass-days, simply disappeared.

The populace stood in blinking wonder; and the devotees adored the
Goddess for the miraculous revelation of her power in a metamorphosis which partook of the shifting pageantry of a dream. Lifting their
hands to heaven, with one voice the beholders rendered testimony to
the lovingkindness of the Goddess thus signally declared. As for me, I **14**
remained nailed to the spot in mute stupefaction; for my wits were scattered by the shock of joy, and I was quite at a loss. What was the right
utterance with which to begin my new life? Where was my voice to
come from? How was I most auspiciously to employ my newborn
tongue? What phrases could I choose to express my gratitude to so
great a Goddess?

But the priest, who by advertisement knew the whole tale of my mis-
fortunes, though wonderstruck at the miracle recovered himself so far as

to signify with gestures that I should be handed a linen garment. For from the moment that the ass stripped me of his wretched skin I had been doing my naked best to hide my privities with the sole naturally supplied veil, the hand, while compressing my thighs. At once one of the initiated pulled off his upper tunic and wrapped me in it; and then the priest, smiling kindly but still staring at my quite-human countenance, thus addressed me:

15   "At last, Lucius, after the long days of disaster and the heavy storms of fortune you have reached the haven of peace and the altar of mercy. Neither your high lineage, nor your pride of place, nor your learning, profited you one jot. You gave yourself to the slavery of pleasure in the lewdness of hot-blooded youth; and you have reaped the reward of your unprospering curiosity. Nevertheless, blind Fortune, persecuting you with horrors and snares, has led you in her shortsighted malice to this beatitude of release. Let her go now and rage as madly as she will; but let her seek another object for her hate. For terror and calamity have no power over him whose life the majesty of our Goddess has claimed for her service.

"What benefit has furying Fortune gained from the robbers, from the wild beasts, from the servitude, from the unending hardships of the way, from the daily fears of death? You are now received into the protection of Fortune, but of Fortune who is open-eyed and who lightens even the other gods with the splendors of her light. Let your face be joyous therefore. Let it be such a face as accords with that white gown you wear. Follow in the train of the Goddess your Savior with steps of triumph. Let the scoffer behold. Let him behold and be shamed, saying in his heart:

" 'Lo, here is Lucius who rejoices in the providence of mighty Isis. Lo, he is loosed from the bonds of misery and victorious over his fate.'

"Yet, that you may be the safer and the surer, enroll your name in this army of holiness, to which you were but a short time past pledged by oath. Dedicate yourself to the service of true religion, and voluntarily bend your neck to the yoke of this ministry. For when you have begun to serve the Goddess you will feel the full fruitfulness of your liberty."

16   When the worthy priest, laboring hard to breathe under the pressure of inspiration, had concluded this speech, I joined the ranks of the religious and followed the procession. All pointed or nodded at me, and cried aloud: "This day has the august power of Almighty Goddess restored him that you see there to human form. Happy, by Hercules, thrice blessed is he who by the purity and faith of his past life has mer-

ited such particular patronage from above! For it is as though he had been set apart from the moment of his second birth (*renatus*) for the ministry of heaven."

Among these ejaculations and the hum of happy prayers, we moved slowly on till we approached the sea. The spot chosen was the very beach where on the preceding day, while yet an ass, I had stabled myself. First, the images of the gods were orderly disposed; and then the high priest dedicated and consecrated to the Goddess a nobly built boat, scribbled all over with the peculiar Egyptian marks, after purifying its torch, flame, egg, and sulphur, and pouring solemn prayers from his sanctified lips.

The shining-white sail of this blessed ship bore a broidered inscription repeating the words of the prayer for this year's prosperous navigation. The mast, when raised, was seen to be a rounded pine-tree of great height with a glittering top that drew all eyes. The prow was curved to represent a goose-neck and covered with flaming gold-plates, while the whole of the polished keel consisted of rich citronwood.

All the people, initiate or lay, zealously piled up winnowing-fans with aromatic scents and other such offerings, and threw libations of milk mixed with crumbs into the sea, until the ship, cargoed with plentiful gifts and auspicious devotions, was let slip from her anchoring ropes. She put out to sea with a mild breeze, all her own; and after she had sailed out of sight into the distance on her course, the bearers of the holy things reassumed their burdens and began a lively return journey to the temple in the same order and propriety as they had come.

On arrival at the temple, the high priest, those who bore the divine *17* figures, and those who had been admitted into the inner light of the cult, collected in the sanctuary of the Goddess. First they put back the breathing images into their right places; then a man, whom all entitled the scribe, took his stand in a high pulpit before the doors, and the Society of the Pastophori—such is the name of the sacred college—was convoked. The scribe thereupon read out of a book a set of patriotic prayers for "the great Prince, the Senate, the Equestrian Order, the Roman people, and all sailors and ships which come under the jurisdiction of Rome." After that he pronounced in the Greek tongue and manner the words "*Laois aphesis.*" The people were dismissed.

The shout that followed showed the popular approval of the day's proceedings; and the congregation began to file out, beaming with joy, carrying boughs of olive and other votive wreaths, and garlanded with flowers. As they left the precincts, they one and all stopped to kiss the feet of a silver image of the Goddess that stood on the steps. But my emotions would not allow me to stir a single inch away from the place. With my eyes fixed upon the image I brooded over my past miseries.

18   Winging rumor, however, let no moss grow on her feathers. The tale of the Goddess's adorable goodness and of my curious adventures very soon had reached my native city; and my servants, friends, and those near to me in blood, at once discarded the sorrow into which the false tidings of my death had plunged them. Overjoyed and surprised, they hastened to visit me with various gifts, looking upon me as a man divinely raised up out of death. I who had shared their grief now shared their pleasure but gratefully refused their gifts, particularly as my servants had luckily taken care to bring me more than enough of clothes and

19 money. Therefore, after I had met these acquaintances politely and told them the full story of my past pains and present prospects, I once more returned to what had become my chief source of delight: the contemplation of the Goddess. Renting a temporary apartment within the temple enclosure I took part in all the services, frequenting the company of the priests and becoming a constant worshiper at the shrine. Nor did a single night pass without some vision visiting my sleep and commanding me to be initiated into the priesthood, to which vocation I had long since been destined.

But though I profoundly desired to take this step, yet a religious qualm held me back. For after careful inquiry I had learned that a consecrated life was full of snags, that the requisite chastity was difficult to observe, and that only the most unrelenting discipline could save the priest from casual pollutions. Turning these doubts over and over in my mind, I kept delaying my initiation, though every day brought me closer to the final decision.

20   One night I had a dream. I thought that the high priest came to me with his bosom full of something or other. I asked him what he was offering me, and he answered, "Presents from Thessaly, for that Snowy Servant of yours has arrived from that province."

When I awoke I pondered over the meaning of this vision, especially as I was sure that I never had a servant of that name. However, I concluded that something to my advantage was portended by the priest offering me presents. Thus, worried and yet hopeful, I awaited the opening of the temple in the morning. At last the white curtains were drawn, and we offered up our prayers before the holy face of the Goddess. The priest went the round of the altars, performed the sacred ceremonial with solemn supplications, and poured out libations of water from the sanctuary-spring. When all these rites were completed, the worshipers saluted the rays of dawn and announced in clear voices that the day had begun.

Then lo, some men who had been in my employ arrived from Hypata, where I had left them on the day when Fotis by her wicked error fitted me for a halter. Accosting them I found that they had brought back my old horse, which had been recovered after changing hands several times and which I identified by a mark on his back. At once I realized how admirably prophetic was my dream; for not only had it foretold gain in a general way but it had actually described the recovery of the horse, my snowy servant.

After this I applied myself even more diligently to attendance on the temple-services; for I considered that the Goddess has vouchsafed sure token of future blessings by her present benignity. Besides, my desire to enter the priesthood increased by bounds every day. Accordingly I had frequent interviews with the high priest, during which I earnestly besought him to initiate me into the mysteries of the Holy Night. But he, a serious-minded man who was noted for his strict observance of his unevangelical religion, checked my implorations with gentle friendliness, as parents get rid of children who come bothering at the wrong moment. At the same time he was careful to soothe me with hopes for the future.

For, he said, the initiation date for each aspirant was given by direct sign from the Goddess; and the officiating priest was selected by the same process—as also the precise sum to be expended on the ceremony. All these details must be awaited with uncomplaining patience, since it was necessary on every count to avoid either forwardness or contumacy, and neither to be slothful when called nor precipitate when not called. Not indeed that there was a single man among them who was so lost to common sense or so foolhardy that he would dare in rank blasphemy to undertake the ministries of the Goddess, which without her consent would be an invocation of destruction. For the gates of shadow as well as the bulwarks of life were under the Goddess's control; and the act of initiation had been compared to a voluntary death with a slight chance of redemption. Therefore the divine will of the Goddess was wont to choose men who had lived their life to the full, who were coming near to the limits of waning light, and who yet could be safely trusted with the mighty secrets of her religion. These men by her divine providence she regenerated and restored to strength sufficient for their new career. Consequently I must await the celestial token, although I had already been manifestly indicated as destined for the blessed ministry. Meanwhile I should abstain from all profane or forbidden foods like the other devotees, that I might hasten the more uprightly into the secret bosom of the faith.

22   Thus spoke the priest; nor did impatience fret my obedient days. For I ambitiously performed the daily tasks of the ministry, intent upon preserving a serenity of soul and a laudable silence. Nor did the mindful love of the Goddess desert me or nail me on a cross of long delay; for there was no darkness in the visions that admonished the darkness of my sleep. She appeared and told me that the day of my desire had arrived, the day which would fulfill my dearest wishes. She also stated the sum of money to be spent on the ceremonial, and appointed the high priest Mithras to preside over my initiation; for, she said, he and I had our destinies mingled by a conjunction of our stars.

Elated by these and other divine commandments of the supreme Goddess, I threw off the coverlet of my sleep, although light was just greying. Hastening straightway to the retreat of the high priest I greeted him just as he was leaving his bedchamber. I had resolved to press my initiation as a thing now due; but the moment that he saw me he began speaking:

"O Lucius, what a happy and blessed man are you, whom the august deity has selected for such direct honors. O why," he cried, "do you stand there idle? Why do you delay a moment? The day you have so constantly desired is come. You are to be initiated into the holy mysteries by these hands of mine in accordance with the divine mandate of the many-titled Goddess."

Thereupon the old man took me by the hand and led me towards the spacious temple; and after he had duly performed the rituals of opening the doors and of making the morning-sacrifice, he produced from the secret recesses of the shrine certain books written in unknown characters. The meaning of these characters was concealed, at times by the concentrated expression of hieroglyphically painted animals, at times by wreathed and twisted letters with tails that twirled like wheels or spiralled together like vine-tendrils—so that it was altogether impossible for any peeping profane to comprehend. From these books the high priest interpreted to me the matters necessary for my mystic preparation.

23   That done, I set about purchasing, partly at my own cost and partly with the aid of friends, all the required commodities. This I did on a larger scale than I had been bidden; and then, at the time that the priest had appointed as most suitable, I was led to the Baths, surrounded by a crowd of devotees. There, after I had taken the usual bath, Mithras himself washed and sprinkled me with pure water, invoking first the pardon of the gods.

Then he led me back once more into the temple and sat me down at the very feet of the Goddess. Two parts of the day had now gone; and after giving me some secret charges, too holy to be uttered, he bade me aloud to fast for the next ten days, eating no flesh and drinking no wine. This fast I reverently observed; and then at last the day arrived when I was to pledge myself to heaven. The sun swung down and drew the evening on; and lo, hosts of people came eagerly from every direction, each man honoring me with various gifts according to the ancient rite. Then, after the uninitiated had withdrawn to a distance and I had donned a new linen gown, the priest grasped my hand and conducted me into the Holy of Holies.

Perhaps, curious reader, you are keen to know what was said and done. I would tell you if it were permitted to tell. But both the ears that heard such things and the tongue that told them would reap a heavy penalty for such rashness. However, I shall not keep you any longer on the cross of your anxiety, distracted as you doubtless are with religious yearning. Hear therefore and believe what I say to be truth.

I approached the confines of death. I trod the threshold of Proserpine; and borne through the elements I returned. At midnight I saw the Sun shining in all his glory. I approached the gods below and the gods above, and I stood beside them, and I worshiped them. Behold, I have told my experience, and yet what you hear can mean nothing to you. I shall therefore keep to the facts which can be declared to the profane without offense.

Morning arrived; and after the due solemnities I came forth sanctified **24** with twelve stoles, an habiliment of deep religious import, but which the bonds of my obligation do not keep me from mentioning, as I was seen by many bystanders. For, by order of the priest, I climbed a wooden pulpit which stood in the middle of the temple before the image of the Goddess. I wore a vestment of linen embroidered with a flower-pattern; a costly cope hung down from my shoulders to my ankles; and from whatever angle you inspected me you saw interesting new animal-shapes among the decorations—here Indian serpents, there Hyperborean griffins, which the Antipodes incubate like birds. This latter garment was what the priests commonly call an Olympic Stole. In my right hand I held a lighted torch; and a comely chaplet was wound round my head, from which the palm-tree leaves jetted like rays of the sun.

Thus decorated like the sun and draped like a statue, the curtains being whisked away, I was suddenly revealed to the gaze of the multitude. After this I celebrated the festal day of initiation, as if it were a birthday, with a sumptuous feasting and merry converse; and the third day was taken up with similar ceremonies, with a ritual-breakfast and the consummation of my priesthood.

Lingering about the temple for several more days, I was granted the delight of viewing the Holy Face: a benefit that no grateful services can ever repay—till at length, after humbly thanking the Goddess, not as she deserved but as I was able, I received her admonition to depart home; and I reluctantly made my preparations. But I could hardly bear to break the ties of intense affection that bound me to the place. Prostrating myself before the Goddess and watering her feet with my tears, I addressed her, gulping back the sobs that disturbed my articulation:

25   "Most holy and everlasting Redeemer of the human race, you munificently cherish our lives and bestow the consoling smiles of a Mother upon our tribulations. There is no day or night, not so much as the minutest fraction of time, that is not stuffed with the eternity of your mercy. You protect men on land and sea. You chase the storms of life and stretch out the hand of succour to the dejected. You can untwine the hopelessly tangled threads of the Fates. You can mitigate the tempests of Fortune and check the stars in the courses of their malice. The gods of heaven worship you. The gods of hell bow before you. You rotate the globe. You light the sun. You govern space. You trample hell. The stars move to your orders, the seasons return, the gods rejoice, the elements combine. At your nod the breezes blow, the clouds collect, seeds sprout, blossoms increase. The birds that fly in the air, the beasts that roam on the hills, the serpents that hide in the earth, the monsters that swim in the ocean, tremble before your majesty.

"O my spirit is not able to give you sufficient praises, nor have I the means to make acceptable sacrifice. My voice has no power to utter what I think of you. Not a thousand mouths with a thousand tongues, not an eternal flow of unwearied declaration, could utter it.

"Howbeit, poor as I am, I shall do all that a truly religious man may do. I shall conjure up your divine countenance within my breast, and there in the secret depths I shall keep divinity forever guarded."

I thus offered my prayer to the supreme Goddess. Then I embraced the priest Mithras, my father in Her; and clinging upon his neck and kissing him oft, I begged his forgiveness that I could not recompense him

26   adequately for the benefits he had heaped upon me. After expressing my sense of obligation at full length, I left him and prepared to revisit my ancestral home from which I had been so long absent.

So, a few days later, as the Goddess admonished, after hastily packing my luggage I went on shipboard and set sail for Rome. Safely and swiftly carried by a favoring breeze, we soon reached the port of Augustus. There I disembarked; and traveling by post-chariot I arrived at the Holy City on the evening of the day before the Ides of December. Nothing now mattered to me so much as to supplicate daily the supreme godhead of Queen Isis, who is propitiated in this city with the deepest veneration as Campensis: a name derived from the site of her temple. In short, I became an unslackening worshiper, a newcomer to this church of hers, but indigenous to her religion.

Now the strong-thewed Sun had passed through all the signs of the circling zodiac, and the year was ended. But the loving insistence of the Goddess once more broke in upon my sleep, once more strongly speaking of mysteries and holy rites. I wondered what was the meaning of this, and what even was foreshadowed. How should I not? For I had thought myself fully initiated already.

After I had reexamined all my religious doubts in the privacy of my 27
own conscience, I consulted a priest. I then learned a new and disturbing thing: that I was initiated into the mysteries of the Goddess, but that I knew nothing of the rites of the mighty God, the supreme Father of the Gods, unconquerable Osiris.

For though there is amity and even unity to be found between the two essences and their religious statement, yet the approach to knowledge of them is by different tracks. So now what I had to do was to await a summons from the great God to his service. Nor was I left long in doubt. During the next night I saw in a dream one of his devotees clad in linen and bearing ivied thyrsi and other objects, which I may not name. He placed his load before my Household Gods; and then, seating himself in my chair, he recited to me the articles necessary for a splendid religious feast—and, in order that I might know him again, he showed me how the heel of his left foot was somewhat hurt, giving him a slight hobble. All the mists of my doubt were cleared by such a manifest sign of the will of the gods.

Therefore, as soon as my matins were finished, I carefully noted the priests, to see if any of them walked like the man in my dream. There he was, the very man. One of the Pastophori closely resembled my midnight visitor in stature and looks as well as in gait. His name, I later found, was Asinius Marcellus, a name asininely suggestive of my late plight. I at once approached the priest, who was not at all surprised at what he heard me say; for he had been similarly admonished as to my initiation into the mysteries of Osiris. On the preceding night, while dress-

ing the garlands on the statue of the Great God, he imagined that the
Mouth, which pronounced the dooms of all mankind, spoke to him. The
message said that a native of Madaura was being sent to him and that he
must impart to this man, poor as he was, the sacraments of the God—
whereby through the God's providence the one would be glorified for
his religious exercises and the other greatly profited.

28   Thus affianced to religion I was yet held back from the full consummation of my desire through the slenderness of my means. For the travel expenses had wasted the remnant of my estate; and the cost of living in
Rome was far ahead of that in the provinces. My poverty thus kept inter-
fering with my plans; and I was left stranded, as the saying goes, between the altar and the block.

Yet the mandates from the God did not weaken their pressure. They
continued to goad me till I became very troubled; and then as the commands grew more incisive, I sold the clothes off my back and scraped up
enough to carry on. This indeed was the course prescribed; for the God
said to me: "If you were hot after some trifle of pleasure, would you hesitate to throw your clothes away? And now, on the brink of initiation, do
you shrink from a poverty that can bring no repentance?"

Everything was thus fully prepared; and now once more I abstained
for ten days from eating flesh. Then, admitted with shaven head to the
nocturnal orgies of the Lord of Gods, I resorted to the ceremonies with
the full confidence that knowledge of a kindred ritual evoked. This occurrence consoled me for my sojourn in a foreign city and also gave me a better chance of earning my livelihood. For, favored by the god Good-Luck,
I managed to subsist on the small fees I gained in the Forum pleading
causes in the Latin tongue.

29   But shortly afterwards I was once more molested by unexpected vi-
sionary commands; and a third time I found myself yearning towards a
mystery. This left me in an oppressively shaken and perplexed state of
mind, uncertain what could be the significance of this new and peculiar
expression of celestial will and what could remain incomplete in my dual
initiation. Surely, thought I, the instructions given me by the two priests
must have been either incorrect or fragmentary; and, by Hercules, I began to suspect them of bad faith. While, however, I was drifting on these
stormy tides of doubt and driven to the verge of distraction, the benign
figure of the God appeared in dream once more.

"To no end," said he, "are you frightened by the continued series of
religious rites, as if something had been previously omitted. Rather, you
should take heart because the deities repeat the tokens of their love for

you. You should exult that you will thrice achieve that which is scarcely even once given to others. And you may rightly conjecture from the number Three that you will remain eternally blessed. Moreover, you will find the ceremony indispensable if you will but realize that the stole of the Goddess with which you were invested in the province is still kept in the temple there. You are thus unable to supplicate at Rome in your stole or to be distinguished by that auspicious garment when you are bidden to don it. Therefore let my command be as glory, happiness, and health to you. Once more joyously become initiated, with the mighty gods for your sponsors."

Thus far did the persuasive majesty of the divine vision announce **30** what I must profitably do. So I did not neglect or weakly postpone the matter. At once I related to a priest what I had seen; and I not only submitted to the yoke of abstinence from meat but voluntarily extended the period beyond the ten days ordained by everlasting law. Then I bought all the necessary articles, considering more the measure of my piety than the narrowness of the regulations. Nor, by Hercules, was I ever sorry for my trouble and expense. And why should I? For now by the generous aid of the gods I was being decently repaid for my forensic labors.

At length, after the lapse of a few days, the Lord Osiris, the most powerful of the great gods, the highest of the greater, the greatest of the highest, and ruler of the greatest, appeared to me in the night, now no longer disguised but deigning to speak to me in his own person and with his own divine voice. He declared that I should rapidly come to the forefront of the legal profession at Rome and that I should not fear the slanders of the malevolent who naturally disliked me on account of the learning I had studiously acquired.

In addition, to enable me to mingle with the throng of devotees and duly serve his mysteries, he appointed me a member of the College of Pastophori—and more, one of the five-yearly decurions; and so, with tonsured crown, I set about joyfully executing my duties in that most ancient society, which had been founded in the period of Sylla, not shading or hiding my baldness but freely exposing it wherever I went.

FLAVIUS JOSEPHUS, *JEWISH ANTIQUITIES (ANTIQUITATES JUDAICAE)*, Book 18.3.4 (65–80)

Near the end of the first century c.e., in his *Jewish Antiquities*, the Jewish historian Josephus (born 37/38 c.e.) reported a scandal that had taken place in 19 c.e. in connection with the worship of Isis in Rome. As Josephus narrates the story, a certain Mundus wished desperately to enjoy the charms of the lady Paulina. When she steadfastly refused, Mundus hatched a plot with a freedwoman Ida and at last managed to spend an entire night with Paulina in the temple of Isis by convincing her that she actually was making love with the Egyptian god Anubis. When the scheme came to light, the emperor Tiberius punished several of the guilty parties with crucifixion and destroyed the temple.

This excerpt from Josephus illustrates well how the early Romans suspected, sometimes persecuted, but yet adored the Egyptian goddess.

This translation is by Louis H. Feldman, *Josephus: IX* (Loeb Classical Library, 1965).

65 About the same time another outrage threw the Jews into an uproar; and simultaneously certain actions of a scandalous nature occurred in connection with the temple of Isis at Rome. I shall first give an account of the daring deed of the followers of Isis and shall then come back to the

66 fate of the Jews. There was a lady Paulina, who because of her descent from noble Romans and because of her own practice of virtue was held in high regard. She also enjoyed the prestige of wealth, had a comely appearance, and was at the age at which women are most exuberant, yet devoted her life to good conduct. She was married to Saturninus, who

67 was fully a match for her in reputation. Decius Mundus, who ranked high among the knights of his day, was in love with her. When he saw that her character was too strong to succumb to gifts, since, even when he sent them abundantly, she scorned them, his passion was inflamed all the more, so that he actually promised to give her 200,000 Attic

68 drachmai if he could share her bed a single time. When even this failed to shake her resolution, he, finding it intolerable not to win his suit, thought that it would be fitting to condemn himself to death by starvation and thus to put an end to the suffering that had overtaken him. And so he decided upon such a death and was actually proceeding to carry

69 out his resolve. Mundus, however, had a freedwoman named Ida, expert in every kind of mischief, whom his father had emancipated. She had no patience with the young man's resolve to die, for it was obvious what he intended. She went to him, used argument to rouse him, and by plausibly undertaking to find a way, held out hope that he might suc-

70 ceed in enjoying intimate relations with Paulina. When he joyfully listened to her importunity, she informed him that she would require no more than 50,000 drachmai to secure the woman. These proposals encouraged the youth, and she received the sum for which she had asked.

She did not, however, proceed by the same course as had previous agents, since she perceived that this woman would never succumb to bribes. But knowing that the lady was very much given to the worship of Isis, Ida devised the following stratagem. She had an interview with 71 some of the priests and promised them every assurance, above all, a sum of money amounting to 25,000 drachmai payable at once and as much more after the success of the plot. She then explained the young man's passionate desire for the woman and urged them to bend every effort to secure her for him. The impact of the money was enough to sway them, 72 and they agreed. The eldest of them hastened to Paulina's house and, on being admitted, requested a private talk with her. This being accorded, he said that he had been sent to her by the god Anubis; the god had fallen in love with her and bade her come to him. The message was what 73 she would most have wished. Not only did she pride herself among her lady friends on receiving such an invitation from Anubis, but she told her husband of her summons to dine with and share the bed of Anubis. Her husband concurred, since he had no doubt of his wife's chastity. Go 74 then she did to the temple. After supper, when it came time to sleep, the doors within the shrine were shut by the priest and the lamps were cleared away. Mundus, for he had been concealed there beforehand, was not rebuffed when he sought intercourse with her. Indeed it was a nightlong service that she performed for him, assuming that he was the god. He departed before the priests, who had been informed of the 75 scheme, had begun to stir. Paulina went early in the morning to her husband and described in detail the divine manifestation of Anubis, and before the ladies, her friends, she put on great airs in talking about him. Those who heard, having regard to the substance of the matter, were in 76 credulous; and yet, on the other hand, finding it impossible not to believe her when they took into consideration her chastity and position in society, they were reducing to marveling. Two days after the incident, 77 Mundus put himself in her way and said: "Well, Paulina, you have indeed saved me 200,000 drachmai which you could have added to your estate, yet you have rendered to perfection the service I urged you to perform. As for your attempt to flout Mundus, I did not concern myself about names, though I did about the pleasure to be derived from the act, so I adopted the name of Anubis as my own." With these words he de- 78 parted. Then she, being now aware for the first time of his dastardly deed, rent her garment; and when she had disclosed to her husband the enormity of the scheme, she begged him not to neglect to obtain redress. He in turn brought the matter to the notice of the emperor. When Tibe- 79

rius had fully informed himself by examining the priests, he crucified
both them and Ida, for the hellish thing was her doing and it was she
who had contrived the whole plot against the lady's honor. Moreover,
he razed the temple and ordered the statue of Isis to be cast into the
80 Tiber River. Mundus's sentence was exile, since Tiberius regarded the
fact that his crime had been committed under the influence of passion as
a bar to a more severe penalty. Such were the insolent acts of the priests
in the temple of Isis.

7
The Roman
Mysteries
of Mithras

7
The Roman
Mysteries
of Mithras

The evolution of the divine Mithras from his origin in the ancient past to his position as bull-slayer in the Roman mysteries is a long, complex, and largely unknown process. Already among the ancient Indo-Iranian peoples, Mithras was known as a god of light, truth, and integrity. In the Vedic literature of India, Mitra is allied with Varuna the god of heaven, and in the Zoroastrian literature of Persia (the *Avesta*), Mithra is associated with Ahura Mazda, the wise lord. According to the *Avesta*, Mithra is the champion of the truth of Ahura Mazda and the warrior against the falsehood of Ahriman. The *Avesta* calls Mithra "the lord of wide pastures" and claims that he provides cattle, prosperity, and life. The priests known as the Magi further developed religious beliefs surrounding Mithra. As the worship of the Magi spread to the west, so did related forms of the worship of Mithras. According to Plutarch, the mysteries of Mithras were in evidence among the pirates based in southeastern Asia Minor during the first century B.C.E.

As we know them, the Mithraic mysteries are a Roman phenomenon that flourished in the Roman Empire from the second century C.E. on. The mysteries of Mithras were mysteries for men. Soldiers, sailors, and imperial officers in particular were attracted to the divine warrior of light, truth, and justice, and this attraction helps to account for the number of Mithraea (sanctuaries of Mithra) located in the frontier provinces where the Roman legions were stationed, as well as in the cities and ports of the empire. The character of Mithras and the Mithraic devotees also helps explain why emperors often favored the worship of this divine warrior.

Those devoted to Mithras entered the Mithraea, designed as caves, and participated in various purifications, initiatory rites, and ceremonial meals. According to the Christian author Tertullian (*On the Crown [De corona]*, 15; *On Baptism [De baptismo]*, 5; *Prescription Against Heretics [De praescriptione haereticorum]*, 40), Mithraic initiates underwent ordeals and tests of valor, were baptized or washed with water, and were sealed on their foreheads. Another Christian author, Justin Martyr (*First Apology,*

66.4), claims that the Mithraic initiates took bread and a cup of water (or a mixed cup of water and wine—these elements may have been symbolic of the body and blood of the bull) and uttered formulas at a holy meal.

The Mithraic rituals were intended to bring about the salvation and transformation of the initiates. In the inscriptions from Santa Prisca the salvific transformation is described as rebirth and creation (or re-creation). Sometimes, as in the literary selection from the Platonist Celsus and in the Mithras Liturgy, texts related to Mithraism suggest that the new life of the initiate was experienced in an ascent of the soul to the realm of the divine (see also Porphyry, *On the Cave of the Nymphs*). The creation or re-creation to be enjoyed applied not only to initiates but also to the cosmos. Mithraic monuments show that the sacrifice of the bull was a moment of creation and life: grain sprouted from the bull's tail or even from the wound itself.

Initiation in the mysteries of Mithras involved progressive stages. Ordinarily, seven are specified: Raven (Corax), Bridegroom (Nymphus; alternately, Occult, Cryphius), Soldier (Miles), Lion (Leo), Persian (Perses), Courier of the Sun (Heliodromus), and Father (Pater). These seven stages correspond well with the archeological evidence of the Mithraeum of Felicissimus at Ostia, Italy, the floor of which has seven stations decorated with symbols appropriate to the seven stages of initiation. Another Mithraeum at Ostia likewise has seven stations marked out with seven arcs; a third has a floor mosaic with seven gates. Note also the account of Celsus and the Mithras Liturgy, in this chapter.

Much of our knowledge of specific features of Mithraic mythology comes from the scenes on such archeological monuments as a bas-relief from Heddernheim, Germany. This stone was carved on both sides and provided with a pivot and socket so that it could be rotated. The front is dominated by the scene of Mithras killing the bull (Mithras *tauroktonos*). As the bull dies, three heads of grain grow from his tail. Mithras has a Phrygian (or Persian) cap on his head, and his cloak is flying behind him. Upon the cloak is perched a raven, a messenger of the sun and a Mithraic grade of initiation. On either side of Mithras *tauroktonos* are the torchbearers (*dadophori*), Cautes (with torch up) and Cautopates (with torch down), symbolic of the coming and going of the sun. Above Mithras is a border with the twelve signs of the zodiac: the border functions both as the ceiling of the cave and, because the cave is a microcosm of the universe, the firmament of heaven. All around the periphery of the stone are mythological scenes from the life of Mithras: he is born from a rock (the sun is born on December 25, at the time of the winter solstice); he shoots an arrow at a rock (to open a spring) and emerges from a tree (compare with the connection of Attis and Osiris to trees); he carries the bull (Mithras *taurophoros*) to be killed; he meets with the Sun (Helios, Sol), who kneels before him; they shake hands in agreement and ride off together in the chariot of the Sun. The four winds and the four seasons are also shown in the corners. The back of this stone from Heddernheim shows the other main scene in Mithraic iconography: the holy meal shared by Mithras and the Sun, who thus commemorate their agreement together by dining, in a cave, around the body of the sacrificed bull.

The interpretation of the literary, epigraphical, and archeological evidence concerning the Mithraic mysteries remains controversial, especially with regard to the possible Zoroastrian background of themes in the Roman mysteries. Clear Persian motifs remain in the initiatory grade of Perses and the attire of Mithras. Whether or not the presence of the snake and the scorpion in the visual representations of Mithras slaying the bull (such as in the Heddernheim monument) indicates a dualistic struggle of good against evil, after the manner of Zoroastrianism, remains uncertain. It is more likely, perhaps, that the evidence suggests some themes that are to be understood in a more astronomical or astrological manner, and that the snake, scorpion, and bull are to be identified with the constellations Hydra, Scorpio, and Taurus. Mithras himself may call to mind the constellation Perseus, dressed in Persian garb and poised with a dagger above Taurus. In this regard the interpretations of Roger Beck and David Ulansey are particularly significant and suggest that Mithraism was a cosmic religion of salvation.

For a further analysis of Mithraism, see Leroy A. Campbell, *Mithraic Iconography and Ideology*, EPRO, tome 11 (Leiden: Brill, 1968); Franz Cumont, *The Mysteries of Mithra* (1903; reprint, New York: Dover, 1956); idem, *Textes et monuments figurés relatifs aux mystères de Mithra*, 2 vols. (Brussels: H. Lamertin, 1896–99); John R. Hinnells, ed., *Mithraic Studies*, 2 vols. (Manchester: Manchester Univ. Press, 1975); Reinhold Merkelbach, *Mithras* (Königstein/Ts.: Hain, 1984); Kurt Rudolph, "Mitra, Mithra, Mithras," *Orientalistische Literaturzeitung* 74 (1979): 309–20; Robert Turcan, *Mithras Platonicus: Recherches sur l'Hellénisation philosophique de Mithra*, EPRO, tome 47 (Leiden, Brill, 1975), and the excellent review article by John Dillon, "The Platonizing of Mithra," *Journal of Mithraic Studies* 2 (1977): 79–85; Maarten J. Vermaseren, *Corpus Inscriptionum et Monumentorum religionis Mithriacae*, 2 vols. (The Hague: M. Nijhoff, 1956–60); idem, *Mithras, the Secret God* (New York: Barnes & Noble, 1963). Now also see

Manfred Clauss, *The Roman Cult of Mithras: The God and His Mysteries*, trans. Richard Gordon (New York: Routledge, 2000). On astronomical interpretations of Mithraism see especially Roger Beck, *Planetary Gods and Planetary Orders in the Mysteries of Mithras*, EPRO, tome 109 (Leiden: Brill, 1988); and David Ulansey, *The Origins of the Mithraic Mysteries* (New York: Oxford University Press, 1989).

LUCIAN OF SAMOSATA, *MENIPPUS (OR, THE DESCENT INTO HADES)*, 6–9

In his inimitable way, the second-century author Lucian presents his dialogue *Menippus* as a satire not only upon those with wealth and might, but also upon those who spend their lives thinking about first causes, final causes, and syllogisms (that is, the philosophers). Menippus the Cynic descends into Hades in order to find out about the best life and the best philosophy and discovers that the good life is not that of the rich and powerful nor that of the philosopher, but rather the common, ordinary life of one who lives well in the present and laughs a great deal. Menippus is able to accomplish his descent into the underworld because of a magical rite performed by one of the Magi, a certain Mithrobarzanes, who lived in Babylon. Lucian's description of the rite is a delightful parody, but it also contains elements that he might have derived from the practices of the Magi: the concern for matters of astronomy, astrology, and magic; the use of purifications, flaming torches (compare with the sacred fire), and such ceremonial foods as water, milk, and honey ("mead," *melikraton*, a drink or libation with honey); the place of ritual, sacrifice, libation, and foreign-sounding chants; and the portrait of the priest (Magos) dressed in Median attire and bearing the name of Mithras in his own name. (For a popular Christian legend about the Magi adoring the infant Jesus, see Matthew 2:1–12.)

This translation is by A. M. Harmon, *Lucian: IV* (Loeb Classical Library, 1969).

MENIPPUS

6 Disappointed, therefore, in this expectation, I was still more uncomfortable than before, although I consoled myself somewhat with the thought that if I was still foolish and went about in ignorance of the truth, at all events I had the company of many wise men, widely renowned for intelligence. So one time, while I lay awake over these problems, I resolved to go to Babylon and address myself to one of the Magi, the disciples and

successors of Zoroaster, as I had heard that with certain charms and cere-
monials they could open the gates of Hades, taking down in safety anyone they would and guiding him back again. Consequently I thought
best to arrange with one of these men for my going down, and then to
call upon Teiresias of Boeotia and find out from him in his capacity of
prophet and sage what the best life was, the life that a man of sense
would choose.

Well, springing to my feet, I made straight for Babylon as fast as I
could go. On my arrival I conversed with one of the Chaldeans, a wise
man of miraculous skill, with grey hair and a very majestic beard; his
name was Mithrobarzánes. By dint of supplications and entreaties, I se-
cured his reluctant consent to be my guide on the journey at whatever
price he would. So the man took me in charge, and first of all, for 7
twenty-nine days, beginning with the new moon, he took me down to
the Euphrates in the early morning, toward sunrise, and bathed me; after which he would make a long address which I could not follow very
well, for like an incompetent announcer at the games, he spoke rapidly
and indistinctly. It is likely, however, that he was invoking certain spirits. Anyhow, after the incantation he would spit in my face thrice and
then go back again without looking at anyone whom he met. We ate
nuts, drank milk, mead, and the water of the Choaspes, and slept out of
doors on the grass.

When he considered the preliminary course of dieting satisfactory,
taking me to the Tigris River at midnight he purged me, cleansed me,
and consecrated me with torches and squills and many other things,
murmuring his incantation as he did so. Then after he had becharmed
me from head to foot and walked all about me, that I might not be
harmed by the phantoms, he took me home again, just as I was, walking
backward. After that, we made ready for the journey. He himself put on 8
a magician's gown very like the Median dress, and speedily costumed
me in these things which you see—the cap, the lion's skin, and the lyre
besides; and he urged me, if anyone should ask my name, not to say
Menippus, but Heracles or Odysseus or Orpheus.

FRIEND

What was his object in that, Menippus? I do not understand the reason either for the costume or for the names.

MENIPPUS

Why, that, at any rate, is obvious and not at all shrouded in mystery.
Since they had been before us in going down to Hades alive, he thought
that if he should make me look like them, I might easily slip by the fron-

tier-guard of Aeacus and go in unhindered as something of an old acquaintance; for thanks to my costume they would speed me along my journey just as they do in the plays.

9   Well, day was just beginning to break when we went down to the river and set about getting under way. He had provided a boat, victims, mead, and everything else that we should need for the ritual. So we shipped all the stores, and at length ourselves

> Gloomily hied us aboard, with great tears falling profusely.

For a space we drifted along in the river, and then we sailed into the marsh and the lake in which the Euphrates loses itself. After crossing this, we came to a deserted, woody, sunless place. There at last we landed with Mithrobarzanes leading the way; we dug a pit, we slaughtered the sheep, and we sprinkled their blood about it. Meanwhile the magician held a burning torch and no longer muttered in a low tone but shouted as loudly as he could, invoking the spirits, one and all, at the top of his lungs; also the Tormentors, the Furies,

> Hecate, queen of the night, and eery Persephoneia.

With these names he intermingled a number of foreign-sounding, meaningless words of many syllables.

PLUTARCH OF CHAERONEA, *LIFE OF POMPEY*, 24.1–8

Plutarch, in his *Life of Pompey*, narrates the story of the grand and violent career of Pompey (b. 106–d. 48 B.C.E.), the ambitious Roman general and politician who triumphed on the battlefield (particularly in the eastern Mediterranean) as well as in the Roman political arena. One of Pompey's impressive military victories was his quick strike against the Cilician pirates in 67 B.C.E. These pirates, operating out of bases in Cilicia and Crete, terrorized people on land and sea by taking cities along the coast, plundering the countryside, kidnapping high officials and wealthy citizens, and controlling the sea lanes. Section 24 of the *Life of Pompey* describes the conduct of the Cilician raiders and suggests that these pirates, being devotees of Mithras, introduced the celebration of the Mithraic mysteries into the Roman world.

The following excerpt is translated by Rex Warner, *Fall of the Roman Republic: Six Lives by Plutarch* (New York: Penguin, 1972).

1   The power of the pirates was originally based on Cilicia and at first the pirate fleets employed hit-and-run tactics. They gained confidence and daring during the period of the Mithridatic war when they took subsi-
2   dies from the King and served in his interest. Then while Romans were

fighting each other in civil wars at the gates of Rome, the sea was left unguarded and so the pirates were gradually enticed further and further on until, instead of confining their operations to attacks on navigation, they began to lay waste islands and cities on the coasts. Soon men of wealth and of good family, men who would claim for themselves exceptional intelligence, began to join the pirate fleets and to share in their enterprises, regarding piracy as a profession in which honor could be gained and ambition satisfied. In many places too there were regular fortified harbors 3 and signal stations for the use of the pirates, and the fleets which put in at these places were admirably equipped for their own work with fine crews, expert pilots, and light, fast ships. They were certainly formidable enough; but what excited most indignation was the odious arrogance of it all—the gilded sails, the purple awnings, the silvered oars—the general impression that they were delighting in this way of life and priding themselves on their evil deeds. Roman supremacy was brought into con- 4 tempt by their flute-playing, their stringed instruments, their drunken revels along every coast, their seizures of high-ranking officials, and the ransoms which they demanded for captured cities. It may be stated as a fact that the pirates had in service more than 1,000 ships and that the cities captured by them amounted to 400. They also attacked and plun- 5 dered sanctuaries and holy places which had never been violated before: Claros, for example, Didyma, and Samothrace; the temple of Chthonian Earth at Hermione; the temple of Asklepios at Epidauros; the temples of Poseidon at the Isthmus, at Taenarum, and at Calauria; the temples of Apollo at Actium and Leucas; and the temples of Hera at Samos, at Argos, and at Lacinium. They themselves offered strange sacrifices of their own at Olympus, where they celebrated secret rites or mysteries, among which were those of Mithras. These Mithraic rites, first celebrated by the pirates, are still celebrated today.

But it was the Romans who suffered most from the insolence of the pi- 6 rates, who would even march inland up the Roman roads from the sea, plundering the country and sacking the country houses on their way. There was one occasion when they captured two praetors, Sextilius and Bellinus, in their official purple-edged robes and carried them off together with their servants and their lictors. Then there was the case of the daughter of Antonius, a man who had celebrated a triumph. She was captured by the pirates while she was on her way to the country and a large ransom had to be paid for her release. But the way in which they treated their prisoners was the most outrageous thing of all. If a prisoner 7 cried out that he was a Roman and gave his name, they would pretend to be absolutely terrified; they would smite their thighs with their hands,

and fall down at his feet, begging him to forgive them. The prisoner, seeing them so humble and hearing their entreaties, would believe that they
meant what they said. They would then put Roman boots on his feet and
clothe him in a Roman toga in order, they said, that there should be no
8   mistake about his identity in the future. And so they would play with
him for some time, getting all the amusement possible out of him until,
in the end, they would let down a ship's ladder when they were far out
to sea and tell him that he was quite free to go and that they wished him
a pleasant journey. If he objected, then they threw him overboard themselves and drowned him.

MITHRAIC INSCRIPTIONS OF SANTA PRISCA

Beneath the Church of Santa Prisca in Rome, a Mithraeum has
yielded a number of inscriptions of considerable importance for our
knowledge of Mithraism in the second century C.E. The inscriptions are
written in Latin (with occasional loan-words), and the Latin lines are po-
etic in nature. Thus, the inscriptions may be lines from Mithraic hymns
or other ritual material that praises or invokes the Mithraic powers. Line
one invokes mother earth under the name Pales. Line four extols a miracle performed by Mithras according to Mithraic mythology, namely
Mithras shooting an arrow at a rock to produce a spring. The mythical
brothers who drink from this spring are the torch-bearers Cautes and
Cautopates. Line seven praises Mithras as the one carrying the bull; line
nine does the same, but uses the first-person singular to portray Mithras
or one representing Mithras as the speaker. Line eleven suggests that
one is reborn (renatum) and created (or re-created, creatum) in the celebration of the mysteries, and the "sweet things" (compare to the nectar of
line four) may refer to the elements in a holy meal within Mithraism.
Line thirteen makes astrological reference to the Ram (Aries) as a sign of
the zodiac. Line fourteen praises Mithras for having slain the bull and
uses terms that closely resemble Christian confessions about the blood of
Christ. Lines sixteen through eighteen recognize representatives of two
Mithraic grades of initiation, Father (Pater) and Lion (Leo); in the last
line the word of acclamation is "hail" (nama), by which the Lions are recognized and greeted within the community of initiates.

This translation of the inscriptions of Santa Prisca is from Hans Dieter
Betz, "The Mithras Inscriptions of Santa Prisca and the New Testament,"
Novum Testamentum 10 (1968):62–80. Betz indicates that several of the
translations he publishes are from M. J. Vermaseren and C. C. van

Essen, *The Excavations in the Mithraeum of the Church of Santa Prisca in Rome* (Leiden: Brill, 1965).

Fertile earth Pales who procreates everything. 1

Rockbound spring that fed the twin-brothers with nectar. 4

This young bull which he carried on his golden shoulders according to his ways. 7

And after I had received (it) I have borne on my shoulders the greatest things of the gods. 9

Sweet are the livers of the birds, but care reigns. 10

him (or: that) who (or: which) is piously reborn and created by sweet things. 11

You must conduct the rite through clouded times together. 12

And here as the first the ram runs exactly on his course. 13

And you saved us after having shed the eternal blood. 14

Accept, O holy Father, accept the incense-burning Lions, through whom we offer the incense, through whom we ourselves are consumed. 16 / 17

Hail to the lions for many and new years. 18

FIRMICUS MATERNUS, *THE ERROR OF THE PAGAN RELIGIONS (DE ERRORE PROFANARUM RELIGIONUM)*, 5.1–2; 20.1

Firmicus Maternus wrote his impassioned work of Christian polemics, *The Error of the Pagan Religions*, with all the zeal of a recent convert anxious to secure the benefits of his conversion. In all likelihood the work was written in the years just before 350 C.E. This work is of enormous interest for the study of religion in general in late antiquity and in particular the study of the mystery religions. In Chapter 5, which deals with Mithraism, Firmicus Maternus begins by alluding to a fiery female potency, portrayed with three faces and entwined with snakes. This female figure is paired with a fiery male potency, and the male figure is identified as Mithras himself. The female figure resembles the goddess Hecate but also calls to mind Anahita, the Persian water goddess. In the same chapter and in Chapter 20, Firmicus Maternus quotes two *symbola*. The first addresses an initiate as one who joins with Mithras in taking cattle and who is welcomed into the Mithraic brotherhood with a handshake from the Father (Pater). The second refers to the birth of Mithras from the rock.

Chapter 19, the beginning of which is missing, probably also offers a Mithraic *symbolon*, partially in the lacuna: . . . *de nymphe, chaire nymphe, chaire neon phos*, ". . . O Bridegroom, hail O Bridegroom, hail new light."

This translation from Firmicus Maternus is by Clarence A. Forbes, *Firmicus Maternus: The Error of the Pagan Religions*, Ancient Christian Writers (New York: Paulist, Newman Press, 1970).

5.1 The Persians and all the Magi who dwell in the confines of the Persian land give their preference to fire and think it ought to be ranked above all the other elements. So they divide fire into two potencies, relating its nature to the potency of the two sexes, and attributing the substance of fire to the image of a man and the image of a woman. The woman they represent with a triform countenance, and entwine her with snaky monsters. This they do so as not to disagree in any way with their sponsor, the devil; they want to have their goddess be sprouting all over with snakes **2** and thus be adorned with the devil's polluted insignia. The male they worship is a cattle rustler, and his cult they relate to the potency of fire, as his prophet handed down the lore to us, saying: *mysta booklopies, syndexie patros agauou* ("initiate of cattle-rustling, companion by handclasp of an illustrious father"). Him they call Mithra, and his cult they carry on in hidden caves, so that they may be forever plunged in the gloomy squalor of darkness and thus shun the grace of light resplendent and serene. O true consecration of a divinity! O repulsive inventions of a barbaric code! Him whose crimes you acknowledge you think to be a god. So you who declare it proper for the cult of the Magi to be carried on by the Persian rite in these cave temples, why do you praise only this among the Persian customs? If you think it worthy of the Roman name to serve the cults of the Persians, the laws of the Persians, . . .

20.1 Another pagan sacrament has the key word *theos ek petras* ("god from a rock"). Why do you adulterate the faith and transfer this holy and worshipful mystery to pagan doings? Different is the stone which God promised He would lay in making strong the foundations of the promised Jerusalem. What the symbol of the worshipful stone means to us is Christ. Why do you with the knavery of a thief transfer to foul superstitions the dignity of a worshipful name? Your stone is one that rain follows and the disastrous collapse of tumbling towers; but our stone, laid by the hand of God, builds up, strengthens, lifts, fortifies, and adorns the grace of the restored work with the splendor of everlasting immortality.

ORIGEN, *AGAINST CELSUS (CONTRA CELSUM)*, 6.22

Near the end of the second century c.e. (ca. 178) the pagan author
Celsus wrote an attack upon Christianity entitled *Alethes Logos* (*True Discourse*). Thanks to the great Christian theologian Origen, who published
his *Contra Celsum* in the mid-third century as a reply to the charges of
Celsus, much of the *Alethes Logos* has survived as quotations in Origen.

The present passage from Origen, which quotes Celsus, describes
the ascent of the soul within the Mithraic mysteries. According to
Celsus, the soul passes through seven heavenly gates, each associated
with a metal and a planet. The planets are listed according to the order of
the days in a week (Saturday is Saturn's day; Friday, Venus's day; Thurs-
day, Jupiter's day; Wednesday, Mercury's day; Tuesday, Mars's day;
Monday, the moon's day; Sunday, the sun's day).

The translation is by Henry Chadwick, *Origen: Contra Celsum* (Cambridge: Cambridge Univ. Press, 1980).

After this from a desire to parade his erudition in his attack on us **22**
Celsus also describes some Persian mysteries, where he says: "These
truths are obscurely represented by the teaching of the Persians and by
the mystery of Mithras which is of Persian origin. For in the latter there
is a symbol of the two orbits in heaven, the one being that of the fixed
stars and the other that assigned to the planets, and of the soul's passage
through these. The symbol is this. There is a ladder with seven gates and
at its top an eighth gate. The first of the gates is of lead, the second of tin,
the third of bronze, the fourth of iron, the fifth of an alloy, the sixth of silver, and the seventh of gold. They associate the first with Kronos (Saturn), taking lead to refer to the slowness of the star; the second with Aphrodite (Venus), comparing her with the brightness and softness of tin;
the third with Zeus (Jupiter), as the gate that has a bronze base and
which is firm; the fourth with Hermes (Mercury), for both iron and Hermes are reliable for all works and make money and are hard-working;
the fifth with Ares (Mars), the gate which as a result of the mixture is un-
even and varied in quality; the sixth with the Moon as the silver gate;
and the seventh with the Sun as the golden gate, these metals resembling their colors."

He next examines the reason for this particular arrangement of the
stars which is indicated by means of symbols in the names of the various
kinds of matter. And he connects musical theories with the theology of
the Persians which he describes. He waxes enthusiastic about these and
gives a second explanation which again contains musical ideas. It

seemed to me that to quote Celsus's words here would be absurd, for it would be to do what he himself has done when, for the purpose of criticizing Christians and Jews, he inappropriately compared their teaching not merely with the remarks of Plato, with which he might have rested content, but also, as he says, with the mysteries of the Persian Mithras and their interpretation of them. Leaving on one side the question whether this is a false or true account of what the Persians say who maintain the doctrines of Mithras, why did he describe these rather than one of the other mysteries with its interpretation? The Greeks do not think the mysteries of Mithras have anything exceptional about them compared with those of Eleusis or with those of Hecate which are revealed to people who are initiated in Aegina. If he wanted to describe barbarian mysteries with their interpretation, why did he not prefer those of the Egyptians on which many pride themselves, or those of the Cappadocians who worship Artemis at Comana, or those of the Thracians, or even those of the Romans themselves who initiate the noblest members of the Senate? But if he thought it inappropriate to bring forward one of these, since they are of no value for the purpose of criticizing Jews or Christians, why did it not also seem inappropriate to him to describe the Mithraic mysteries?

PORPHYRY, *ON THE CAVE OF THE NYMPHS (DE ANTRO NYMPHARUM)*, 6–7

The prolific author Porphyry (b. 232 or 233–d. ca. 305 C.E.), a disciple and editor of the Neoplatonist philosopher Plotinus, wrote a large number of works on religion and philosophy, including the present essay *On the Cave of the Nymphs*. In this essay Porphyry offers an interpretation of a portion of Homer's *Odyssey* (13.102–12) that depicts a lovely cave, sacred to the nymphs. In Homer's description the cave contained stores of honey and flowing water, and two gates gave humans and immortals access to the cave. Porphyry writes his commentary on the Homeric passage in the form of allegorical exegesis. Homer's cave of the nymphs becomes a symbol of the cosmos, and the souls descend into the *genesis* ("generation" or "coming into being") of the cosmos, and ascend from it into the immortal realm.

De antro nympharum 6–7 applies Porphyry's allegorical understanding of the cave of the nymphs to the cave within which the Mithraic rites were celebrated. Elsewhere in the essay Porphyry also comments upon the use of honey in the mysteries of Mithras (15–16; compare, perhaps, the nectar and the "sweet things" mentioned in the inscriptions of Santa

Prisca, lines 4 and 11), and the sword of Aries wielded by Mithras (24; see the ram [i.e., Aries] in the inscriptions of Santa Prisca, line 13).

The following translation by Marvin W. Meyer is based upon the Greek text in the Teubner edition (August Nauck, ed., *Porphyrii Philosophi Platonici Opuscula Selecta* [Leipzig: Teubner, 1886]). For a good English translation of the entire essay, with additional bibliography, see Robert Lamberton, *Porphyry: On the Cave of the Nymphs* (Barrytown, N.Y.: Station Hill, 1983).

Thus the Persians, as mystagogues, initiate the *mystes* by teaching him the downward way of the souls and their way back, and calling the place a grotto. First, as Euboulos says, in the mountains near Persia Zoroaster dedicated a natural grotto, flowery and with springs, to the honor of Mithras, the maker and father of all, because [for him] the grotto was an image of the cosmos that Mithras created, and the things arranged symmetrically within were symbols of the cosmic elements and regions. Then, after Zoroaster, the habit of performing the mysteries in caves and grottos, either natural or artificial, prevailed also with others. For as they founded temples, abodes, and altars for the Olympian gods, sacrificial hearths for deities of the earth (*chthonioi*) and heroes, and trenches and pits for deities under the earth (*hypochthonioi*), so also they founded caves and grottos for the cosmos, and similarly for the nymphs, on account of the waters that pour down or come up in caves. And the Naiads, as we shall go through a little later, are nymphs set over the waters. **6**

As we said, not only have they made the cave a symbol of the [generated], perceptible cosmos, but they also have used the cave as a symbol of all the unseen powers, since the caves are dark, and that which is the essence of the powers is invisible. Thus Kronos prepares a cave for himself in the ocean, and there he hides his children. Similarly, Demeter brings up Kore in a cave along with nymphs; and one will find many other such things if one goes over the works of the theologians. **7**

THE MITHRAS LITURGY

The so-called Mithras Liturgy is one of the most interesting and perplexing of texts concerning the worship of Mithras in late antiquity. Occupying lines 475–834 of the Great Magical Papyrus of Paris (see also the Isis Love Spell in Chapter 6), the Mithras Liturgy manifests a syncretistic piety that makes use of astrology and magic in order to provide a liturgical spell for the ecstatic ascent of the soul to god. Although we cannot agree with Albrecht Dieterich that the Mithras Liturgy preserves the highest sacrament of Mithraic initiation, the text does contain several clearly Mithraic themes. Most impressive among the Mithraic themes are the mention of "the great god Helios Mithras" (line 482), the portrayal of fire-breathing Aion (lines 587–616), the description of Helios the Sun (lines 635–37), and the depiction of the highest god (lines 693–703). The appearance of the highest god (a young god wearing the *anaxyrides*, or trousers, which were typical of Middle Eastern attire, and projecting astral power) closely resembles portraits of Mithras himself from Mithraic monuments.

The Mithras Liturgy may be divided into two sections: a liturgical mystery for the ascent of the soul (lines 475–750) and instructions for the use of the liturgy (lines 751–834). The liturgical mystery presents seven stages of ascent:

1) The four elements
2) The lower powers of the air
3) Aion and his powers
4) Helios, the sun
5) The seven Fates
6) The seven Pole-Lords
7) The highest god, portrayed like Mithras

The encounter with the highest god, the Mithras Liturgy promises, will produce divine revelation and will culminate in an experience of immortalization (*apathanatismos*).

The magical components in the text include descriptions of breathing techniques, recipes, magical rites, amulets, and magical words of power (*voces magicae*). The magical words at times are onomatopoetic (such as PPP—popping like thunder), symbolic (such as AEEIOYO, which uses the seven Greek vowels in a series), or glossolalic (speaking in tongues). Some magical words derive from such foreign languages as Egyptian (ARARMACHES, "Harmachis," or PHRE, "Re") and Hebrew (SEMESILAM, "Eternal Sun," or IAO, the ineffable name of God, Yahweh). The letters of the magical words also may be manipulated for the sake of power (for example, IAO OAI AIO, permutations of the ineffable name of God in Hebrew, and PSINOTHER NOPSITHER THERNOPSI, permutations of the phrase "the son of God" in Egyptian).

The Mithras Liturgy is translated and edited by Marvin W. Meyer, in Hans Dieter Betz, ed., *The Greek Magical Papyri in Translation* (Chicago: Univ. of Chicago Press, 1986), and in Marvin W. Meyer, ed. and trans., *The "Mithras Liturgy,"* Society of Biblical Literature Texts and Transla-

tions, no. 10 (Missoula, Mont.: Scholars, 1976). On the Mithras Liturgy
see especially Albrecht Dieterich, *Eine Mithrasliturgie*, 3d ed. (Darmstadt:
Wissenschaftliche Buchgesellschaft, 1966). Several of the quotations in
the spells at the end of the Mithras Liturgy are taken from Homer's *Iliad*.

B̲e gracious to me, O Pronoia and Psyche, as I write these mysteries   475
handed down ⟨not⟩ for gain but for instruction; and for an only child I
request immortality, O initiates of this our power—furthermore, it is
necessary for you, O daughter, to take the juices of herbs and spices,   480
which will ⟨be made known⟩ to you at the end of my holy treatise—
which the great god Helios Mithras ordered to be revealed to me by his
archangel, so that I alone may ascend into heaven as an inquirer and be-   485
hold the universe.

    This is the invocation of the ceremony:
First origin of my origin, AEEIOYO,
first beginning of my beginning, PPP SSS PHR[   ],
spirit of spirit, the first of the spirit in me, MMM,   490
fire given by god to my mixture of the mixtures in me, the first of the fire
    in me, EY EIA EE,
water of water, the first of the water in me, OOO AAA EEE,
earthy substance, the first of the earthy substance in me, YE YOE,   495
my complete body—I, NN whose mother is NN—which was formed by
    a noble arm and an incorruptible right hand in a world without light
    and yet radiant, without soul and yet alive with soul, YEI AYI EYOIE:
now if it be your will, METERTA PHOTH—METHARTHA PHERIE, in   500
    another place—IEREZATH,
give me over to immortal birth and, following that, to my underlying na-
    ture,
so that, after the present need which is pressing me exceedingly, I may
    gaze upon the immortal beginning with the immortal spirit,   505
    ANCHREPHRENESOYPHIRIGCH,
with the immortal water, ERONOYI PARAKOYNETH,
with the most steadfast air, EIOAE PSENABOTH;
that I may be born again (*metagen⟨n⟩etho*) in thought, KRAOCHRAX R
    OIM ENARCHOMAI,
and the sacred spirit may breathe in me, NECHTHEN APOTOY   510
    NECHTHIN ARPI ETH;
so that I may wonder at the sacred fire, KYPHE;
that I may gaze upon the unfathomable, awesome water of the dawn,
    NYO THESO ECHO OYCHIECHOA,

515 and the vivifying and encircling aether may hear me, ARNOMETHPH;
     for today I am about to behold, with immortal eyes—
     I, born mortal from mortal womb, but transformed by tremendous
520   power and an incorruptible right hand!—
     and with immortal spirit, the immortal Aion and master of the fiery dia-
        dems—
     I, sanctified through holy consecrations!—
     while there subsists within me, holy, for a short time, my human soul-
        might,
525 which I will again receive after the present bitter and relentless necessity
        which is pressing down upon me—
     I, NN whose mother is NN, according to the immutable decree of god,
        EYE YIA EEI AO EIAY IYA IEO!
530 Since it is impossible for me, born mortal, to rise with the golden bright-
        nesses of the immortal brilliance, OEY AEO EYA EOE YAE OIAE,
     stand, O perishable nature of mortals,
     and at once ⟨receive⟩ me safe and sound after the inexorable and press-
535   ing need.
     For I am the son PSYCHO[N] DEMOY PROCHO PROA,
     I am MACHARPH[ ]N MOY PROPSYCHON PROE!

     Draw in breath from the rays, drawing up three times as much as you
540 can, and you will see yourself being lifted up and ascending to the
     height, so that you seem to be in midair. You will hear nothing either of
     man or of any other living thing, nor in that hour will you see anything of
     mortal affairs of earth, but rather you will see all immortal things. For in
545 that day and hour you will see the divine order of the skies: the presid-
     ing gods rising into heaven, and others setting. Now the course of the
     visible gods will appear through the disk of god, my father; and in simi-
550 lar fashion the so-called "pipe," the origin of the ministering wind. For
     you will see it hanging from the sun's disk like a pipe. You will see the
     outflow of this object toward the regions westward, boundless as an east
     wind, if it be assigned to the regions of the East—and the other (viz. the
555 west wind), similarly, toward its own regions. And you will see the gods
     staring intently at you and rushing at you.
        So at once put your right finger on your mouth and say:
        Silence! Silence! Silence!
        Symbol of the living, incorruptible god!
560   Guard me, Silence, NECHTHEIR THANMELOY!

     Then make a long hissing sound, next make a popping sound, and say:

PROPROPHEGGE MORIOS PROPHYR PROPHEGGE NEMETHIRE
ARPSENTEN   PITETMI   MEOY   ENARTH   PHYRKECHO
PSYRIDARIO TYRE PHILBA.   565

Then you will see the gods looking graciously upon you and no longer
rushing at you, but rather going about in their own order of affairs.

So when you see that the world above is clear and circling, and that   570
none of the gods or angels is threatening you, expect to hear a great
crash of thunder, so as to shock you. Then say again:

Silence! Silence!—the prayer.
I am a star, wandering about with you,
and shining forth out of the deep, OXY O XERTHEYTH.   575

Immediately after you have said these things the sun's disk will be ex-
panded. And after you have said the second prayer, where there is "Silence! Silence!" and the accompanying words, make a hissing sound
twice and a popping sound twice, and immediately you will see many   580
five-pronged stars coming forth from the disk and filling all the air. Then
say again:

Silence! Silence!

And when the disk is open, you will see the fireless circle, and the fiery
doors shut tight.

At once close your eyes and recite the following prayer. The third   585
prayer:

Give ear to me,
hearken to me, NN whose mother is NN,
O Lord, you who have bound together with your breath the fiery bars
    of the fourfold root,   590
O Fire-Walker, PENTITEROYNI,
Light-Maker—others: Encloser, SEMESILAM,
Fire-Breather, PSYRINPHEY,
Fire-Feeler, IAO,
Light-Breather, OAI,
Fire-Delighter, ELOYRE,
Beautiful Light, AZAI,
Aion, ACHBA,
Light-Master, PEPPER PREPEMPIPI,   595
Fire-Body, PHNOYENIOCH,
Light-Giver,
Fire-Sower, AREI EIKITA,

Fire-Driver, GALLABALBA,
Light-Forcer, AIO,
Fire-Whirler, PYRICHIBOOSEIA,
Light-Mover, SANCHEROB,
600 Thunder-Shaker, IE OE IOEIO,
Glory-Light, BEEGENETE,
Light-Increaser, SOYSINEPHIEN,
Fire-Light-Maintainer, SOYSINEPHI ARENBARAZEI
    MARMARENTEY,
Star-Tamer:
open for me, PROPROPHEGGE EMETHEIRE
    MORIOMOTYREPHILBA,
605 because, on account of the pressing and bitter and inexorable neces-
    sity, I invoke the immortal names, living and honored, which never
    pass into mortal nature and are not declared in articulate speech by
610 human tongue or mortal speech or mortal sound:
EEO OEEO IOO OE EEO EEO OE EO IOO OEEE OEE OOE IE EO
OO OE IEO OE OOE IEO OE IEEO EE IO OE IOE OEO EOE OEO
615 OIE OIE EO OI III EOE OYE EOOEE EO EIA AEA EEA EEEE EEE
EEE IEO EEO OEEEOE EEO EYO OE EIO EO OE OE EE OOO
YIOE.

Say all these things with fire and spirit, until completing the first utter-
620 ance; then, similarly, begin the second, until you complete the seven immortal gods of the world. When you have said these things, you will
hear thundering and shaking in the surrounding realm; and you will likewise feel yourself being agitated. Then say again:

Silence!—the prayer.

625 Then open your eyes, and you will see the doors open and the world of
the gods which is within the doors, so that from the pleasure and joy of
the sight your spirit runs ahead and ascends.
    So stand still and at once draw breath from the divine into yourself,
630 while you look intently. Then when your soul is restored, say:

Come, Lord, ARCHANDARA PHOTAZA PYRIPHOTA ZABYTHIX
ETIMENMERO PHORATHEN ERIE PROTHRI PHORATHI.

When you have said this, the rays will turn toward you; look at the cen-
635 ter of them. For when you have done this, you will see a youthful god,
beautiful in appearance, with fiery hair, and in a white tunic and a scar-

let cloak, and wearing a fiery crown. At once greet him with the fire-greeting:

Hail, O Lord,
Great Power, Great Might, King, Greatest of gods, Helios, the Lord of 640
    heaven and earth, God of gods:
mighty is your breath;
mighty is your strength, O Lord.
If it be your will,
announce me to the supreme god,
the one who has begotten and made you:
that a man—
I, NN whose mother is NN, who was born from the mortal womb of 645
    NN and from the fluid of semen,
and who, since he has been born again from you today, has become
    immortal out of so many myriads in this hour according to the wish
    of god the exceedingly good—
resolves to worship you, 650
and prays with all his human power,
that you may take along with you the horoscope of the day and hour
    today, which has the name THRAPSIARI MORIROK,
that he may appear and give revelation during the good hours, EORO
    RORE ORRI ORIOR ROR ROI OR REORORI EOR EOR EOR EORE! 655

After you have said these things, he will come to the celestial pole, and you will see him walking as if on a road.

Look intently, and make a long bellowing sound, like a horn, releasing all your breath and straining your sides; and kiss the amulets and 660 say, first toward the right:

Protect me, PROSYMERI!

After saying this, you will see the doors thrown open, and seven virgins coming from deep within, dressed in linen garments, and with the faces of asps. They are called the Fates of heaven, and wield golden 665 wands. When you see them, greet them in this manner:

Hail, O seven Fates of heaven, O noble and good virgins, O sacred
    ones and companions of MINIMIRROPHOR, O most holy guard-
    ians of the four pillars!
Hail to you, the first, CHREPSENTHAES! 670
Hail to you, the second, MENESCHEES!
Hail to you, the third, MECHRAN!
Hail to you, the fourth, ARARMACHES!

Hail to you, the fifth, ECHOMMIE!
Hail to you, the sixth, TICHNONDAES!
Hail to you, the seventh, EROY ROMBRIES!

675 There also come forth another seven gods, who have the faces of black bulls, in linen loin-cloths, and in possession of seven golden diadems. They are the so-called Pole-Lords of heaven, whom you must greet in the same manner, each of them with his own name:

Hail, O guardians of the pivot, O sacred and brave youths,
680   who turn at one command the revolving axis of the vault of heaven,
       who send out thunder and lightning and jolts of earthquakes and thunderbolts against the nations of impious people,
       but to me, who am pious and god-fearing, you send health and sound-
685   ness of body, and acuteness of hearing and seeing, and calmness in the present good hours of this day,
       O my Lords and powerfully ruling Gods!
Hail to you, the first, AIERONTHI!
Hail to you, the second, MERCHEIMEROS!
Hail to you, the third, ACHRICHIOYR!
690 Hail to you, the fourth, MESARGILTO!
Hail to you, the fifth, CHICHROALITHO!
Hail to you, the sixth, ERMICHTHATHOPS!
Hail to you, the seventh, EORASICHE!

695 Now when they take their place, here and there, in order, look in the air and you will see lightning-bolts going down, and lights flashing, and the earth shaking, and a god descending, a god immensely great, having a bright appearance, youthful, golden-haired, with a white tunic and a
700 golden crown and trousers, and holding in his right hand a golden shoulder of a young bull: this is the Bear which moves and turns heaven around, moving upward and downward in accordance with the hour. Then you will see lightning-bolts leaping from his eyes and stars from his body.

705 And at once produce a long bellowing sound, straining your belly, that you may excite the five senses: bellow long until the conclusion, and again kiss the amulets, and say:

MOKRIMO PHERIMOPHERERI, life of me, NN:
stay!
710 Dwell in my soul!
Do not abandon me, for one entreats you, ENTHO PHENEN THROPIOTH.

And gaze upon the god while bellowing long; and greet him in this manner:

Hail, O Lord, O Master of the water!
Hail, O Founder of the earth!
Hail, O Ruler of the wind!
O Bright Lightener, PROPROPHEGGE EMETHIRI ARTENTEPI   715
  THETH MIMEO YENARO PHYRCHECHO PSERI DARIO PHRE
  PHRELBA!
Give revelation, O Lord, concerning the matter of NN.
O Lord, while being born again (*palingenomenos*), I am passing away;
while growing and having grown, I am dying;   720
while being born from a life-generating birth, I am passing on, re-
  leased to death—
as you have founded,
as you have decreed,
and have established the mystery.
I am PHEROYRA MIOYRI.

After you have said these things, he will immediately respond with a revelation. Now you will grow weak in soul and will not be in yourself,   725
when he answers you. He speaks the oracle to you in verse, and after speaking he will depart. But you remain silent, since you will be able to comprehend all these matters by yourself; for at a later time you will re-   730
member infallibly the things spoken by the great god, even if the oracle contained myriads of verses.

If you also wish to use a fellow-initiate, so that he alone may hear with you the things spoken, let him remain pure together with you for ⟨seven⟩ days and abstain from meat and the bath. And even if you are   735
alone, and you undertake the things communicated by the god, you speak as though prophesying in ecstasy. And if you also wish to show him, then judge whether he is completely worthy as a man: treat him   740
just as if in his place you were being judged in the matter of immortalization and whisper to him the first prayer, of which the begin-ning is "First origin of my origin, AEEIOYO." And say the successive things as an initiate, over his head, in a soft voice, so that he may   745
not hear, as you are anointing his face with the mystery. This immortalization takes place three times a year. And if anyone, O child, after the teaching, wishes to disobey, then for him it will no longer be   750
in effect.

Instruction for the ritual:
Take a sun-scarab which has twelve rays, and make it fall into a deep,

turquoise cup, at the time when the moon is invisible; put in together
755 with it the seed of the lotometra, and honey; and, after grinding it, prepare a cake. And at once you will see it (viz. the scarab) moving forward
and eating; and when it has consumed it, it immediately dies. Pick it up
and throw it into a glass vessel of excellent rose oil, as much as you wish;
760 and spreading sacred sand in a pure manner, set the vessel on it, and say
the formula over the vessel for seven days, while the sun is in mid-
heaven:

> I have consecrated you,
> that your essence may be useful to me, to NN alone, IE IA E EE OY
> EIA,
765 that you may prove useful to me alone.
> For I am PHOR PHORA PHOS PHOTIZAAS—others: PHOR PHOR
> OPHOTHEI XAAS.

On the seventh day pick up the scarab and bury it with myrrh and wine
from Mendes and fine linen, and put it away in a flourishing bean-field.
770 Then, after you have entertained and feasted together, put away, in a
pure manner, the ointment for the immortalization.
   If you want to show this to someone else, take the juice of the herb
called "kentritis," and smear it, along with rose oil, over the eyes of the
775 one you wish; and he will see so clearly that he will amaze you. I have
not found a greater spell than this in the world. Ask the god for what
you want, and he will give to you.
   Now presentation before the great god is like this: obtaining the
780 above-mentioned herb kentritis, at the conjunction (viz. of the sun and
the moon) occurring in the Lion, take the juice and, after mixing it with
honey and myrrh, write on a leaf of the persea tree the eight-letter formula, as is mentioned below. And keeping yourself pure for three days
785 before, set out early in the morning toward the East, lick off the leaf
while you show it to the Sun, and then he (viz. the sun god) will listen to
you attentively. Begin to consecrate this at the divine new moon, in the
Lion. Now this is the formula:

> I EE OO IAI.

790 Lick this up, so that you may be protected; and rolling up the leaf, throw
it into the rose oil. Many times have I used the spell, and have wondered
greatly.
> But the god said to me:
> Use the ointment no longer,
> but, after casting it into the river,

⟨you must⟩ consult while wearing the great mystery of the scarab revi-   **795**
    talized through the twenty-five living birds,
and consult once a month, at full moon, instead of three times a year.

The kentritis plant grows from the month of Payni, in the regions of
the black earth, and is similar to the erect verbena. This is how to recog-   **800**
nize it: an ibis-wing is dipped at its black tip and smeared with the juice,
and the feathers fall off when touched. After the Lord pointed this out, it   **805**
was found in Menelaitis in Phalagry, at the river banks, near the Besas
plant. It is of a single stem, and reddish down to the root; and the leaves
are rather crinkled and have fruit like the tip of wild asparagus. It is simi-   **810**
lar to the so-called talapes, like the wild beet.

Now the amulets require this procedure: copy the right one onto the
skin of a black sheep, with myrrh-ink, and after tying it with sinews of   **815**
the same animal, put it on; and copy the left one onto the skin of a white
sheep, and use the same procedure. The left one is very full of
"PROSTHYMERI," and has this text: **820**

"So speaking, he drove through the trench the single-hoofed horses."
"And men gasping among grievous slaughters."
"And they washed off their profuse sweat in the sea."
"You will dare to lift up your mighty spear against Zeus."

Zeus went up the mountain with a golden bullock and a silver dag-   **825**
ger. Upon all he bestowed a share, only to Amara did he not give, but he
said:

"Let go of what you have,
and then you will receive, PSINOTHER NOPSITHER THERNOPSI,"
    and so on, as you like.
"So Ares suffered, when Otos and mighty Epialtes . . . him."   **830**

Spell for restraining anger:
"You will dare to lift up your mighty spear against Zeus."

For friends:
"Let . . . seize . . . , lest we become a source of joy for our enemies."

8
The Mysteries
within Judaism
and Christianity

8
The Mysteries within Judaism and Christianity

During the time of the Roman Empire, several Jewish religious traditions, and especially early Christianity, showed remarkable similarities to the mystery religions. Like the Greco-Roman mysteries, Judaism and Christianity were in large part religions of choice, and Jewish and Christian initiates, like many of their counterparts in the mysteries, underwent purifications, fasts, baptism and lustrations (that is, proselyte baptism and Christian baptism), and other ceremonial rites (such as circumcision and anointing the forehead with oil) in order to be admitted into the community. From the time of Paul, Christian baptism commonly was understood as a death experience and the emergence from the water was taken as the beginning of new life. Once admitted into the church, Christian initiates entered a brotherhood and sisterhood in which, ideally speaking, "there is neither Jew nor Greek, there is neither slave nor free person, there is not male and female" (Galatians 3:28). Many ceremonies celebrated in Jewish and Christian communities were meant specifically for the initiated, and one such ceremony was the holy meal, namely, the Jewish Seder and the Christian Eucharist. The Seder is a sacred feast reenacting the Exodus from Egypt, and the Eucharist is a sacramental meal commemorating the death of Christ. By eating of the bread and drinking the wine that typified the body and blood of the crucified Christ, believers participated in Christ's passion. In some Jewish and Christian communities, mysticism was as prominent a feature of religious life as in the mystery religions: Jewish mystics sought a vision of the divine Throne-Chariot (the Merkabah), Christian mystics sought union with Christ. Thus, Christians realized their salvation through an encounter with their dying and rising Savior; they lived "in Christ," as Paul puts it, or were "born again" (or "from above"), as John declares.

This quick sketch of Judaism and early Christianity, deliberately drawn in order to stress points of similarity with the mystery religions, clarifies why students of religion in the ancient world and in more recent times have considered some expressions of Judaism and numerous manifestations of Christianity to be quite in harmony with the mystery religions. As the readings in this chapter illustrate, a Greco-Roman author (Plutarch) could examine Judaism and conclude that the Hebrew god Yahweh was to be identified with the Greek god Dionysos; an ancient Jewish philosopher (Philo) could describe a mystical Jewish group with terms from the mysteries; and early Christian writers (the author of the *Gospel of Philip*, and Clement of Alexandria) could employ mystery language to proclaim the gospel of Christ.

Scholars have proposed several theories to account for the obvious similarities between Christianity and the mystery religions. Theories of dependence frequently have been proposed. Early Christian authors noted the similarities between Christianity and Mithraism and charged that the mysteries were godless, demonically inspired imitations of true Christianity (Justin Martyr, *First Apology*, 66.4; idem, *Dialogue with Trypho*, 70.1; Tertullian, *Prescription Against Heretics*, 40). Some modern scholars, conversely, have suggested that early Christianity (even before the fourth century C.E., when Christianity began to adopt the practices of its non-Christian neighbors with vigor) borrowed substantially from the mystery religions all around. According to these suggestions, Paul's proclamation of the cross and resurrection and John's statement of rebirth are comprehensible as Christian adaptations of mystery cult theology.

Today, however, most scholars are considerably more cautious about the parallels between early Christianity and the mysteries and hesitate before jumping to conclusions about dependence. To be sure, one religious tradition may appropriate themes from another, and so it must have been with early Christianity and the mystery religions. Yet Judaism, Christianity, and the mysteries were equally parts of the religious milieu of the Greco-Roman world, and this explains many of their similarities. As Greco-Roman religions they sometimes faced similar challenges, proposed similar ways of salvation, and shared similar visions of the way to light and life.

The bibliography on the relationship between Christianity and the mystery religions is extensive. The following are among the more important works: Gustav Anrich, *Das antike Mysterienwesen in seinem Einfluss auf das Christentum* (Göttingen: Vandenhoek und Ruprecht, 1894); Wilhelm Bousset, *Kyrios Christos* (1913; reprint, Nashville: Abingdon, 1970); Raymond E. Brown, *The Semitic Background of the Term "Mystery" in the New Testament*, Facet Books, Biblical Series, no. 21 (Philadelphia: Fortress, 1968); Edwin Hatch, *The Influence of Greek Ideas on Christianity* (1888;

reprint, New York: Harper & Brothers, 1957); Gary Lease, "Mithraism and Christianity: Borrowings and Transformations," in *Aufstieg und Niedergang der römischen Welt*, ed. Hildegard Temporini and Wolfgang Haase (Berlin: Walter de Gruyter, 1980), Band II. 23.2, 1306–32; Bruce M. Metzger, "Methodology in the Study of the Mystery Religions and Early Christianity," in *Historical and Literary Studies: Pagan, Jewish, and Christian*, New Testament Tools and Studies, vol. 8 (Leiden: Brill, 1968), 1–24; Arthur Darby Nock, *Early Gentile Christianity and Its Hellenistic Background* (1927; reprint, New York: Harper, 1964); idem, "Hellenistic Mysteries and Christian Sacraments," in *Essays on Religion and the Ancient World*, ed. Zeph Stewart, vol. 2 (Cambridge: Harvard Univ. Press, 1972), 791–820; Hugo Rahner, "The Christian Mystery and the Pagan Mysteries," in *The Mysteries*, ed. Joseph Campbell, Bollingen Series, no. 30, Papers from the Eranos Yearbooks (Princeton: Princeton Univ. Press, 1955), 337–401; Jonathan Z. Smith, *Drudgery Divine: On the Comparison of Early Christianities and the Religions of Late Antiquity*, Jordan Lectures in Comparative Religion, 14 (Chicago: University of Chicago Press, 1990).

For additional Jewish and Christian texts that employ terminology similar to that of the mysteries, see the Dead Sea Scrolls (e.g., the Community Rule [or Manual of Discipline, lQS] and the Angelic Liturgy [representing Jewish Merkabah mysticism]); the Book of Joseph and Asenath (esp. chapters 8 and 16); the Gospel of John 2–3 (Jesus performs a Dionysian "sign" by changing water to wine, and discusses what it means when one is born anew, or born from above, *gennethe anothen*); 1 Corinthians 15 (Paul presents the *mysterion* of resurrection by comparing the life-cycles of grain and of people, 15:36; cp. also John 12:24).

PLUTARCH OF CHAERONEA, *TABLE-TALK (QUAESTIONES CONVIVALES)*, Book 4, Question 6.1–2 (671C–672C)

In this excerpt from a dialogue, Plutarch of Chaeronea presents his speakers as they are enjoying a symposium and discussing the identity of the Jewish god. One of the speakers, Moeragenes, proposes that there is reason to equate the Jewish god (often addressed in Hebrew as Adonai, "my Lord"—compare to Adonis) with the Greek god Dionysos. Moeragenes gives a Greek interpretation of such Hebrew festivals as the Feast (not "Fast") of Tabernacles (or Booths, *Sukkoth* in Hebrew) and cites various passages in the Hebrew Scriptures, but the conclusions sometimes are based upon a misunderstanding of Judaism. The suggested etymologies of *Levites* and *Sabbath*, for instance, are hardly to be taken seriously. Moeragenes asserts that the exact nature of Jewish worship in the temple remains unknown, but in his opinion the observance may very well be Bacchic in character.

On the cry Saboi ("followers of Sabos," that is, Sabazios) in a Bacchic context, compare Plutarch's version with that of Demosthenes: initiates of Sabazios, often identified with Dionysos, parade through the streets, with snakes, and shout, "*Euoi Saboi*," and "*Hyes Attes! Attes Hyes!*" (Demosthenes, *On the Crown* [*De Corona*], 260).

The following passage is translated by Herbert B. Hoffleit, *Plutarch's Moralia: VIII* (Loeb Classical Library, 1969).

Who the god of the Jews is
Speakers: Symmachus, Moeragenes, and others

1   Symmachus, surprised at this last statement, asked, "Lamprias, are you enrolling your national god in the calendar of the Hebrews and insinuating into their secret rites 'him of the orgiastic cry (Euios), exciter of women, Dionysos, glorified with mad honors'? Is there actually some tradition that demonstrates identity between him and Adonis?" Moeragenes interposed, "Never mind him. I as an Athenian can answer you and say that the god is no other. Most of the relevant proofs can lawfully be pronounced or divulged only to those of us who have been initiated into the Perfect Mysteries celebrated every other year, but what I am going to speak of is not forbidden in conversation with friends, especially over after-dinner wine, while we are enjoying the god's own bounty. I am ready to speak if these gentlemen urge me."

2   At this, all did urge him and beg him to go on. "First," he said, "the time and character of the greatest, most sacred holiday of the Jews clearly befit Dionysos. When they celebrate their so-called Fast, at the height of the vintage, they set out tables of all sorts of fruit under tents and huts plaited for the most part of vines and ivy. They call the first of the two days Tabernacles. A few days later they celebrate another festival, this time identified with Bacchos not through obscure hints but plainly called by his name, a festival that is a sort of 'Procession of Branches' or 'Thyrsus Procession,' in which they enter the temple each carrying a thyrsus. What they do after entering we do not know, but it is probable that the rite is a Bacchic revelry, for in fact they use little trumpets to invoke their god as do the Argives at their Dionysia. Others of them advance playing harps; these players are called in their language Levites, either from 'Lysios' or, better, from 'Euios.'

"I believe that even the feast of the Sabbath is not completely unrelated to Dionysos. Many even now call the Bacchantes 'Saboi' and utter that cry when celebrating the god. Testimony to this can be found in Demosthenes and Menander. You would not be far off the track if you attributed the use of this name Saboi to the strange excitement (*sobesis*) that possesses the celebrants. The Jews themselves testify to a connection with Dionysos when they keep the Sabbath by inviting each other to drink and enjoy wine; when more important business interferes with this custom, they regularly take at least a sip of neat wine. Now thus far one might call the argument only probable; but the opposition is quite demolished, in the first place by the High Priest, who leads the procession at their festival wearing a miter and clad in a gold-embroidered fawnskin, a robe reaching to the ankles, and buskins, with many bells attached to his clothes and ringing below him as he walks. All this corresponds to our custom. In the second place, they also have noise as an element in their nocturnal festivals, and call the nurses of the god 'bronze rattlers.' The carved thyrsus in the relief on the pediment of the Temple and the drums (provide other parallels). All this surely befits (they might say) no divinity but Dionysos.

"Further, the Jews use no honey in their religious services because they believe that honey spoils the wine with which it is mixed; and they used honey as libation and in place of wine before the vine was discovered. Even up to the present time those of the barbarians who do not make wine drink mead, counteracting the sweetness somewhat by the use of winelike bitter roots. The Greeks, on the other hand, offer the same libations as 'sober libations' and *melisponda* on the principle that there is a particular opposition between honey and wine. To show that what I have said is the practice of the Jews we may find no slight confirmation in the fact that among many penalties employed among them the one most disliked is the exclusion of a convicted offender from the use of wine for such a period as the sentencing judge may prescribe. Those thus punished . . .

PHILO OF ALEXANDRIA, *ON THE CONTEMPLATIVE LIFE (DE VITA CONTEMPLATIVA)*, 11 (83–90)

Philo Judaeus, or Philo of Alexandria (b. ca. 30 B.C.E.–d. 45 C.E.), was a leader of the large Jewish community in Alexandria, Egypt, and a Hellenistic Jewish philosopher and theologian. His writings, which are numerous, reflect upon the relationship between Greek philosophical thought and Judaism. *On the Contemplative Life* describes the virtues of the Therapeutae who, in contrast to the Essenes, pursue the life of contemplation. (For Philo, the Essenes represent the life of activity.) The Therapeutae (known only from Philo) were Jewish mystics and ascetics who lived especially in the area around Alexandria, near Lake Mareotis. That they were Jewish is not to be doubted, in spite of the efforts of Eusebius of Caesarea to present them as Christians (*History of the Church*, 2.17, citing Philo). Philo notes that the Therapeutae above all desire to see, to have a vision of the true Being; so intense is their passion that Philo compares them to Bacchoi/Bacchai or Korybantes (12). For this reason the Therapeutae ordinarily live solitary lives of simplicity and rigorous piety, but at the time of a festival like the Feast of Pentecost (Shavuoth, "Weeks") they put on white robes and gather together as a community for worship and a common meal. Afterwards they celebrate a sacred vigil by forming two choirs, a men's chorus and a women's chorus, and sing hymns and dance throughout the evening. Then, "having drunk as in the Bacchic rites of the strong wine of God's love" (85), they become a single choir and commemorate the Exodus event. Just as a choir of Israelites, with Moses and Miriam leading them, praised God at the time of the Exodus (Exod. 15:1–21), so also the choir of Therapeutae sings all night long, until at sunrise they face the east and greet the rising sun.

Thus the Therapeutae participated in ceremonies resembling some of those in the mystery religions. Philo also portrays them with terms derived from the mysteries, especially the Bacchic mysteries.

This selection from *De vita contemplativa* is translated by F. H. Colson, *Philo: IX* (Loeb Classical Library, 1941).

83 After the supper they hold the sacred vigil which is conducted in the following way. They rise up all together and standing in the middle of the refectory form themselves first into two choirs, one of men and one of women, the leader and precentor chosen for each being the most

84 honored amongst them and also the most musical. Then they sing hymns to God composed of many measures and set to many melodies, sometimes chanting together, sometimes taking up the harmony antiphonally, hands and feet keeping time in accompaniment, and rapt with enthusiasm reproduce sometimes the lyrics of the procession, sometimes of the halt and of the wheeling and counter-wheeling of a

85 choric dance. Then when each choir has separately done its own part in the feast, having drunk as in the Bacchic rites of the strong wine of God's love they mix and both together become a single choir, a copy of the choir set up of old beside the Red Sea in honor of the wonders

86 there wrought. For at the command of God the sea became a source of salvation to one party and of perdition to the other. As it broke in twain and withdrew under the violence of the forces which swept it

back there rose on either side, opposite to each other, the semblance of solid walls, while the space thus opened between them broadened into a highway smooth and dry throughout on which the people marched under guidance right on until they reached the higher ground on the opposite mainland. But when the sea came rushing in with the returning tide, and from either side passed over the ground where the dry land had appeared, the pursuing enemy were submerged and perished. This wonderful sight and experience, an act transcending word **87** and thought and hope, so filled with ecstasy both men and women that forming a single choir they sang hymns of thanksgiving to God their Savior, the men led by the prophet Moses and the women by the prophetess Miriam.

It is on this model above all that the choir of the Therapeutae of either **88** sex, note in response to note and voice to voice, the treble of the women blending with the bass of the men, create a harmonious concent, music in the truest sense. Lovely are the thoughts, lovely the words, and worthy of reverence the choristers, and the end and aim of thoughts, words, and choristers alike is piety. Thus they continue till dawn, drunk with **89** this drunkenness in which there is no shame, then not with heavy heads or drowsy eyes but more alert and wakeful than when they came to the banquet, they stand with their faces and whole body turned to the east and when they see the sun rising they stretch their hands up to heaven and pray for bright days and knowledge of the truth and the power of keen-sighted thinking. And after the prayers they depart each to his private sanctuary once more to ply the trade and till the field of their wonted philosophy.

So much then for the Therapeutae, who have taken to their hearts the **90** contemplation of nature and what it has to teach, and have lived in the soul alone, citizens of Heaven and the world, presented to the Father and Maker of all by their faithful sponsor Virtue, who has procured for them God's friendship and added a gift going hand in hand with it, true excellence of life, a boon better than all good fortune and rising to the very summit of felicity.

CLEMENT OF ALEXANDRIA, "TO THEODORE"

Professor Morton Smith reports that in 1958, while he was visiting the Greek Orthodox Monastery of Mar Saba in Palestine, he discovered part of a letter of Clement of Alexandria (b. ca. 150–d. ca. 215) to a certain Theodore. Clement of Alexandria was a Christian convert, and an Alexandrian theologian of note whose writings include the *Miscellanies* (or *Stromateis*, mentioned at the opening of the present text) and the *Exhortation to the Greeks* (part of which is given in this chapter). The letter, which has generated much discussion and controversy, denounces the Carpocratians (a Gnostic sect), and in so doing mentions a hitherto unknown edition of the Gospel according to Mark, namely the Secret Gospel of Mark. Clement calls the Secret Gospel "a more spiritual Gospel," and utilizes terms derived from the mysteries (such as "the hierophantic teaching of the Lord," "mystagogue," "the innermost sanctuary" [*adyton*], "those who are being initiated into the great mysteries" [*ta megala mysteria*]).

Recent studies of the Secret Gospel of Mark suggest that this edition, known only from the letter of Clement, in fact may antedate the edition received into the New Testament canon. The two passages unique to the Secret Gospel are to be inserted immediately after Mark 10:34, and at Mark 10:46. See John Dominic Crossan, *Four Other Gospels: Shadows on the Contours of Canon* (Minneapolis: Seabury, Winston Press, 1985), 89–121; Charles W. Hedrick with Nikolaos Olympiou, "Secret Mark: New Photographs, New Witnesses," *The Fourth R* 13 (2000): 3–16; Helmut Koester, "History and Development of Mark's Gospel (From Mark to *Secret Mark* and 'Canonical' Mark)," in *Colloquy on New Testament Studies: A Time for Reappraisal and Fresh Approaches*, ed. Bruce Corley (Macon, Ga.: Mercer University Press, 1983), 35–57; Marvin W. Meyer, *Secret Gospels: Essays on Thomas and the Secret Gospel of Mark* (Harrisburg, Pa.: Trinity Press International, 2003), including the chapter "The Naked Youths in the Villa of the Mysteries, Canonical Mark, and Secret Mark"; and Hans-Martin Schenke, "The Mystery of the Gospel of Mark," *The Second Century* 4 (1984): 65–82.

The translation of this excerpt is by Morton Smith, *Clement of Alexandria and a Secret Gospel of Mark* (Cambridge: Harvard Univ. Press, 1973). See also Smith, *The Secret Gospel: The Discovery and Interpretation of the Secret Gospel According to Mark* (New York: Harper & Row, 1973). Smith recently has given an assessment of the scholarship on the Secret Gospel in "Clement of Alexandria and Secret Mark: The Score at the End of the First Decade," *Harvard Theological Review* 75 (1982): 449–61.

1.1   From the letters of the most holy Clement, the author of the *Stromateis*. To Theodore.

You did well in silencing the unspeakable teachings of the Carpocratians. For these are the "wandering stars" referred to in the prophecy, who wander from the narrow road of the commandments

into a boundless abyss of the carnal and bodily sins. For, priding them-   5
selves in knowledge, as they say, "of the deep things of Satan," they do
not know that they are casting themselves away into "the nether world
of the darkness" of falsity, and, boasting that they are free, they have become slaves of servile desires. Such men are to be opposed in all ways
and altogether. For, even if they should say something true, one who
loves the truth should not, even so, agree with them. For not all true
things are the truth, nor should that truth which merely seems true ac-   10
cording to human opinions be preferred to the true truth, that according
to the faith.

Now of the things they keep saying about the divinely inspired Gospel according to Mark, some are altogether falsifications, and others,
even if they do contain some true elements, nevertheless are not reported truly. For the true things, being mixed with inventions, are falsi-
fied, so that, as the saying goes, even the salt loses its savor.   15

As for Mark, then, during Peter's stay in Rome he wrote an account
of the Lord's doings, not, however, declaring all of them, nor yet hinting
at the secret ones, but selecting what he thought most useful for increasing the faith of those who were being instructed. But when Peter died a
martyr, Mark came over to Alexandria, bringing both his own notes and
those of Peter, from which he transferred to his former book the things   20
suitable to whatever makes for progress toward knowledge. Thus he
composed a more spiritual Gospel for the use of those who were being
perfected. Nevertheless, he yet did not divulge the things not to be uttered, nor did he write down the hierophantic teaching of the Lord, but
to the stories already written he added yet others and, moreover,
brought in certain sayings of which he knew the interpretation would, as 25
a mystagogue, lead the hearers into the innermost sanctuary of that
truth hidden by seven veils. Thus, in sum, he prepared matters, neither
grudgingly nor incautiously, in my opinion, and, dying, he left his com-
position to the church in Alexandria, where it even yet is most carefully 2.1
guarded, being read only to those who are being initiated into the great
mysteries.

But since the foul demons are always devising destruction for the
race of men, Carpocrates, instructed by them and using deceitful arts, so   5
enslaved a certain presbyter of the church in Alexandria that he got from
him a copy of the secret Gospel, which he both interpreted according to
his blasphemous and carnal doctrine and, moreover, polluted, mixing
with the spotless and holy words utterly shameless lies. From this mixture is drawn off the teaching of the Carpocratians.   10

To them, therefore, as I said above, one must never give way; nor, when they put forward their falsifications, should one concede that the Gospel is by Mark, but should even deny it on oath. For, "Not all true things are to be said to all men." For this reason the Wisdom of God,
15 through Solomon, advises, "Answer the fool from his folly," teaching that the light of the truth should be hidden from those who are mentally blind. Again it says, "From him who has not shall be taken away," and, "Let the fool walk in darkness." But we are "children of light," having been illuminated by "the dayspring" of the spirit of the Lord "from on high," and "Where the Spirit of the Lord is," it says, "there is liberty," for "All things are pure to the pure."

To you, therefore, I shall not hesitate to answer the questions you
20 have asked, refuting the falsifications by the very words of the Gospel. For example, after "And they were in the road going up to Jerusalem," and what follows, until "After three days he shall arise," the secret Gospel brings the following material word for word: "And they come into Bethany. And a certain woman whose brother had died was there. And, coming, she prostrated herself before Jesus and says to him, 'Son of
25 David, have mercy on me.' But the disciples rebuked her. And Jesus, being angered, went off with her into the garden where the tomb was, and
3.1 straightway a great cry was heard from the tomb. And going near Jesus rolled away the stone from the door of the tomb. And straightway, going in where the youth was, he stretched forth his hand and raised him, seiz-
5 ing his hand. But the youth, looking upon him, loved him and began to beseech him that he might be with him. And going out of the tomb they came into the house of the youth, for he was rich. And after six days Jesus told him what to do and in the evening the youth comes to him, wearing a linen cloth over his naked body. And he remained with him
10 that night, for Jesus taught him the mystery of the kingdom of God. And thence, arising, he returned to the other side of the Jordan."

After these words follows the text, "And James and John come to him," and all that section. But "naked man with naked man," and the other things about which you wrote, are not found.

And after the words, "And he comes into Jericho," the secret Gospel
15 adds only, "And the sister of the youth whom Jesus loved and his mother and Salome were there, and Jesus did not receive them." But the many other things about which you wrote both seem to be and are falsifications.

Now the true explanation and that which accords with the true philosophy . . .

GOSPEL OF PHILIP, Pages 67–75, 81–86

The *Gospel of Philip* is the third tractate in Codex II of the Nag Hammadi Library. The Nag Hammadi Library is a collection of thirteen codices (books) containing some fifty-two tractates, all of them written in the Coptic language and many of them proclaiming Christian Gnosticism. The *Gospel of Philip*, dating from the second or third century C.E., is a collection of mystical meditations about Gnostic spirituality.

The *Gospel of Philip* declares that the mature Gnostic, unlike the immature Christian, becomes so intimately joined to Christ that "this person is no longer a Christian but a Christ." To accomplish such a transformation one must gain a proper Gnostic understanding of the symbols and images of the truth and thereby attain to the truth. For that purpose, the *Gospel of Philip* continues, one partakes of the holy sacraments: "The Lord [did] everything in a mystery (*mysterion*), a baptism and a chrism and a eucharist and a redemption and a bridal chamber" (67,27–30). By participating in these sacramental rituals the Gnostic participates in mysteries and realizes heavenly rest.

In the *Gospel of Philip* the highest sacrament is the bridal chamber, the "true mystery" by means of which one transcends the divisions that separate Adam from Eve, man from woman, and the divine from the human. When one has experienced this, one becomes "a son of the bridal chamber" and may behold what is secret and hidden "in a perfect day and a holy light" (86,17–18).

The following excerpt is translated by Wesley W. Isenberg, "Gospel of Philip," in *The Nag Hammadi Library in English*, eds. James M. Robinson and Marvin W. Meyer (Leiden: Brill; San Francisco: Harper & Row, 1977). For further discussion see Jorunn Jacobson Buckley, "A Cult-Mystery in *The Gospel of Philip*," *Journal of Biblical Literature* 99 (1980): 569–81; Robert M. Grant, "The Mystery of Marriage in the Gospel of Philip," *Vigiliae Christianae* 11 (1961): 129–40.

T̲ruth did not come into the world naked, but it came in types and im- **67,10** ages. One will not receive truth in any other way. There is a rebirth and an image of rebirth. It is certainly necessary that they should be born again through the image. What is the resurrection? The image must rise **15** again through the image. The ⟨bridegroom⟩ and the image must enter through the image into the truth: this is the restoration. It is appropriate that those who do have it not only acquire the name of the Father and **20** the Son and the Holy Spirit, but that they have acquired it on their own.

If one does not acquire the name for himself, the name ("Christian") will also be taken from him. But one receives them in the aromatic unction of 25 the power of the cross. This power the apostles called "the right and the left." For this person is no longer a Christian but a Christ.

The Lord [did] everything in a mystery, a baptism and a chrism and a 30 eucharist and a redemption and a bridal chamber.

[The Lord] said, "I came to make [the things below] like the things [above, and the things] outside like those [inside. I came to unite] them 35 in that place." [He revealed himself in] this place through [types and images]. Those who say, "[There is a heavenly man and] there is one above 68,1 [him," are wrong. For] he who is revealed [in heaven is] that [heavenly man], the one who is called "the one who is below"; and he to whom the hidden belongs is that one who is above him. For it is good that they 5 should say, "The inner and the outer, with what is outside the outer." Because of this the Lord called destruction "the outer darkness": there is not another outside of it. He said, "My Father who is in secret." He said, 10 "Go into your chamber and shut the door behind you, and pray to your Father who is in secret," the one who is within them all. But that which 15 is within them all is the fullness. Beyond it there is nothing else within it. This is that of which they say, "That which is above them."

Before Christ some came from a place they were no longer able to en- 20 ter, and they went where they were no longer able to come out. Then Christ came. Those who went in he brought out, and those who went out he brought in.

When Eve was still in Adam death did not exist. When she was sepa- 25 rated from him death came into being. If he again becomes complete and attains his former self, death will be no more.

"My God, my God, why, O Lord, have you forsaken me?" It was on the cross that he said these words, for it was there that he was divided. 30 [Everyone] who has been begotten through him who [destroys did not emanate] from God.

The [Lord rose] from the dead. [He became as he used] to be, but now [his body was] perfect. [He did indeed possess] flesh, but this 35 [flesh] is true flesh. [Our flesh] is not true, but [we possess] only an image of the true.

69,1   A bridal chamber is not for the animals, nor is it for the slaves, nor for the defiled women; but it is for the free men and virgins.

5   Through the Holy Spirit we are indeed begotten again, but we are begotten through Christ in the two. We are anointed through the Spirit. When we were begotten we were united. None shall be able to see 10 himself either in water or in a mirror without light. Nor again will you

be able to see in light without water or mirror. For this reason it is fitting
to baptize in the two, in the light and the water. Now the light is the
chrism.

There were three buildings specifically for sacrifice in Jerusalem. The   15
one facing west was called "the Holy." Another facing south was called
"the Holy of the Holy." The third facing east was called "the Holy of the   20
Holies," the place where only the high priest enters. Baptism is "the
Holy" building. Redemption is "the Holy of the Holy." "The Holy of the
Holies" is the bridal chamber. Baptism includes the resurrection [and   25
the] redemption; the redemption (take place) in the bridal chamber. But
the bridal chamber is in that which is superior to [it and the others, be-
cause] you will not find [anything like] it. [Those who are familiar with
it] are those who pray in "the Holy" in Jerusalem. [There are some in] Je-   30
rusalem who pray [only in] Jerusalem, awaiting [the kingdom of
heaven]. These are called "the Holy of the Holies," [because before the]   35
veil was rent [we had no] other bridal chamber except the image [of the
bridal chamber which is] above. Because of this its veil was rent from top   70,1
to bottom. For it was fitting for some from below to go upward.

The powers do not see those who are clothed in the perfect light, and   5
consequently are not able to detain them. One will clothe himself in this
light sacramentally in the union.

If the woman had not separated from the man, she would not die   10
with the man. His separation became the beginning of death. Because of
this Christ came to repair the separation which was from the beginning
and again unite the two, and to give life to those who died as a result of   15
the separation and unite them. But the woman is united to her husband
in the bridal chamber. Indeed those who have united in the bridal chamber will no longer be separated. Thus Eve separated from Adam because   20
she was never united with him in the bridal chamber.

The soul of Adam came into being by means of a breath, which is a
synonym for [spirit]. The spirit given him is his mother. His soul was re-   25
placed by a [spirit]. When he was united (to the spirit), [he spoke] words
incomprehensible to the powers. They envied him [because they were
separated from the] spiritual union. [   ] hidden [   ]. This [separa-   30
tion] afforded them the opportunity [to fashion] for themselves [the sym-
bolic] bridal chamber so that [men would be defiled].

Jesus revealed [himself at the] Jordan: it was the [fullness of the king-   35
dom] of heaven. He who [was begotten] before everything was begotten   71,1
anew. He [who was] once [anointed] was anointed anew. He who was
redeemed in turn redeemed (others).

Is it permitted to utter a mystery? The Father of everything united

5   with the virgin who came down, and a fire shone for him on that day.
    He appeared in the great bridal chamber. Therefore, his body came into
10 being on that very day. It left the bridal chamber as one who came into
    being from the bridegroom and the bride. So Jesus established every-
15 thing in it through these. It is fitting for each of the disciples to enter into
    his rest.

    Adam came into being from two virgins, from the Spirit and from the
20 virgin earth. Christ, therefore, was born from a virgin to rectify the fall
    which occurred in the beginning.

    There are two trees growing in Paradise. The one bears [animals], the
25 other bears men. Adam [ate] from the tree which bore animals. He be-
    came an animal and he brought forth animals. For this reason the chil-
    dren of Adam worship [animals]. The tree [whose] fruit [Adam ate] is
30 [the tree of knowledge. That] is why [sins] increased. [If he] ate the [fruit
    of the other tree, that is to say, the] fruit of the [tree of life, the one which]
35 bears men, [then the gods would] worship man. [For in the begin-
72,1 ning] God created man. [But now men] create God. That is the way it is
    in the world—men make gods and worship their creation. It would be fit-
    ting for the gods to worship men!

5   Surely what a man accomplishes depends on his abilities. We even re-
    fer to one's accomplishments as "abilities." Among his accomplishments
10 are his children. They originate in a moment of ease. Thus his abilities de-
    termine what he may accomplish, but this ease is clearly evident in the
    children. You will find that this applies directly to the image. Here is the
15 man made after the image accomplishing things with his physical
    strength, but producing his children with ease.

    In this world the slaves serve the free. In the kingdom of heaven the
20 free will minister to the slaves: the children of the bridal chamber will
    minister to the children of the marriage. The children of the bridal cham-
    ber have [just one] name. Together they [share] rest. They need take no
25 (other) form [because they have] contemplation, [comprehending by in-
    sight]. They are numerous [because they do not put their treasure] in the
    things [below, which are despised, but] in the glories which [are above,
    though they did] not (yet) [know] them.

30   Those [who will be baptized go] down into the water. [But Christ, by
    coming] out (of the water), will consecrate it, [so that] they who have [re-
    ceived baptism] in his name [may be perfect]. For he said, "[Thus] we
73,1 should fulfill all righteousness."

    Those who say they will die first and then rise are in error. If they do
    not receive the resurrection while they live, when they die they will re-

ceive nothing. So also when speaking about baptism they say, "Baptism   5
is a great thing," because if people receive it they will live.

Philip the apostle said, "Joseph the carpenter planted a garden be-   10
cause he needed wood for his trade. It was he who made the cross from
the trees which he planted. His own offspring hung on that which he
planted. His offspring was Jesus and the planting was the cross." But the   15
tree of life is in the middle of the garden. However, it is from the olive
tree that we get the chrism, and from the chrism, the resurrection.

This world is a corpse-eater. All the things eaten in it themselves die   20
also. Truth is a life-eater. Therefore no one nourished by [truth] will die.
It was from that place that Jesus came and brought food. To those who   25
so desired he gave [life, that] they might not die.

God [planted] a garden. Man [was put into the] garden. There were
[many trees there for him], and man [lived] in [this place] with the [bless-   30
ing and in the image] of God. The things which are in [it I will eat as] I
wish. This garden [is the place where] they will say to me, "[O man, eat]   35
this or do not eat [that, just as you] wish." This is the place where I will   74,1
eat all things, since the tree of knowledge is there. That one killed Adam,
but here the tree of knowledge made men alive. The law was the tree. It   5
has power to give the knowledge of good and evil. It neither removed
him from evil, nor did it set him in the good, but it created death for
those who ate of it. For when he said, "Eat this, do not eat that," it be-   10
came the beginning of death.

The chrism is superior to baptism, for it is from the word "chrism"
that we have been called "Christians," certainly not because of the word   15
"baptism." And it is because of the chrism that "the Christ" has his
name. For the Father anointed the Son, and the Son anointed the apostles, and the apostles anointed us. He who has been anointed possesses
everything. He possesses the resurrection, the light, the cross, the Holy   20
Spirit. The Father gave him this in the bridal chamber; he merely accepted (the gift). The Father was in the Son and the Son in the Father.
This is [the] kingdom of heaven.

The Lord said it well: "Some have entered the kingdom of heaven   25
laughing and they have come out." [They do not remain there—the] one
because he is [not] a Christian, [the other because he regrets (his action)]
afterward. And as soon as [Christ went down into] the water he came
[out laughing at] everything (of this world), [not] because [he considers   30
it] a trifle, but [because he is full of] contempt for it. He who [wants to en-
ter] the kingdom of [heaven will attain it]. If he despises [everything (of   35
this world)] and scorns it as a trifle, [he will come] out laughing. So it

75,1 is also with the bread and the cup and the oil, even though there is another one superior to these.

5 The world came about through a mistake. For he who created it
wanted to create it imperishable and immortal. He fell short of attaining
his desire. For the world never was imperishable, nor, for that matter,
10 was he who made the world. For things are not imperishable, but sons
are. Nothing will be able to receive imperishability if it does not first become a son. But he who has not the ability to receive, how much more
will he be unable to give?

15 The cup of prayer contains wine and water, since it is appointed as
the type of the blood for which thanks is given. And it is full of the Holy
20 Spirit, and it belongs to the wholly perfect man. When we drink this, we
shall receive for ourselves the perfect man. The living water is a body. It
is necessary that we put on the living man. Therefore, when he is about
to go down into the water, he unclothes himself, in order that he may
put on the living man.

81,15 There is the Son of man and there is the son of the Son of man. The
Lord is the Son of man, and the son of the Son of man is he who is cre-
20 ated through the Son of man. The Son of man received from God the capacity to create. He also has the ability to beget. He who has received the
ability to create is a creature. He who has received the ability to beget is
an offspring. He who creates cannot beget. He who begets also has
25 power to create. Now they say, "He who creates begets." But his so-
called "offspring" is merely a creature. [Therefore] his children are not
offspring but [creatures]. He who creates works openly and he himself is
30 visible. He who begets begets in [private] and he himself is hidden,
[since he is superior to every] image. He who creates [creates] openly.
35 But one who begets [begets] children in private. No [one will be able] to
82,1 know when [the husband] and the wife have intercourse with one another except the two of them. Indeed marriage in the world is a mystery
for those who have taken a wife. If there is a hidden quality to the mar-
5 riage of defilement, how much more is the undefiled marriage a true
mystery! It is not fleshly put pure. It belongs not to desire but to the will.
10 It belongs not to the darkness or the night but to the day and the light. If
a marriage is open to the public, it has become prostitution, and the
bride plays the harlot not only when she is impregnated by another man
15 but even if she slips out of her bedroom and is seen. Let her show herself
only to her father and her mother and to the friend of the bridegroom
and the sons of the bridegroom. These are permitted to enter every day
20 into the bridal chamber. But let the others yearn just to listen to her voice

and to enjoy her ointment, and let them feed from the crumbs that fall from the table, like the dogs. Bridegrooms and brides belong to the bridal chamber. No one shall be able to see the bridegroom with the   25
bride unless [one become] one.

When Abraham [rejoiced] that he was to see what he was to see, [he circumcised] the flesh of the foreskin, teaching us that it is proper to destroy the flesh.

[Most things] in the world, as long as their [inner parts] are hidden,   30
stand upright and live. [If they are revealed] they die, as is illustrated by the visible man: [as long as] the intestines of the man are hidden, the man is alive; when his intestines are exposed and come out of him, the   83,1
man will die. So also with the tree: while its root is hidden it sprouts and grows. If its root is exposed, the tree dries up. So it is with every birth   5
that is in the world, not only with the revealed but with the hidden. For so long as the root of wickedness is hidden, it is strong. But when it is recognized it is dissolved. When it is revealed it perishes. That is why the   10
word says, "Already the ax is laid at the root of the trees." It will not merely cut—what is cut sprouts again—but the ax penetrates deeply un-   15
til it brings up the root. Jesus pulled out the root of the whole place, while others did it only partially. As for ourselves, let each one of us dig down after the root of evil which is within one, and let one pluck it out of   20
one's heart from the root. It will be plucked out if we recognize it. But if we are ignorant of it, it takes root in us and produces its fruit in our   25
heart. It masters us. We are its slaves. It takes us captive, to make us do what we do [not] want; and what we do want we do [not] do. It is powerful because we have not recognized it. While it exists it is active. Igno-   30
rance is the mother of [all evil]. Ignorance will eventuate in [death, because] those that come from [ignorance] neither were nor [are] nor shall   35
be. [But those who are in the truth] will be perfect when all the truth is re-   84,1
vealed. For truth is like ignorance: while it is hidden it rests in itself, but when it is revealed and is recognized, it is praised inasmuch as it is   5
stronger than ignorance and error. It gives freedom. The word said, "If you know the truth, the truth will make you free." Ignorance is a slave.   10
Knowledge is freedom. If we know the truth, we shall find the fruits of the truth within us. If we are joined to it, it will bring our fulfillment.

At the present time we have the manifest things of creation. We say,   15
"The strong are they who are held in high regard. And the obscure are the weak who are despised." Contrast the manifest things of truth: they are weak and despised, while the hidden things are strong and held in   20
high regard. The mysteries of truth are revealed, though in type and image. The bridal chamber, however, remains hidden. It is the holy in the

25 holy. The veil at first concealed how God controlled the creation, but when the veil is rent and the things inside are revealed, this house will be left desolate, or rather will be [destroyed]. But the whole inferior

30 Godhead will not flee [from] these places into the holies [of the] holies, for it will not be able to mix with the unmixed [light] and the [flawless]

35 fullness, but will be under the wings of the Cross [and under] its arms.

85,1 This ark will be [its] salvation when the flood of water surges over them. If some belong to the order of the priesthood they will be able to go

5 within the veil with the high priest. For this reason the veil was not rent at the top only, since it would have been open only to those above; nor was it rent at the bottom only, since it would have been revealed only to

10 those below. But it was rent from top to bottom. Those above opened to us who are below, in order that we may go in to the secret of the truth. This truly is what is held in high regard, since it is strong! But we shall go

15 in there by means of lowly types and forms of weakness. They are lowly indeed when compared with the perfect glory. There is glory which surpasses glory. There is power which surpasses power. Therefore the perfect things have opened to us, together with the hidden things of truth.

20 The holies of the holies were revealed, and the bridal chamber invited us in.

As long as it is hidden, wickedness is indeed ineffectual, but it has not been removed from the midst of the seed of the Holy Spirit. They are

25 slaves of evil. But when it is revealed, then the perfect light will flow out on every one. And all those who are in it will [receive the chrism]. Then the slaves will be free [and] the captives ransomed. "[Every] plant

30 [which] my father who is in heaven [had not] planted [will be] plucked out." Those who are separated will be united [and] will be filled. Every one who will [enter] the bridal chamber will kindle the [light], for [it

35 burns] just as in the marriages which are [observed, though they] hap-

86,1 pen at night. That fire [burns] only at night and is put out. But the mysteries of this marriage are perfected rather in the day and the light. Nei-

5 ther that day nor its light ever sets. If anyone becomes a son of the bridal chamber, he will receive the light. If anyone does not receive it while he is in these places, he will not be able to receive it in the other place. He who will receive that light will not be seen, nor can he be detained. And

10 none shall be able to torment a person like this even while he dwells in the world. And again when he leaves the world he has already received the truth in the images. The world has become the aion, for the aion is

15 fullness for him. This is the way it is: it is revealed to him alone, not hidden in the darkness and the light, but hidden in a perfect day and a holy light.

CLEMENT OF ALEXANDRIA, *EXHORTATION TO THE GREEKS* (*PROTREPTIKOS PROS HELLENAS*), 2.11–24; 12.118–20

Near the end of the second century C.E., Clement of Alexandria wrote this attack on the myths and mysteries of his day. Clement speculates about the etymology of the word *mysterion* and the origin of the mysteries themselves, but his speculative efforts must be taken as polemical. Clement admits that he is about to divulge the secret things of the mysteries in order to lay bare their unholy and outrageous character. He proceeds to expose what he judges to be the scandal of "the mysteries of the atheists"—the violence, the licentiousness, the murder, the utter shamelessness—but in the process he cites *symbola* and traditions that deserve our careful attention as we attempt to reconstruct the mysteries of the Greco-Roman world.

In Chapter 12 of the *Exhortation to the Greeks*, Clement presents Christianity as a mystery religion, with "truly sacred mysteries" that offer pure light and a vision of the one God. Clement urges his reader to avoid what he calls the corruption and destruction of the Greek religious heritage, and instead to turn to the Christian gospel: "Then thou shalt have the vision of my God, and shalt be initiated in those holy mysteries, and shalt taste the joys that are hidden away in heaven, preserved for me, 'which neither ear hath heard nor have they entered into the heart' of any man" (*Exhortation to the Greeks*, 12.118; the quotation is from 1 Corinthians 2:9).

The *symbola* quoted in the *Protreptikos* are discussed in the appropriate chapters.

These selections from Clement are translated by G. W. Butterworth, *Clement of Alexandria* (Loeb Classical Library, 1968).

Do not therefore seek diligently after godless sanctuaries, nor after   **2.11**
mouths of caverns full of jugglery, nor the Thesprotian caldron, nor the Cirrhaean tripod, nor the Dodonian copper. As for the old stump honored by the desert sands, and the oracular shrine there gone to decay with the oak itself, abandon them both to the region of legends now grown old. The Castalian spring, at least, is all silent. So is the spring of Colophon; and the rest of the prophetic streams are likewise dead. Stripped of their absurd pretensions, though none too soon, they are at last thoroughly exposed; the waters have run dry together with the legends attached to them. Relate to me the utterly vain utterances of that other form of divination—I should rather say hallucination—the oracles of Apollo, Clarian, Pythian, and Didymean, and those of Amphiaraus

and Amphilochus; and, if you will, devote to destruction along with them the soothsayers, augurs, and interpreters of dreams. At the same time, take and place by the side of Pythian Apollo those who divine by flour, and by barley, and the ventriloquists still held in honor among the multitude. Yes, and let the sanctuaries of Egypt and the Tuscan oracles of the dead be delivered over to darkness. Homes of hallucination in very truth they are, these schools of sophistry for unbelieving men, these gambling-dens of sheer delusion. Partners in this business of trickery are goats, trained for divination; and ravens, taught by men to give oracular responses to men.

12   But what if I were to recount the mysteries for you? I will not burlesque them, as Alcibiades is said to have done, but will thoroughly lay bare, in accordance with the principle of truth, the trickery they conceal; and as for your so-called gods themselves, to whom the mystic rites belong, I will display them on the stage of life, as it were, for the spectators of truth. The raving Dionysos is worshiped by Bacchantes with orgies, in which they celebrate their sacred frenzy by a feast of raw flesh (omophagia). Wreathed with snakes, they perform the distribution of portions of their victims, shouting the name of Eva (Eua), that Eva through whom error entered into the world; and a consecrated snake is the emblem of the Bacchic orgies. At any rate, according to the correct Hebrew speech, the word "hevia" with an aspirate means the female snake. Deo and Kore have come to be the subject of a mystic drama, and Eleusis celebrates with torches the rape of the daughter and the sorrowful wandering of the mother.

13   Now it seems to me that the terms "orgy" and "mystery" must be derived, the former from the wrath (orge) of Deo against Zeus, and the latter from the pollution (mysos) that took place in connection with Dionysos. But even if they are named after a certain Myus of Attica, who according to Apollodorus was killed in hunting, I make no objection. Your mysteries have received the glory of funeral honors! You may also, in another way, suppose them to be hunting-stories (mytheria), since the letters correspond; for as surely as there are men who hunt wild beasts, so do legends like these hunt the rudest among Thracians, the silliest among Phrygians, and the daimon-fearers among Greeks. A curse then upon the man who started this deception for mankind, whether it be Dardanus, who introduced the mysteries of the Mother of the Gods; or Eetion, who founded the Samothracian orgies and rites; or that Phrygian Midas, who learnt the artful deceit from Odrysus and then passed it on to his subjects. For I could never be beguiled by the claims of the islander Cinyras, of Cyprus, who had the audacity to transfer the lascivious or-

gies of Aprodite from night to day, in his ambition to deify a harlot of his own country. Others say that it was Melampus the son of Amythaon who brought into Greece from Egypt the festivals of Deo, that is, the story of her grief celebrated in hymns. These men I for my part would call originators of mischief, parents of godless legends and deadly daimon-worship, seeing that they implanted the mysteries in human life to be a seed of evil and corruption.

But now—and high time too—I will convict your orgies themselves of **14** being full of deception and jugglery, and if you have been initiated you will smile the more at these legends you are wont to honor. I will tell openly the secret things, and will not shrink from speaking of what you are not ashamed to worship. There is, then, the "foam-born" "Cyprus-born" goddess, the darling of Cinyras. I mean Aphrodite, who received the name Philomedes because she was born from the *medea*, those lustful members that were cut off from Ouranos and after the separation did violence to the wave. See how lewd are the members from which so worthy an offspring is born! And in the rites which celebrate this pleasure of the sea, as a symbol of her birth, the gift of a cake of salt and a phallus is made to those who are initiated in the art of fornication; and the initiated bring their tribute

The mysteries of Deo commemorate the amorous embraces of Zeus **15** with his mother Demeter, and the wrath of Deo—I do not know what to call her for the future, mother or wife—on account of which she is said to have received the name Brimo; also the supplications of Zeus, the drink of bile, the tearing out the heart of the victims, and unspeakable obscenities. The same rites are performed in honor of Attis and Kybele and the Korybantes by the Phrygians, who have spread it abroad how that Zeus tore off the testicles of a ram, and then brought and flung them into the midst of Deo's lap, thus paying a sham penalty for his violent embrace by pretending that he had mutilated himself. If I go on further to quote the symbols of initiation into this mystery they will, I know, move you to laughter, even though you are in no laughing humor when your rites are being exposed. "I ate from the drum; I drank from the cymbal; I carried the sacred dish; I stole into the bridal chamber." Are not these symbols an outrage? Are not the mysteries a mockery? But what if I were to add **16** the rest of the story? Demeter becomes pregnant; the Maiden (Kore) grows up; and this Zeus who begat her has further intercourse, this time with Persephone herself, his own daughter, after his union with her mother Deo. Totally forgetful of his former pollution Zeus becomes the ravisher as well as the father of the maiden, meeting her under the form of a serpent, his true nature being thus revealed. At any rate, in the

Sabazian mysteries the sign given to those who are initiated is "the god over the breast"; this is a serpent drawn over the breast of the votaries, a proof of the licentiousness of Zeus. Persephone also bears a child, which has the form of a bull. To be sure, we are told by a certain mythological poet that

> The bull begets a snake, the snake a bull;
> On hills the herdsman bears his mystic goad—

17 the herdsman's goad being, I think, a name for the wand which the Bacchantes wreathe. Would you have me also tell you the story of Persephone gathering flowers, of her basket, and how she was seized by Aidoneus, of the chasm that opened in the earth, and of the swine of Eubouleus that were swallowed up along with the two deities, which is the reason given for the custom of casting swine into the sacred caverns at the festival of the Thesmophoria? This is the tale which the women celebrate at their various feasts in the city, Thesmophoria, Scirophoria, Arretophoria, where in different ways they work up into tragedy the rape of Persephone.

The mysteries of Dionysos are of a perfectly savage character. He was yet a child, and the Kouretes were dancing around him with warlike movement, when the Titans stealthily drew near. First they beguiled him with childish toys, and then—these very Titans—tore him to pieces, though he was but an infant. Orpheus of Thrace, the poet of the Initiation, speaks of the

> Top, wheel and jointed dolls, with beauteous fruit
> Of gold from the clear-voiced Hesperides.

18 And it is worth while to quote the worthless symbols of this rite of yours in order to excite condemnation: the knuckle-bone, the ball, the spinning-top, apples, wheel, mirror, fleece! Now Athena made off with the heart of Dionysos, and received the name Pallas from its palpitating. But the Titans, they who tore him to pieces, placed a caldron upon a tripod, and casting the limbs of Dionysos into it first boiled them down; then, piercing them with spits, they "held them over Hephaistos." Later on Zeus appeared; perhaps, since he was a god, because he smelt the steam of the flesh that was cooking, which your gods admit they "receive as their portion." He plagues the Titans with thunder and entrusts the limbs of Dionysos to his son Apollo for burial. In obedience to Zeus, Apollo carries the mutilated corpse to Parnassus and lays it to rest.

19 If you would like a vision of the Korybantic orgies also, this is the

story. Two of the Korybantes slew a third one, who was their brother, covered the head of the corpse with a purple cloak, and then wreathed and buried it, bearing it upon a brazen shield to the skirts of Mount Olympus. Here we see what the mysteries are, in one word, murders and burials! The priests of these mysteries, whom such as are interested in them call "Presidents of the Princes' rites," add a portent to the dismal tale. They forbid wild celery, root and all, to be placed on the table, for they actually believe that wild celery grows out of the blood that flowed from the murdered brother. It is a similar custom, of course, that is observed by the women who celebrate the Thesmophoria. They are careful not to eat any pomegranate seeds which fall to the ground, being of the opinion that pomegranates spring from the drops of Dionysos's blood. The Korybantes are also called by the name Kabeiroi, which proclaims the rite of the Kabeiroi. For this very pair of fratricides got possession of the chest in which the virilia of Dionysos were deposited, and brought it to Tuscany, traders in glorious wares! There they sojourned, being exiles, and communicated their precious teaching of piety, the virilia and the chest, to Tuscans for purposes of worship. For this reason not unnaturally some wish to call Dionysos Attis, because he was mutilated.

Yet how can we wonder if Tuscans, who are barbarians, are thus con- 20
secrated to base passions, when Athenians and the rest of Greece—I blush even to speak of it—possess that shameful tale about Deo? It tells how Deo, wandering through Eleusis, which is a part of Attica, in search of her daughter the Maiden, becomes exhausted and sits down at a well in deep distress. This display of grief is forbidden, up to the present day, to those who are initiated, lest the worshipers should seem to imitate the goddess in her sorrow. At that time Eleusis was inhabited by aborigines, whose names were Baubo, Dysaules, Triptolemos, and also Eumolpos and Eubouleus. Triptolemos was a herdsman, Eumolopos a shepherd, and Eubouleus a swineherd. These were progenitors of the Eumolpidai and of the Heralds (Kerykes), who form the priestly clan at Athens. But to continue; for I will not forbear to tell the rest of the story. Baubo, having received Deo as a guest, offers her a draught of wine and meal (kykeon). She declines to take it, being unwilling to drink on account of her mourning. Baubo is deeply hurt, thinking she has been slighted, and thereupon uncovers her secret parts and exhibits them to the goddess. Deo is pleased at the sight, and now at last receives the draught— delighted with the spectacle! These are the secret mysteries of the Athe- 21
nians! These are also the subjects of Orpheus's poems. I will quote you the very lines of Orpheus, in order that you may have the originator of the mysteries as witness of their shamelessness:

This said, she drew aside her robes, and showed
A sight of shame; child Iacchos was there,
And laughing, plunged his hand below her breasts.
Then smiled the goddess, in her heart she smiled,
And drank the draught from out the glancing cup.

And the formula of the Eleusinian mysteries is as follows: "I fasted; I drank the draught; I took from the chest; having done my task, I placed in the basket, and from the basket into the chest." Beautiful sights indeed, and fit for a goddess! Yes, such rites are meet for the night and torch fires, and for the "great-hearted"—I should rather say empty-headed—people of the Erechtheidai, with the rest of the Greeks as well, "whom after death there await such things as they little expect." Against whom does Heracleitus of Ephesus utter this prophecy? Against "night-roamers, magicians (*magoi*), Bacchantes, Lenaean revellers, and devotees of the mysteries (*mystai*)." These are the people whom he threatens with the penalties that follow death; for these he prophesies the fire. "For in unholy fashion are they initiated into the mysteries customary among men."

The mysteries, then, are mere custom and vain opinion, and it is a deceit of the serpent that men worship when, with spurious piety, they turn towards these sacred initiations that are really profanities, and solemn rites that are without sanctity. Consider, too, the contents of the mystic chests; for I must strip bare their holy things and utter the unspeakable. Are they not sesame cakes, pyramid and spherical cakes, cakes with many navels, also balls of salt and a serpent, the mystic sign of Dionysos Bassareus? Are they not also pomegranates, fig branches, fennel stalks, ivy leaves, round cakes, and poppies? These are their holy things! In addition, there are the unutterable symbols of Ge Themis, marjoram, a lamp, a sword, and a woman's comb, which is a euphemistic expression used in the mysteries for a woman's secret parts. What manifest shamelessness! Formerly night, which drew a veil over the pleasures of temperate men, was a time for silence. But now, when night is for those who are being initiated a temptation to licentiousness, talk abounds, and the torch-fires convict unbridled passions. Quench the fire, thou priest. Shrink from the flaming brands, torchbearer (*dadouchos*). The light convicts your Iacchos. Suffer night to hide the mysteries. Let the orgies be honored by darkness. The fire is not acting a part; to convict and to punish is its duty.

These are the mysteries of the atheists. And I am right in branding as atheists men who are ignorant of the true God, but shamelessly worship a child being torn to pieces by Titans, a poor grief-stricken woman, and parts of the body which, from a sense of shame, are truly too sacred to speak of. It is a twofold atheism in which they are entangled; first, the atheism of being ignorant of God, since they do not recognize the true God; and then this second error, of believing in the existence of beings that have no existence, and calling by the name of gods those who are not really gods—nay more, who do not even exist, but have only got the name. No doubt this is also the reason why the Apostle convicts us, when he says, "And ye were strangers from the covenants of the promise, being without hope and atheists in the world."

Blessings be upon the Scythian king, whoever he was. When a countryman of his own was imitating among the Scythians the rite of the Mother of the Gods as practised at Cyzicus, by beating a drum and clanging a cymbal, and by having images of the goddess suspended from his neck after the manner of a priest of Kybele (Menagyrtes), this king slew him with an arrow, on the ground that the man, having been deprived of his own virility in Greece, was now communicating the effeminate disease to his fellow Scythians. All this—for I must not in the least conceal what I think—makes me amazed how the term atheist has been applied to Euhemerus of Acragas, Nicanor of Cyprus, Diagoras and Hippo of Melos, with that Cyrenian named Theodorus and a good many others besides, men who lived sensible lives and discerned more acutely, I imagine, than the rest of mankind the error connected with these gods. Even if they did not perceive the truth itself, they at least suspected the error; and this suspicion is a living spark of wisdom, and no small one, which grows up like a seed into truth. One of them thus directs the Egyptians: "If you believe they are gods, do not lament them, nor beat the breast; but if you mourn for them, no longer consider these beings to be gods." Another, having taken hold of a Heracles made from a log of wood—he happened, likely enough, to be cooking something at home—said: "Come, Heracles, now is your time to undertake this thirteenth labor for me, as you did the twelve for Eurystheus, and prepare Diagoras his dish!" Then he put him into the fire like a log.

Let us then shun custom; let us shun it as some dangerous headland, **12.118** or threatening Charybdis, or the Sirens of legend. Custom strangles man; it turns him away from truth; it leads him away from life; it is a snare, an abyss, a pit, a devouring evil.

Wide of that smoke and wave direct, O helmsman, thy vessel.

Let us flee, comrades, let us flee from this wave. It belches forth fire; it is an island of wickedness heaped with bones and corpses, and she who sings therein is pleasure, a harlot in the bloom of youth, delighting in her vulgar music.

Hither, renowned Odysseus, great glory of all the Achaeans:
Bring thy ship to the land, that a song divine may entrance thee.

She praises thee, sailor, she calls thee renowned in song; the harlot would make the glory of the Greeks her own. Leave her to roam among the corpses; a heavenly wind comes to thine aid. Pass by pleasure; she beguiles.

Let not thy heart be deceived by a woman with trailing garment,
Coaxing with wily words to find the place of thy dwelling.

Sail past the song; it works death. Only resolve, and thou hast vanquished destruction; bound to the wood of the cross thou shalt live freed from all corruption. The Word of God shall be thy pilot and the Holy Spirit shall bring thee to anchor in the harbors of heaven. Then thou shalt have the vision of my God, and shalt be initiated in those holy mysteries, and shalt taste the joys that are hidden away in heaven, preserved for me, "which neither ear hath heard nor have they entered into the heart" of any man.

And lo! methinks I see a pair of suns
And a double Thebes,

said one (viz. Pentheus) who was revelling in frenzy through idols, drunk with sheer ignorance. I would pity him in his drunkenness, and would appeal to him to return from this madness to sober salvation, seeing that the Lord also welcomes the repentance, and not the death, of a sinner. Come, thou frenzy-stricken one, not resting on thy wand (thyrsus), not wreathed with ivy! Cast off thy headdress; cast off thy fawnskin; return to soberness! I will show thee the Word, and the Word's mysteries, describing them according to thine own semblance of them. This is the mountain beloved of God, not a subject for tragedies, like Cithaeron, but one devoted to the dramas of truth, a wineless mountain, shaded by hallowed groves. Therein revel no Maenads, sisters of "thunder-smitten" Semele, who are initiated in the loathsome distribution of raw flesh, but the daughters of God, the beautiful lambs, who declare the solemn rites of the Word, assembling a sober company. The righteous form this company, and their song is a hymn in praise of the King of all. The maidens play the harp, angels give glory, prophets speak, a noise of music rises; swiftly they pursue the sacred band (*thiasos*), those who have been called hasting with eager longing to receive the Father. Come to me, old man, come thou too! Quit Thebes; fling away thy prophecy and Bacchic revelry and be led by the hand to truth. Behold, I give thee the wood of the cross to lean upon. Hasten, Teiresias, believe! Thou shalt have sight. Christ, by whom the eyes of the blind see again, shineth upon thee more brightly than the sun. Night shall flee from thee; fire shall fear thee; death shall depart from thee. Thou shalt see heaven, old man, though thou canst not see Thebes.

O truly sacred mysteries! O pure light! In the blaze of the torches I **120** have a vision of heaven and of God. I become holy by initiation. The Lord reveals the mysteries; He marks the worshiper with His seal, gives light to guide his way, and commends him, when he has believed, to the Father's care, where he is guarded for ages to come. These are the revels of my mysteries! If thou wilt, be thyself also initiated, and thou shalt dance with angels around the unbegotten and imperishable and only true God, the Word of God joining with us in our hymn of praise. This Jesus being eternal, one great high priest of one God who is also Father, prays for men and encourages men: " 'Give ear, ye myriad peoples,' or rather, so many of mankind as are governed by reason, both barbarians and Greeks; the whole race of men I call, I who was their Creator by the Father's will. Come to me, that ye may be marshalled under one God and the one Word of God; and do not surpass the irrational creatures in reason only, for to you alone of all mortal beings I offer the fruit of immortality. I desire, yea, I desire to impart to you even this gracious favor, supplying in its fullness the good gift of incorruption. And I freely give you divine reason, the knowledge of God; I give you Myself in perfection. For this is Myself, this is God's desire, this is the concord, this the harmony of the Father: this is the Son, this is Christ, this is the Word of God, the arm of the Lord, the might of the universe, the Father's will. O ye who of old were images, but do not all resemble your model, I desire to conform you to the archetype, that you may become even as I am. I will anoint you with the ointment of faith, whereby you cast away corruption; and I will display unveiled the figure of righteousness, whereby you ascend to God. 'Come unto Me, all ye that labor and are heavy laden, and I will give you rest. Take My yoke upon you and learn of Me; for I am meek and lowly in heart, and ye shall find rest unto your souls. For My yoke is easy and My burden is light.' "

Epilogue

Dying and Rising in Christianity and the Other Mysteries

Clement of Alexandria claimed that Christianity may be understood as a mystery religion, and he may well be right. "O truly sacred mysteries!" he writes in his *Exhortation to the Greeks* (quoted above). "O pure light! In the blaze of the torches I have a vision of heaven and of God. I become holy by initiation. The Lord reveals the mysteries"—the Christian mysteries, Clement asserts, the only true mysteries. Clement puts his own Christian spin on his understanding of the mysteries, and he balances his condemnation of the excesses of the revels of the Greco-Roman mysteries with his adoration of initiation into the mysteries of Christ.

Paul the apostle of Christ also describes the Christian gospel as a mystery. In 1 Corinthians 15 Paul cites an early Christian creed to highlight the essence of the gospel as he understands it: Christ died, Christ was raised. For Paul, and for countless Christian believers after Paul, Christ is preeminently a dying and rising savior, and those who follow Christ participate in the crucifixion and resurrection of Christ. We have died with Christ, Paul proclaims, and we shall be raised with Christ—Paul maintains his eschatological reservation by keeping the resurrection of believers a matter of future expectation and hope. When Paul explains the nature of the resurrection in 1 Corinthians 15, he employs images familiar to devotees of the mystery religions, for example the Eleusinian mysteries of Demeter and Kore. The resurrected body, he emphasizes, is like a seed of wheat or some other grain that dies and then rises. For the initiates into the Eleusinian mysteries, this cycle of grain was dramatized in the death and new life of Kore and, by extension, the initiates into the mysteries. For the early Christians envisioned by Paul, this cycle of grain was used as a metaphor for the death and resurrection of Christ as the firstfruits of the resurrection of Christians.

In large part Paul's vision of Christ as a dying and rising savior, reminiscent of other savior figures in other Greco-Roman mystery religions, has carried the day as the dominant formulation of the Christian gospel.

To be sure, from the beginning of the Christian movement there have been a variety of Christianities and a variety of ways of interpreting the significance of Christ, and some of these still present viable christological options. Jesus may be understood in other ways than a dying and rising savior, but for many believers the gospel of the cross and resurrection has proved to be a compelling formulation of the Christian message. To this day Christian churches are recognized by the cross that typically marks them. Within most churches the dominant piece of furniture is the altar, which witnesses in different ways, in Roman Catholic, Orthodox, and Protestant congregations, to the death of Jesus as a sacrifice. In the springtime of each liturgical year the Christian holy week is observed with grief for the death of Jesus, on Good Friday, and with celebration for the resurrection of Jesus, on Easter Sunday.

This prominent Christian focus on Jesus as a dying and rising savior comes as somewhat of a surprise in that it seems to minimize or even ignore the life of the historical Jesus, the Jewish teacher of wisdom and faith healer in whose name and memory Christianity was founded. Jesus traversed Galilee teaching and preaching that God's realm is close at hand and can be discovered in the surprises evident in everyday life and in the wholeness that comes in a fractured world. Jesus encouraged people to seek and find, and he told stories, now frequently termed parables, to illustrate how people might seek and find God and God's realm. From the teachings of Jesus come provocative utterances describing the life of the followers of Jesus. Do to others as you would have them do to you. Love your neighbor as yourself. Love even your enemies. Turn the other cheek, go the extra mile, give your last garment. Be shrewd as snakes and innocent as doves. Be like children.

Of course, Jesus the Jewish teacher did die, as the Christian gospel states. So did Socrates, Buddha, and others, yet their deaths were not proclaimed to be the saving event that Jesus' death was said to be. But the story of the death of Jesus in Christian thought resembles more closely the stories of the deaths of savior figures in the mystery religions. The story of the dying and rising deity is one of the oldest stories in the world, and fertility deities like Baal embody the dying and rising of crops as recounted in the mythic cycles of death and rebirth. As we have seen throughout this volume, in the mystery religions and in early Christianity these interests in death and rebirth are applied to human life, so that it is said that the dying and rising of the divine savior figures may be realized in the lives of the human beings who die and rise with them.

Some scholars have argued that the image of the dying and rising gods and goddesses in the mystery religions is fanciful, and that these deities do not actually rise as Jesus is said to have risen. They may indeed die, like Jesus, but thereafter they stay where they belong, that is, dead. Such a critique of dying and rising deities may well be motivated by apologetic concerns designed to maintain the uniqueness of the resurrected Christ. In fact, the deities in the mystery religions provide ample evidence for the proclamation of the continuation of life and the manifestation of new life in the mysteries. Here a few examples cited in this volume must suffice. Like the grain, Kore returns mythically to the land of the living from her yearly sojourn in the realm of Hades. Osiris exists in the realm of the dead as the ruler of that realm, and the "grain Osiris" proclaims the growth or rebirth of grain and of Osiris. When Lucius is initiated into the mysteries of Isis, according to Apuleius, he undergoes a nocturnal death experience by passing through the realm of death, the realm of Osiris, and emerging in the morning, dressed like the rising sun, to celebrate his initiation after the manner of a birthday. Archeological monuments show the Mithraic bull also anticipating new life, and heads of grain grow from the dying bull. The Mithraic inscriptions from Santa Prisca include references to one that "is piously reborn and created by sweet things." Similar references to rebirth are to be found in Apuleius, in the inscription of 376 C.E. on the *taurobolium* and *criobolium*, and in the Mithras Liturgy. Attis too provides a hint of new life after his death: his body does not decay, his hair continues to grow, and his little finger (his penis?) remains in motion. During the spring the death of Attis is observed on the Day of Blood, and new life may be celebrated in the Hilaria.

Which brings us back to Clement of Alexandria's claim that Christianity is a mystery religion: "O truly sacred mysteries! O pure light!" It may well be that Christianity witnesses to the triumph of Baal, Kore, and all the other dying and rising gods and goddesses in the proclamation of the death and resurrection of Christ. In Christianity the ancient story of the dying and rising of the divine, of crops, of humans, of all, may reach a powerful conclusion, and the piety of the mysteries may achieve a final vindication. In Christianity the pure light that shines, according to Clement, may be the light of those enlightened by the ancient mysteries.

GLOSSARY

Abydos	Egyptian city with shrine of Osiris.
Acdestis	Agdistis.
Acheron	A river leading into the Greek underworld.
Adamas	Primal human.
Adonis	"Lord" (Semitic), lover of Aphrodite, a youth who dies and is resurrected.
Aeacus	Greek judge of the dead.
Agdistis	Androgynous child (or alter ego) of Kybele.
Aidoneus	"Unseen One" (Greek), epithet of Hades.
Aion	(Aeon). God of time, boundless time, especially within Mithraism; often he is leontocephalic, he holds keys to heaven, and he may breathe fire. In Gnostic literature, the personification of an age or power.
Amenthes	The West, i.e., the realm of darkness and death in Egyptian thought.
Anubis	Egyptian jackal-headed god of mummification.
Aphrodite	Greek goddess of love (Canaanite goddess Astarte).
Apis	Greek name for Egyptian Hapi.
Apollo	Greek god of wisdom, beauty, and law, associated with the sun; twin brother of Artemis; often equated with the Egyptian god Horus.
Apollo Karneios	God worshiped in the Andanian mysteries; see Karneios.
Ares	Greek god of war.
Arretophoria	Athenian children's festival in which young girls bear sacred things to the temple of Aphrodite.
Artemis	Greek goddess of the wilds, goddess of Ephesus; identified with Roman goddess Diana; sometimes associated with Cappadocian goddess Ma.
Aroueris	(Haroeris). Greek form of the name for the Egyptian god Horus the Elder.
Asklepios	(Aesculapius). Greek hero and god of healing.

Athena	Greek matron goddess of Athens, born from the head of Zeus.
Attis	Phrygian eunuch, lover of the Great Mother.
Bacchae	(Bacchai). Bacchantes, female followers of Bacchos, or Dionysos.
Bacchos	(pl., Bacchoi). Dionysos; a person (especially a male) possessed by Dionysos.
Bacchus	(pl., Bacchi). Latinized form of Bacchos.
Bassareus	From the Greek or Thracian word "fox," an epithet of Dionysos.
Baubo	Mythical peasant woman of Eleusis who amuses Demeter with obscene gestures according to Clement of Alexandria, *Exhortation to the Greeks*; see also Iambe.
Bear	Constellation Ursa Major, known as the Bull or the Bull's Foreleg in Egypt.
Belf	Magical figure in Egyptian tradition.
Bellona	Roman goddess of war, sometimes identified with Cappadocian goddess Ma.
Brimo	"Strong One," "Terrible One" (Greek), epithet of goddess of the underworld (e.g., Demeter, Kore, Hecate).
Brimos	"Strong One," "Terrible One" (Greek), epithet of Dionysos.
Bromios	"Thunderer," "Boisterous One" (Greek), epithet of Dionysos.
Cadmus	Mythical founder of Thebes.
Carpocratians	Libertine Gnostic followers of the second-century C.E. teacher Carpocrates of Alexandria.
Cautes, Cautopates	Mythological torch-bearers in the mysteries of Mithras.
Cecropian Minerva	Roman goddess of arts and crafts; Cecropian is an adjective formed from Cecrops, the name of the founder of Athens, according to Greek mythology; "sprung from the earth itself."
Ceres	Roman goddess of grain, identified with the Greek goddess Demeter.
Choes	Pitcher feast, part of Anthesteria, the Athenian flower festival in honor of Dionysos.
Cupid	Roman god of love.
Cybele	Latinized form of Kybele.

Dadouchos	Torch-bearer, a priest especially in the Eleusinian mysteries; the dadouchos at Eleusis was appointed from the Kerykes.
Demeter	"Grain Mother" (or, less plausibly, "Earth Mother") of Greek mysteries, especially the Eleusinian mysteries.
Demophon	Mythical son of Keleos and Metaneira.
Deo	Demeter.
Derketo	Atargatis, Syrian goddess.
Deucalion	Greek hero of the story of the great flood.
Diana Dictynna	Diana is the Roman goddess of fertility, wooded places; identified with the Greek goddess Artemis and the Cretan goddess Britomartis (also called Dictynna, goddess of the nets).
Dindymus	Mountain in Anatolia, linked to worship of Kybele.
Dionysos	Greek god of fertility, ecstasy, and wine; also called Bacchos.
Dioskouroi	"Sons of Zeus" (Greek), Kastor and Polydeukes (Castor and Pollux).
Dysaules	Mythical peasant of Eleusis, husband of Baubo; see Clement of Alexandria, *Exhortation to the Greeks.*
Endymion	A beautiful young man loved by Selene in Greek mythology.
Erechtheidai	Members of the family or tribe of Erechtheus, the legendary king of Athens; thus, a term for Athenians.
Eros	Greek god of love.
Eubouleus	(Euboulos). "Good counselor" (Greek), the mythical herder of swine in the myth of Demeter and Kore; sometimes a title of Hades or Dionysos.
Euios	(Evius). Epithet of the Greek god Dionysos, from the cry Euoi.
Eumolpos	"One who sings well" (Greek), the mythical ancestor of the Eumolpidai, the Eleusinian family from which the hierophant of the mysteries was chosen; see also Kerykes.
Euoi	(Euai, Eua, Eva, Evohe). Cry of worshipers of Dionysos.
Fates	Divine powers (feminine) in Mithras Liturgy,

these powers are similar to the seven Hathors in Egyptian thought; sometimes associated with the constellation Ursa Major, or the Pleiades.

Father	Cp. Pater.
Four pillars	Egyptian concept of four pillars supporting heaven; the pillars are the arms and legs of Nut.
Gaia	(Ge). Greek goddess, the earth.
Gallus	(pl., Galli). Eunuch of the Great Mother of Anatolia or Syria.
Glykon	Serpent, incarnation of Asklepios in the mysteries founded by Alexander of Abonoteichos.
Great Goddesses	Goddesses (Demeter and Kore?) worshiped in the Andanian mysteries according to Pausanias.
Great Gods	Gods worshiped in the Andanian mysteries; a title of the Kabeiroi.
Hades	Greek god of the underworld; also called Plouton.
Hagne	(Hagna). "Holy One," "Pure One" (Greek), a goddess (and a fountain) in the Andanian mysteries; an epithet of goddesses, e.g. Demeter.
Hapi	Sacred bull of Memphis, Egypt; called Apis by the Greeks.
Harmachis	"Horus who is on the horizon," Greek form of Egyptian epithet of Horus.
Harpocrates	"Horus the child," the son of Isis and Osiris.
Hecate	Ancient earth goddess with lunar and magical features.
Helios	"Sun," the sun god; often associated with Mithras.
Hephaistos	(Hephaestus). Greek god of fire, the divine smith; often equated with the Egyptian god Ptah.
Hermes	Greek messenger of the gods; equated with Thoth, the Egyptian moon god.
Horus	One of several Egyptian gods, often the son of Isis and Osiris; equated with the Greek god Apollo.
Ia	Bride-to-be of Attis.
Iacchos	Ritual cry in the Eleusinian mysteries, personified as a god and finally identified with Bacchos (Dionysos).
Iambe	Mythical maid of Eleusis who amuses Demeter ac-

	cording to the *Homeric Hymn to Demeter*; see also Baubo.
Ida	Mountain in Anatolia, home of Kybele; also the name of a mountain in Crete (adjective : Idaean, Idaian).
Iobacchos	(pl., Iobacchoi). Worshiper of Bacchos, especially in an Athenian club (the term is formed by combining the cry "Io" with the name "Bacchos").
Isis	Egyptian goddess of the royal throne; wife of Osiris.
Juno	Ancient Italian goddess of light, marriage, and childbirth; identified with the Greek goddess Hera.
Kabeiroi	Gods of Samothrace, linked with the "Great Gods" and the Dioskouroi.
Karneios	Ancient god worshiped in the Andanian mysteries and other festivals; often associated with the Greek god Apollo (adjective: Karnasian).
Keleos	Mythical king of Eleusis.
Kerykes	"Heralds" (Greek), the Eleusinian family from which priests of the mysteries were chosen; see also Eumolpos.
Kore	"Maiden" (Greek) of grain, the daughter of Demeter in Greek mysteries, especially the Eleusinian mysteries.
Korybantes	Ecstatic celebrants often linked with Kybele and Phrygia.
Korybas	Divine prototype of the Korybantes.
Kouretes	Ecstatic celebrants originally linked with Zeus and Crete.
Kronos	Ruler of the Titans, husband of Rhea and father of several Olympian deities; equated with Geb, the Egyptian earth god.
Kybele	Phrygian Great Mother.
Kykeon	Ceremonial drink in the Eleusinian mysteries, consisting of barley water and pennyroyal; possibly alcoholic or hallucinogenic.
Lenaean	"Of the wine-press" (Greek), from Lenaios, epithet of Dionysos.

Leo	"Lion," a Mithraic grade of initiation; also a constellation and sign of the zodiac.
Lethe	Oblivion, plain and spring in the Greek underworld.
Liber	Latin god of fertility and wine; see also Dionysos.
Liknites	"Of the liknon" (Greek), epithet of Dionysos.
Liknon	Winnowing basket, cradle in mysteries of Dionysos.
Lion	Cp. Leo.
Lysios	"One who releases" (Greek), epithet of Dionysos.
Ma	Cappadocian Mother, goddess of fertility and nature.
Maenads	Women in a Dionysian frenzy.
Magos	(pl., Magoi). Persian priest; more generally, magician; often Latizined as Magus (pl., magi).
Memphis	Capital city of Egypt.
Men	Phrygian god, linked with the moon.
Menagyrtes	Mendicant priest of Kybele; see also Metragyrtes.
Metaneira	Mythical queen of Eleusis.
Metragyrtes	(pl., Metragyrtai). Mendicant priest of Kybele; see also Gallus.
Minerva	Roman goddess of arts and crafts, identified with the Greek goddess Athena.
Mithras	(Mithra). Persian god of light and truth; god of the Mithraic mysteries, with solar associations.
Mnemosyne	Memory, spring in the Greek underworld.
Mneuis	(Mnevis). Greek name for sacred bull of Heliopolis, Egypt.
Mousaios	Legendary singer in Orphic mysteries.
Nabin	Egyptian goddess mentioned in the magical papyri; loved by Thoth.
Naiads	Greek nymphs of rivers and springs.
Nana	Daughter of Sangarius of Phrygia ("Mama"?).
Nemesis	Greek goddess associated with wild animals and divine retribution.
Nephthys	Egyptian goddess, "lady of the house," sister of Isis.
Oannes	Mesopotamian god of wisdom, part man and part fish.

Onnophris	(Un-nefer). Egyptian epithet for Osiris; it may mean "Good One."
Orpheus	Legendary Thracian singer, founder of Orphic mysteries.
Osiris	Egyptian god of moisture, underworld; husband of Isis.
Ouranos	(Uranus). "Sky" or "Heaven" (Greek), the divine father of Kronos and the Titans; he was castrated by his son Kronos.
Pales	Italian goddess of flocks and herds.
Pallas	Epithet of the Greek goddess Athena; probably means "Maiden," otherwise, "one who brandishes" a spear or "one who springs" from the head of Zeus.
Pan	Greek god of the wild, half man and half goat.
Papas	Attis ("Papa"?).
Pastophori	Shrine-bearers, officials in the mysteries of Isis.
Pater	"Father," a Mithraic grade of initiation.
Persephone	Greek goddess, queen of the underworld, identified with Kore.
Pessinuntia	Phrygian Mother of the Gods, from Pessinus.
Pessinus	Town in Phrygia, the center of the worship of Kybele.
Phoebus	"Bright One" (Greek: Phoibos), epithet of Greek god Apollo.
Plouton	(Pluto). "Wealthy One," the Greek god of the underworld; see also Hades.
Pole-Lords	Heavenly powers (masculine) in Mithras Liturgy, guardians of the polestar; cp. the constellation Ursa Minor.
Pronoia	"Providence" (Greek).
Proserpine	(Proserpina). Latin for Persephone.
Psyche	"Soul" (Greek), a goddess in love with Eros according to the Greek myths.
Re	Egyptian sun god.
Rhamnusia	Epithet of the Greek goddess Nemesis (from her shrine at Rhamnus in Attica).
Rhea	Titaness, wife of Kronos and mother of several Olympian deities; identified with the Great

Mother; also equated with Nut, the Egyptian sky goddess.

Sabazios (Sabazius). Phrygian god, linked with snakes.

Saboi (Sabi). Followers of Sabos (Sabazios); part of the cry "Euoi Saboi."

Sangarius King, or river, of Phrygia in the myth of Kybele and Attis.

Sarapis (Serapis). Osiris-Apis, Egyptian god with features of Osiris and the Apis bull of Memphis; given Greek features during the Hellenistic period.

Scarab Scarab beetle, Egyptian amulet and symbol of Khepera, the god of the rising sun.

Scirophoria Athenian summer festival in honor of Demeter, Kore, and especially Athena; parasols probably were carried, and pigs and fertility charms may have been thrown into caves in the ground.

Selene Greek goddess of the moon.

Semele Mother of Dionysos according to some Greek myths.

Semiramis Daughter of the Syrian goddess.

Silenus Spirit of the wild, an old man often portrayed with horse ears.

Sistrum (pl., sistra). Egyptian rattle, often made of metal, used for the worship of the goddess Isis.

Styx A river of the Greek underworld (adjective: Stygian).

Teiresias Old, blind seer, follower of Dionysos in Euripides' *Bacchae*.

Themis Greek goddess closely linked to Gaia (Ge).

Therapeutae "Healers" or "Worshipers" (Greek), Jewish mystics and ascetics living near Alexandria, Egypt.

Thesmophoria Greek agricultural festival honoring Demeter, celebrated in the autumn by women.

Thesmophoros "Lawgiver" (Greek), epithet of Demeter (and Isis), also used to describe Dionysos in the Orphic Hymns.

Thoth Egyptian god of truth and intelligence, moon god; sometimes considered the father of Isis.

Thoueris (Taueret). Egyptian hippopotamus goddess, sometimes associated with Set.

Throne-Chariot	(Merkabah). Hebrew term for the Throne of God; see Ezekiel 1, 10.
Thyrsus	(pl., thyrsi). Dionysian staff with ivy or vine leaves at the tip.
Titans	In Greek mythology, older gods who preceded the Olympian deities and competed with them for power.
To	Egyptian power mentioned in the magical papyri; the name may be related to the Egyptian words for "land" or "great."
Triptolemos	"Thrice Warring One" or "Thrice Plowing One" (Greek), the mythical plower in the Eleusinian mysteries.
Typhon	Monster of Greek mythology, often equated with Egyptian god Set.
Venus	Roman goddess of love; sometimes identified with the Greek goddess Aphrodite.
Zeus	Greek father god.
Zoroaster	(Zarathustra). Prophet of ancient Persia and founder of Zoroastrianism.

ACKNOWLEDGMENTS

Acknowledgment is made as follows for permission to reprint previously published material.

Ares Publishers: Rule of the Iobacchoi, trans. Marcus N. Tod, *Ancient Inscriptions: Sidelights on Greek History,* © 1974. Used by permission.

E. J. Brill: Mithraic Inscriptions of Santa Prisca, trans. Hans Dieter Betz, Maarten J. Vermaseren, and C. C. van Essen, *Novum Testamentum* 10 (1968): 62-80. Used by permission.

Cambridge University Press: Excerpt from Origen, *Against Celsus,* trans. Henry Chadwick, *Origen: Contra Celsum,* © 1980. Used by permission.

Doubleday & Company, Inc.: Excerpt from *Alexander the False Prophet,* trans. Lionel Cassian, *Selected Satires of Lucian,* © 1962 Lionel Cassian. Used by permission of Doubleday, a division of Bantam Doubleday Dell Publishing Group.

Grafton Books (Collins Publishing Group): Catullus, Poem 63, trans. C. H. Sisson, *The Poetry of Catullus,* © 1966 C. H. Sisson. Used by permission.

Harper & Row, Publishers, Inc.: Excerpts from the *Gospel of Philip,* trans. Wesley W. Isenberg, *Nag Hammadi Library in English,* © 1978, 1988 E. J. Brill. Used by permission of HarperCollins Publishers.

Harvard University Press: Clement of Alexandria, "To Theodore," trans. Morton Smith, *Clement of Alexandria and a Secret Gospel of Mark,* © 1973 President and Fellows of Harvard College. Used by permission of the publishers.

Harvard University Press: Excerpts from Achilles Tatius, trans. S. Gaselee, © 1917; Clement of Alexandria, *Exhortation to the Greeks,* trans. G. W. Butterworth, © 1919; Diodorus Siculus, trans. C. H. Oldfather, © 1939; Josephus, trans. Louis H. Feldman, © 1965; Lucian, *Menippus,* trans. A. M. Harmon, © 1925; Pausanias, *Description of Greece,* Book 4, *Messenia,* trans. W. H. S. Jones and H. A. Ormerod, © 1926; Pausanias, *Description of Greece,* Book 6, *Elis,* trans. H. H. S. Jones, © 1933; Philo, trans. G. H. Colson, © 1941; Plutarch, *Progress in Virtue,* trans. Frank Cole Babbitt, ©1936; Plutarch, *Table Talk,* trans. Herbert B. Hoffleit, © 1969. Reprinted by permission of the publishers and the Loeb Classical Library.

Indiana University Press: Excerpts from Apuleius, *The Golden Ass*, trans. Jack Lindsay, © 1932. Used by permission.

Macmillan Publishing Company: Isis Aretalogy, trans. Frederick C. Grant, *Hellenistic Religions: The Age of Syncretism*, © 1953 Macmillan Publishing Company, renewed 1981 Estate of Frederick C. Grant. Used by permission of Prentice-Hall, Inc.

Modern Library: Excerpt from Plato, *Republic*, trans. B. Jowett, 1941. Used by permission of Oxford University Press.

New American Library, Inc. (Mentor): Excerpt from Aristophanes, *The Frogs*, trans. Richmond Lattimore, *Four Plays by Aristophanes*, © 1962 William Arrowsmith. Used by permission of Dutton Signet, a division of Penguin Putnam, Inc.

Oxford University Press (Clarendon Press): Excerpts from Hippolytus, *Refutation of All Heresies*, trans. Werner Foerster, *Gnosis*, © 1971 Artemis Verlag, Zurich. Used by permission of Artemis Publishers.

Paulist Press (Newman Press): Excerpts from Arnobius of Sicca, *The Case Against the Pagans*. trans. George E. McCracken, © 1949; Firmicus Maternus, *The Error of the Pagan Religions*, trans. Clarence A. Forbes, © 1970. Used by permission of Paulist Press.

Penguin Books: Excerpts from Herodotus, trans. Aubrey de Sélincourt, *Herodotus: The Histories*, © 1954 Estate of Aubrey de Sélincourt; Livy, *History of Rome* 39.8-19, trans. Henry Bettenson, *Livy: Rome and the Mediterranean*, © 1976 Henry Bettenson; Livy, *History of Rome* 29.10-14, trans. Aubrey de Sélincourt, *Livy: The War with Hannibal*, © 1965 Estate of Aubrey de Sélincourt; Plutarch, *Life of Pompey*, trans. Rex Warner, *Plutarch: Fall of the Roman Republic*, © 1958 Rex Warner. Used by permission of Penguin Books Ltd.

Scholars Press (Society of Biblical Literature): Homeric Hymn to Demeter, trans. David G. Rice and John E. Stambaugh, *Sources for the Study of Greek Religion*, © 1979; excerpts from Lucian of Samosata, *The Syrian Goddess*, trans. Harold W. Attridge and Robert A. Oden, © 1976; Mithras Liturgy, trans. Marvin W. Meyer, *The "Mithras Liturgy"*, © 1976; Orphic Hymns, trans. Apostolos N. Athanassakis, *The Orphic Hymns*, © 1977. Used by permission of Scholars Press.

Thames & Hudson, Inc.: Excerpt from Prudentius, trans. Maarten J. Vermaseren, *Cybele and Attis*, © 1977. Used by permission.

University of Chicago Press: Excerpts from Euripides, *The Bacchae*, trans. William Arrowsmith, © 1959; Mithras Liturgy and Isis love spell, trans. Marvin W. Meyer, *The Greek Magical Papyri in Translation*, ed. Hans Dieter Betz, © 1986. Used by permission.

CPSIA information can be obtained at www.ICGtesting.com
Printed in the USA
BVOW08s2035100215

387225BV00001B/1/P